DECEIVERS AND DECEIVED

A publication of

THE INSTITUTE OF PUBLIC POLICY ANALYSIS
Stanford University

DECEIVERS AND DECEIVED

Observations on Confidence Men and Their
Victims, Informants and Their Quarry,
Political and Industrial Spies
and Ordinary Citizens

By

RICHARD H. BLUM

Program Director
Joint Program in Drug, Crime and Community Studies
Institute of Public Policy Analysis
Consulting Professor of Psychology
Stanford University
Stanford, California

CHARLES C THOMAS • PUBLISHER
Springfield · Illinois · U.S.A.

Published and Distributed Throughout the World by
CHARLES C THOMAS • PUBLISHER

BANNERSTONE HOUSE
301-327 East Lawrence Avenue, Springfield, Illinois, U.S.A.
NATCHEZ PLANTATION HOUSE
735 North Atlantic Boulevard, Fort Lauderdale, Florida, U.S.A.

With THOMAS BOOKS *careful attention is given to all details of
manufacturing and design. It is the Publisher's desire to present books
that are satisfactory as to their physical qualities and artistic possibilities
and appropriate for their particular use.* THOMAS BOOKS *will be true
to those laws of quality that assure a good name and good will.*

Printed in the United States of America
W-2

THIS BOOK IS dedicated to all those law enforcement personnel who have been working to bring criminological and social science research together with police planning and practice. It is particularly dedicated to our deceased colleague in the Cell, Ed Comber, and to the Cell's members Fabbri, Guidici, Kimble, Lewis, Pomeroy and Ross, along with our sometime visitors, Beal, Ingersoll and McLaren. It is also dedicated to those leaders, former Chief Justice Earl Warren and former Attorney General Ramsey Clark, whose example and personal encouragement have meant so much to us.

ACKNOWLEDGMENTS

I WISH TO ACKNOWLEDGE support for our work by the President's Commission on Law Enforcement and the Administration of Justice and the Federal Bureau of Narcotics and Dangerous Drugs of the United States Department of Justice. I thank the following persons for their cooperation during various phases of the work reported here: Thomas Cahill, former Chief of Police, San Francisco; Herschel Elkins, Deputy Attorney General, State of California; and Earl Whitmore, Sheriff of San Mateo County, California.

My special thanks go to the following people who served as working colleagues on this study: Lauraine Braunstein, Marguerite Crouse, John Fabbri, Kay Gilman, Gideon Jean-Jacques, James Hurley, Nick Munson, Wesley Pomeroy, Martha Rosman, Jane Trotman and Keith Trotman.

CONTENTS

DECEIVERS AND DECEIVED

Chapter I

OVERVIEW

THIS BOOK PRESENTS A series of observations of people who have consistently deceived others or who, as victims, have been deceived. The aim in undertaking these inquiries was to learn something of the settings, personalities and interpersonal transactions which are productive of violations of trust, to learn something of the chain of events leading to and comprising deception and to gain some perspective in an arena of human conduct which is emotionally charged, as the words "treason," "fink," "squealer," "Judas" and "betrayer" imply. This endeavor was not intended to encompass the whole range of human deception nor judgments thereof, nor was it embarked upon with the idea that only one set of factors would be identified as accounting for trust violation. To the contrary, the initial premise was that trust violations, like most forms of human congress, arise from varied circumstances and serve several possible interpersonal functions. It was not and it is not now the intent to enumerate all of these but rather to identify some aspects of trust violation which might not already be known in the wisdom of folklore, practical politics, or the human sciences.

Some of the people and actions observed and reported here constitute criminological cases. Implicit in that classification of criminality is that an individual knowingly intended to steal from another, as in defrauding through bunco games, and that the perpetrator planned or engaged in the wrongdoing itself. Implicit in that criminality is the notion of a victim of the crime, one presumed innocent, on whose behalf the state as law enforcer and prosecutor stands ready to act through its agents. The observations on confidence men contained in this book are instances of that criminal deception. Complementary observations on the victims of confidence men are also presented. The

results, it will be seen, make the innocence of the victim, especially his psychological innocence, a matter of some question.
We sought additional evidence of criminal trust violation by
comparing embezzlers with confidence men and with other
randomly selected criminals. That inquiry, which reviewed social
and psychiatric records of every identified confidence man and
embezzler processed through the prison system of northern
California, revealed little except that embezzlers, unlike confidence men, were more often said to be gamblers and were less
often described as having (poor relations) with their wives and
parents. Because such facts as these contribute little to our
understanding of the embezzler's trust violation, we do not
further report that study here. Similarly, we sought among
smugglers information that would yield us insights into their
deceptions. What we learned was the (cleverness) of modern
smugglers and the (foolishness) of amateurs but nothing that be-
spoke etiology and dynamics of deception as a psychological,
as opposed to an operational, matter.

Observations on political defectors are of a different order.
We have two samples; first, persons defecting from the United
States and NATO countries to the Iron Curtain lands and second,
those from the Iron Curtain coming West. In either East or
West, their acts are usually judged according to criminal statutes
(but of a different sort,) since the State conceives itself as victim
as well as prosecutor (given the chance for the latter to take
place). These political offenses are usually thought of as ideological matters, and because of that component of idealism and
imputed morality, viewers may respond with sympathy and
admiration even if the offender is a traitor. Yet it will be seen
that preconceptions may be erroneous. Especially among the
defectors from the West, the individual histories are so strongly
suggestive of sociopathy and unpremeditated entry into the
espionage business that ideological or political motivation is
difficult to show. In consequence, we shall reason that the
careers of most traitors evolve from personal difficulties and
situational pressures—as well as opportunities—rather than burning political convictions or even an explicit intent to "spy." On
the other hand, the Iron Curtain defectors, especially Soviet,

may more often be idealists. Since spies are cast as criminals in their homeland because of their defection, the average Western viewer is not only likely to approve their conduct but in examining their careers as presented here, will find less evidence for deviant personality, delinquency or the exploitation of trust for personal gain. That does not rule out a history of deception in their lives, especially since life in the Soviet Union appears to require deception for survival.

A third and limited set of observations presented here concerns persons involved in events which are on the borderline between civil as opposed to criminal violations of trust. Civil complaints are those in which the state adjudicates, determining where injury or negligence has occurred, but does not prosecute on behalf of an injured party. Such grievances come to court as torts. Our data focus on persons alleged or found to have engaged in industrial espionage. A broader population of deceivers could have been obtained had we studied adultery in marriage or contract violation in business. The prospects of either endeavor as a focus of study were overwhelming, although some information on cheating in marriage and in business is presented in our survey of a sample of ordinary citizens. As to the study of industrial spies, it began accidentally from opportunities arising during a preliminary work on character and managerial competence. We tried to use the opportunity to learn if there were differences in the personal histories and presumed character of those engaged in industrial trust violations in comparison with their peers not known to have engaged in trust violation.

Two other borderline groups had been planned for inclusion in the work, but both were frustrated. We had learned from reading Hubner (1965) that many credit risks would be careless, immature people; others we suspected of more planned theft. The records of credit bureaus proved inadequate for our purposes, whereas our funds and energy were insufficient for beginning a credit risk study without a case-finding base. Consumer fraud was also to be included, but unexpected ambiguity stood in our way and because of it we foundered. Prosecutions were so few that judicial decisions could not serve as criteria for defining criminal violation of trust. Citizen complaints were more common, but records of these were poor at best. And we found at the outset that a customer complaint might be evidence only of disappointment or occasionally a deceptive device on the part of the customer himself who sought aggressively to avoid payment of bills. For example, is an allegedly poor job of roof oiling the result of criminal intent or is it the bad luck of a customer stuck with an incompetent contractor? Might it even be the bad luck of the contractor stuck with a litigious customer?

Another set of observations presented here comprises yet a different classification of trust violations. The persons involved are rarely accused of criminal deception or of being criminal. No political coloring is involved in their cases. An intentional failure in contractual obligations is not implied. Most often there is not even awareness on the part of the one deceived that Mr. X is his betrayer. Who are the cases? Police informants. These may play their part by virtue of being the confidants of criminals, in which case the nicer word used to describe them in our American culture which claims (usually inconsistently at best and sometimes hypocritically) to abhor tattling is "double dealer." Other words are fink, rat, stoolie, informer, snitch and squealer. An informer, it will be shown, may not be acting perfidiously to mine confessions of secret things; he may simply observe or overhear enough to convince him that the police should hear what he has seen or heard. If he reports it, he is an upright citizen doing his civic duty. If he remains in a privileged place so as to continue to observe such goings-on, as barkeeps, cab drivers, prostitutes or wives of racketeers may do, and should he or she become a regular and reliable information source, then one has an informant in the law-enforcement sense of the word, or an agent-in-place as the intelligence community would call him. Does such a person deceive? There will be argument about it, less so if it can be shown that the informant seeks such privy places so as to exploit them, more so if the informant himself is exploited by those upon whom he informs or by those to whom he gives the information. It will be seen that the informant is rarely a simple "rat." Rather his act of betrayal, if it is decided to call it that, is also (as with the other trust violators in this study) the result of a sequence of events and a play of forces which may call into question the degree of choice or responsibility which an informant can exercise as he is propelled into his sometimes desperate position.

⁓We also asked a sample of the quarry of informants what they thought their nemesis to be moved by and to be like. The quarry—a group of drug dealers—offered accurate if unextraordinary descriptions of the snitches they knew or thought they knew. What was extraordinary was what we took to be their blind spots, in contrast to the insights as to motives and relationships between victim (quarry) and fink as recounted both by the police handling snitches and the snitches themselves. These discrepancies led us to speculate on hidden complexities underlying some (trust violations,) our thesis being that betrayal is engendered in situations where the victim insists on being unrealistic about a relationship, failing to comprehend enmity for himself and affection for his enemies on the part of someone close, and that one becoming the betrayer. The thesis also proposes that the betrayal itself can be a means whereby the angry weak instruct the strong in their hostility and, in doing so, reorder the relationship among the lives of all concerned.

The question of responsibility, indeed of awareness, can be raised for other conduct which may also be considered a violation of trust. To pursue it, we sought to identify two rather different groups; first, the "inside men" used by more sophisticated safecrackers and burglars to provide intelligence for their "stings," and second, missing persons. We found some inside men, too few, though, to justify a full chapter here but sufficient to remind us of the complexities of our subject. "Inside men" are often simply unwitting(employees adroitly pumped for information—) by Don Juan behavior by the burglar to dazzle a payroll secretary, companions at the next barstool, or other seemingly casual conversationalists.) The aware kind exist, of course, such as the disloyal employee paid for his help, a criminal cohort documented so as to be hired by a jewelry store as sales help or, cleverly, the silent long-time partner who does the filing of safe and payroll data for the insurance company covering the store.

But the ones who most likely shake preset judgments about whose trust is being violated are those inside men who are also the owners of the store; they themselves hired the burglar.

As for missing persons, we mention our venture but shall not report it further. We cannot say whether or not missing persons have violated trust because we could not find them! Why not? Not because they were missing but because they had returned. We took records of every missing person reported in a major city for one year—2,631 of them. Within half a year, only eleven were still gone. Of these, there were only four adults, three of them believed dead and the fourth a chap who left his wife meanly but not mysteriously. Review of the cases of returning prodigals showed that most adults had left a mate (heterosexual or homosexual, married or otherwise) after fighting. Most juveniles were truants, eloping, going off with a divorced parent, or seeking the high life. Whether or not trust had been violated, no one could be sure. For many, there had been no binding compact perceived, and consequently, responsibility and awareness for anything as profound as betrayal remained in doubt.

Clearly, the study of violations of trust is made difficult by the problems of case definition and of case finding. It is made difficult by the complexity of the psychodynamic, interpersonal, institutional, economic and political levels involved. It is also made difficult, but very pertinently, by the inevitable intrusion of moral and ideological matters. Case-finding rests at a primary level upon the moral stance of the participants. At the secondary, or removed, scientific level, it still rests upon a moral stance. We propose that violations of trust are mostly moral matters and more intensely these, than they are problems of law, of politics or of social science. These latter are but external forms classifying what happens between people. The real process of trust violation, its raw material, is deception between people.

Betrayal, once that word is invoked by some party to the process, is the emotional characterization attendant upon discovery that a relationship has not been what it ought, morally, to be. The charge of betrayal then, of being "had," is an exclamation of moral outrage which comes first among humans. Only later does one come to actions at law, political speculation or the beginning of scientific inquiry. The point needs stressing; there will be no understanding of trust violation which ignores its moral-emotional dimension and the primacy of that in defining those events which are considered as trust violations.

As to determining forces (the roots and antecedents of trust violation), we shall see that these are a mix of the history and circumstance of the person, his groups, his situation, the politics of his times, the relationship between victim and deceiver, the psychodynamics of them both and, in addition, the morality and the predilections of the observer. The latter is noted because we shall demonstrate a relationship between being a deceiver and being deceived and between these correlated experiences and sensitivity to corruption and deception in others. One sees many parallels in this mix of antecedents and correlates with findings from other research on lives, on crisis behavior, on person appraisal, on psychopathology, on criminal careers and the like. We conclude initially that trust violations are the same order of conduct as other complicated human interactions and endeavors. We also call attention to the possibility that part of the communality of explanation—that ubiquitous social science assertion of multideterminism and multiple levels of correlates and functions—may rest not within the events observed but with our means and fashions for accounting for human conduct. The limitations of criminology in particular and the social/behavior sciences in general are such that investigators and clinicians use much the same tools and concepts in looking at and talking about one form of social conduct as another.

As there is no single cause for trust violation, there is no uniform phenomenon which is trust violation. Deception is the practice of falsehood on another, a process between people we propose, but it has many guises. Betrayal is the reaction to a discovery of a relationship where moral/emotional expectations have been disappointed, but the characterization embraces varied enterprises. Indeed, both definitions are pale enough to bespeak the complexity of events when trust is given (perhaps) and trust is abused (perhaps). At best, the events judged to be trust violation have in common the judgment by someone that someone else should not have acted, given the confidences involved, as he did. A rule has been broken, a wrong has occurred, even though the rule may never have been written or even discussed. Nevertheless, the person wronged assumes that both parties have subscribed to the rule and that it was a fundamental one for continuing human intercourse. The essence of that "rule" would appear to be that persons who enter into socially defined relationships with one another (or with plural "others," as in organizations or nation-states) which require for their function and continuation the giving and receiving of confidences, engage not to reveal or exploit their knowledge, position or advantages to bring harm to the other. The giver of confidence is vulnerable because the deceiver appears to have accepted the usually unstated obligation to protect the self-interest of the other. The reaction on the part of the one betrayed is outrage or sorrow. That reaction seems predicated at the very least on the feeling that harm should not come from an unanticipated source pledged personally or obligated by custom to do no harm and to get no self-gain from the vulnerability arising from the granting of trust. If harm is to come not only from outsiders or identified competitors, predators and the like but also from those in whom one engages in special trusting relationships, relationships where most of the emotional business of life is transacted, then is not the core of one's life jeopardized? Trust is given to those one is close to, those one needs something from, those on whom one depends—the co-workers in living; if they violate trust, have they not torn out the heart of one's hopes and satisfactions? Ironically it must be in these needful and exposed circumstances that any betrayal arises, simply because by definition and opportunity it is within the family, between lovers, or within the combat group, the business partnership or the intelligence unit that one person can exploit the confidence of another to his own ends. There is, further, the likelihood that a person's vanity as well as his confidence in himself and his social universe can be traumatically shocked by trust badly placed; that is, but not realizing that one is or is about to be "had." We can understand how such an event could undermine one's self-trust at being able to judge others, to read the signs of loyalty or love or to defend oneself from the expected beasts in the jungle of human affairs. Such a failure to estimate accurately the intentions and capabilities of others vis-à-vis oneself can well be a fundamental threat to anyone's sense of security as well as to that core of vanity which, inside us, would have us believe that all others ought to love and serve us. If such failures are repeated, that is, if a person is repeatedly deceived—and we shall see that some victims are repeaters just as violators can be chronic ones—must not the victim also begin to hear an inner voice which tells him of his own culpability? May there not be some compulsion to enter into relationships based on fantasy, magical thinking or exploitative lying? Perhaps, after all, naiveté is a commitment to the irrational. In any event, recognition that one's plight is one's own doing is not likely to lessen the intensity with which others are blamed for what has transpired.

It will be seen, as one compares our working conceptions of trust violation with the popular definitions which came out of our study of the experience of ordinary folk with deception (see Chapter XII), that our definition is the more elaborate but does not contradict popular themes and does contain the elements present in most folk definitions. Our definition, like our methods, will be useful at best for a brief span of time and ought soon to be replaced by better. This book will serve its ends if only it stimulates others to consider the problems of trust violation and out of that to develop further means for a better understanding of one domain of human conduct.

Chapter II

CONFIDENCE MEN: A BRIEF INTRODUCTION

THE CONFIDENCE MAN is no stranger to mankind, and so it is that history as well as fiction, biography, police annals and, much more recently, criminology and its social, scientific or medical contributors, is filled with examples. Was not Hermes himself a charming trickster, our earliest example and god to thieves? The confidence man's essence, whether illustrated in the biography of Kreuger, the match king; *The Yellow Kid Weil*, Herman Melville's complex novel; or as observed by Maurer or other scholars, is theft by guile in a person-to-person relationship. A first cousin to the confidence man, indeed usually the con man himself wearing another face, is the salesman perpetrating fraud upon the consumer. The difference is that the latter is, as is to be expected in these days of mass media, mass organizations and mass sales, impersonal in approach. It is also the case that whereas the confidence man usually provides no material objects in exchange for his victim's money, the consumer's exploiter may deliver a product, albeit not the one desired.

We shall not burden the reader with a review of the literature on confidence men and their operations, although we do cite the following works for those seeking further references: Aydelotte, 1968; Barbash, 1952; Brannan, 1948; Bromberg, 1941; Bromberg and Keiser, 1938; Brunswick, 1943; Campion, 1957; Gibney, 1960; Janney, 1942; Jenkens, 1954; Karpman, 1949; MacDonald, 1939; Maurer, 1940; Norfleet, 1924; Podalsky, 1957; Roebuck and Johnson, 1964; Scarne, 1961; Schmideberg, 1958; Schur, 1948; Shaplen, 1960; and Wile, 1942. Among these, there are only a few which count as objective studies, Maurer's being the classic, and their findings are limited to some extent by the prevalence of lower-class offenders as the popuation studied. The biographies of Kreuger and the Yellow Kid are exceptions. A common thread in all of the observations is that profit-making is but one of the motives to be inferred in the confidence man. Confidence men also are busy acting out their fantasied desires to be (more accurately to *appear* to others to be) persons of importance. They are also enjoying the development and exercise of power over their victims, repetitively "proving" their cleverness and superiority. A further recurring feature is that of the "big spender," for whom money is important only insofar as one demonstrates one's worth in its spending and, not incidentally, shows oneself to be a "swinger," that is a generous, risk-taking, pleasure-loving, free-and-easy sort of chap. Also central to the confidence man as portrayed in biographies and studies is his chronic violation of a wide range of criminal laws, almost all of them property crimes (ranging from pickpocketing to income tax evasion), and his disregard for ordinary interpersonal conventions. Psychologists would speak of a general socialization failure; that is, confidence men do not grow up with a proper conscience. Instead, they learn a set of skills which allow them to prey on their fellow men, not to live with them under the set of rules which requires honest work and respect for others as basic ingredients for life in the community.

The descriptions of their inner life, that is of the psychodynamic components of their personalities, are necessarily more tentative. There is general agreement that as confidence men can be seen to differ from respectable citizens on the surface by being less honest and more disdainful of their fellow men, so there are psychological features which either account for or are accompaniments to that visible deviation. Most psychiatrists and psychologists who have studied them emphasize the presence of psychopathology, either in the form of neuroses or character disorders. The agreement among diagnosticians ceases there. Some call attention to psychosexual conflicts and their expression through the seduction of victims, which becomes a way of mastering the inner inability of the confidence man to enjoy normal loving relationships with others. Some diagnosticians note the prevalence of depression, of self-destructive behavior, or poor reality contact as evidenced by grandiose fantasies, i.e. the con man comes to believe he really is as important as he tells others he is. The importance of lying is to be stressed; the Roebuck and Johnson (1964) study is richly illustrative of the use of lies by cons when they were children. The evidence is for lies being learned as a psychological defense against the sexual indiscretions of parents or of heavy involvement of the (male) children in Oedipal-complex situations with their mothers. Implicit here is that deception as an adult way of life has beginnings in early neuroses. The use of the lie as a technique for sharing fantasies, for it is a sharing between con man and his victim, may reflect an earlier sharing of lies between the child and his parents. It is also possible that the impersonation which is so much a part of con man activities is an outgrowth, a repetition, of a much earlier childhood fantasy in which the con man as a child imagined himself to be in a position of power and sexual supremacy vis-à-vis his father and mother. If so, the narcissism, the inability to tolerate frustration, the distortions of reality, the inability to be emotionally close to others, and the other adult defects observed must be presumed to be the result of very early failures in psychological development. If that is the case, we would expect the confidence men whom we set out to study also to show pervasive personality disorder. We shall see that such is indeed the case.

It is well not to overlook how "normal" it is to be a confidence man or swindler. In our society, salesmanship is valued, commerce is based on the ability of people to persuade others whom they do not know that their products are worthy. The promise of gain is central to our—and to most—societies. It is not in itself abnormal to offer to others "opportunities" which will make them richer, handsomer, happier, more successful and the like. It is also not extraordinary to lie, nor to misrepresent and to deceive in ordinary business. Viewed in this light, what the confidence man does is simply an extreme expression of normal business dealings. In this sense and in his rejection of violence, his pursuit of status, his reliance on team work, the practice of a skilled trade and aggressively competitive behavior (granted it is against his clients rather than other con men), the swindler embraces the values of the larger society. His need to appear honest or to assuage guilty feelings is also to be inferred, for he rationalizes his dishonesty by claiming that the swindle is the fault of the victim because it is the victim's greed which is to blame for his succumbing to the blandishments of the con game. Both victim and con man are thus the same, he claims, and there is no innocent man to stand in contrast to the guilty. Some of those who have described swindles accept the con man's justification, agreeing that victims are larcenous and are cheated only because they are so busy cheating. Others disagree and call attention to the innocent victim who is perfectly honest in seeking a bargain or in taking advantage of an opportunity for a clever but not evidently dishonest gain.

As far as special techniques for the identification and successful persuasion of victims, there is no evidence in the literature which suggests that con men have any special sensitivity or gifts of insight into the minds of others. The assumption of the con man to the effect that everyone is larcenous and that anyone who is not a con must therefore be a mark (victim) certainly provides them with enough potential victims—nearly the whole of society. The con man's own assurance, freedom from remorse or conventional morality, lack of affection or empathy for others, enjoyment of acting and theater, skilled salesmanship, and time-tested effectiveness of the various con game scams (scenarios, plots) are all assets in operations. When there is added to these a systematized approach, as for example the use of mass advertisements, the preparation of the marks with props, shills and impersonation, the employment of criminal specialists as prospect-hunters and ropers (aides), it is not surprising that marks are indeed found and do provide a living for whatever number of confidence men this society supports.

As for victims, the literature provides us no clues except Norfleet (1924), who was a remarkable one-time victim who spent his life in pursuit of his original exploiters. Norfleet described himself as by no means motivated by greed or willing to be dishonest, just a trusting Texas rancher doing what any American would do to capitalize on a money-making opportunity which appeared to be falling into his lap. His own part was not crooked, although Norfleet did engage in small conspiracies (using his name to bet the stock exchange "president's" interests as required by the scam and thus implicating himself in what appeared dishonest—although unknown to Norfleet *qua* victim, no bet was ever made). Insofar as Norfleet was a typical victim, he was certainly no example of the "every man a crook" philosophy argued by swindlers; to the contrary, he counted himself more honest than many of the official protectors of the criminal law; he singled out politicians and police involved in corruption and the "fix" as illustrations of what he had in mind. What is clear about victims is that for the con game to work at all, the victim must be willing to strike up acquaintances with new people, to develop trust in others and to be ready to invest money and emotion in an acquaintance's project. The victim must also be ready—in the case of con games rather than consumer fraud or swindles—to accept the conditions of the investment opportunity, namely to enter into a conspiracy against another person, to agree to secrecy, and to be willing to live with confusion without demanding clarity (for the more complicated con games, called long cons, have as their hallmark confusing activity with a fast presentation of characters, ready but inadequate explanations and a continuing switch of topics and characters).

For many victims, a sensitivity to embarrassment is also present, for the failure to complain, which forestalls calling in the police, can only be described as an unwillingness to stand out as a dupe. That failure to complain once the thief has gone may imply more than embarrassment, for in some cases, even after the ball is over, the victim may admire and even protect the man who has cheated him. Campion and others give examples of victims refusing to believe ill of their swindler, no matter how great the evidence. We must call this a delusion. As Campion (1957) says, it is not the story alone which the victim buys but its telling as well. It is the relationship to the con man which, in the long con, provides the substance. In the quick operation, called the short con, that is not the case. The Yellow Kid (1948) emphasizes the importance of the con man to the victim when he speaks of seduction and romance, of an invitation to mystery and of the con man as the weaver of spells who provides the victim with an opportunity to live out his fantasies. In the long con, which requires an intense relationship between con man and victim over time, the con man must be more than a business opportunity in the eyes of his mark. He is more than a story-teller too, for he is a magician who guides the victim into a world of pleasant dreams. Those dreams are not solely of the future, the bait of money or joy at some later time but are in the present, for it is in the present moment that there occurs the hope, the excitement, the dispelled loneliness and the sense of importance in association with prestigeful men (the con man wearing his mask), which constitute the early returns on the victim's investment in the con man. There is another ingredient as well, and this is deference at the social level. The victim does not challenge the genuinity of the con man. "Give me your trust," demanded Melville's (1954) confidence man, and his victims responded as required. It can also be termed subordination or dependency; these are implied in the "mesmerism" of which Norfleet spoke. Contemporary research on hypnotism suggests that an essential ingredient in hypnotism is the willingness of the subject to subordinate himself to the hypnotized. There is, one would expect, a readiness among victims to subordinate their trust to the con man.

We have, in setting forth these characteristics of con man and victim, gone beyond what others have found or claimed. We have deduced, we have speculated and we have sought to introduce our own findings. These are presented in much more detail in the following two chapters.

Chapter III

CONFIDENCE MEN AND THEIR OPERATIONS

I get out of bed in the morning and I put up my antenna to listen to what the day will say to me. Maybe it tells me a good day is coming and so I thank Jesus Christ for that, I thank Him for another day to scheme and beat the tricks.

They say crime doesn't pay, but I believe it does.

(Remarks during our interviews.)

METHOD OF ANALYSIS

In THIS CHAPTER we will present our observations on confidence men with respect to their methods, points of view, interests and certain features of personality. Our first task was to find a sample of confidence men. Earlier we had drawn a sample for records' analysis from inmates identifiable as confidence men in the California Department of Corrections files. It became clear from that analysis that a prison sample would not suffice, since few confidence men were identifiable from prison records, few were in prison and those who were identified and still incarcerated were spread widely over the state. Another reason for not relying on jail or prison populations was the inability to observe the con man at work in his natural habitat. Furthermore, in prison there is not much opportunity to safeguard oneself against lies, whereas on the outside, what a man says can at least be checked against what he does, and he can also be checked for consistency over time. Consequently, our endeavor was to obtain a sample of confidence men working on the outside; that is, living their natural lives.

To obtain the sample, we worked with the Fraud Detail of a major city police department. Through their contacts, working con men were identified. In some cases, identification was made while the man was in jail; interview and observations were delayed until his release. A number of cases were identified

18

through other police departments in the area, although only one of these was included in our sample. In two cases, confidence men were found to be in nearby prisons, and in both cases, because of the institution's (reputation for excellence,) the men were interviewed there in spite of our preference for free-setting contact. In one of those two cases, the inmate did not cooperate, so that no information of value was obtained.

Each con man was identified as such on the basis of (a) his rap sheet, (b) the judgment of the two fraud detail inspectors who worked as research assistants on the project and (c) his own description of himself as a con man. In some cases, he was also identified by his colleagues—other confidence men—as a professional criminal and con man.* In only one case did a con man deny his "profession" during our interview; he was an internationally known professional whose rap sheet extended back to 1913. His "colleagues" and his own family agreed that he was a con man. He was 89 years old when we interviewed him in the hospital where it was feared he was dying. In this special case, there was no opportunity for behavior observations nor for that kind of informal interview which usually led to frankness. It was also quite possible that an 89-year-old thief who thought he was dying (he did not or has not yet) wished to present himself in as angelic a way as possible. It is quite likely that he was rehearsing on us the story he was preparing to lay on St. Peter.

Thirty-four confidence men and one con woman were identified and approached by us during the study; an additional four, well-known to the senior investigator from prior contacts, were subject to intensive case reviews as we developed the interview schedule. Eight of the bunco artists were gypsies who were

---

* An important feature to be noted in the definition of the confidence man is that this role does not exclude either being expert in other forms of criminal expertise, nor does it exclude a legitimate occupation. Although most of the cons in our sample supported themselves primarily through fraud, one had "retired" and was working as a businessman (with occasional "fencing") and another was working as a legitimate salesman while he awaited trial on a marriage bunco charge. Most of the cons in our sample had held some kind of legitimate employment at one time in their lives, and conversely, all had engaged in other criminality aside from fraud.

observed and interviewed but who refused to cooperate by being frank with us. Eleven of the remaining group were considered to be, after initial observation, unrewarding for intensive study; two of these were pitchmen operating a gift-box lottery "scam" (confidence game) from a "store" (fixed location complete with props), one was a card shark and gambling con, eight were "block hustlers" (sellers of fake jewelry, fake perfume, phony "hot" items, etc.). One pigeon dropper refused to cooperate. The remaining fourteen comprised an intensive sample who were interviewed, who were cooperative and who were competent thieves, experienced in a variety of con games.

Interviews were conducted by the senior investigator, by the two fraud-detail research assistants or by all three; and in one case the interview was conducted by a police sergeant. A guided interview schedule was employed; interviews ranged from two to twenty hours (spread over many weeks) in length. The intensive sample was also examined in terms of background data (rap sheets and supplemental fraud detail records) and for those out of jail, observations. When conducted by the fraud inspectors, these were routine procedures. When done by the senior investigator, they involved being with the con man while he selected and approached a victim and laid on the story. When it was apparent that the story was being accepted by the victim, contact was broken off and suitable excuses made. An additional and critically important set of observations were made in the case of those con men working with the senior investigator, for in each case, the con man laid a story on the investigator and attempted to victimize him. Another unusual set of observations was made possible by a two-man team of con men who, over a period of time, would rehearse their stories in the presence of the investigator. Observations were also made on non-sample professional criminals while accompanying members of the bunco gypsy and pickpocket squads during their ordinary work rounds.

Twelve men and one woman took psychological tests. In several cases, the test results were invalid and could not be incorporated in our analysis. Tests given were the Minnesota Multiphasic Inventory (MMPI) and the Strong Vocational Interest Blank (Strong Test).

We had hoped to provide two control samples to compare with our con men. One group were to have been legitimate promoters who were much like confidence men in that they were (a) primarily salesmen or new business organizers, (b) without any permanent business or organizational affiliation of their own, (c) opportunists in the sense they took business opportunities where they found them and (d) relied on themselves, their wits, for success. The legitimate promoters, by our definition, differ from con men in that they were not known to violate criminal laws and in their operations did not intend to defraud. Our second proposed sample was to consist of "shady promoters" who were like the legitimate ones except that they intended to defraud and who, on the basis of past investigations by regulatory commissions, grand juries and the like, had been accused of violating codes and statutes.

After conducting interviews with legitimate promoters and with "shady" ones, it became apparent that we could not proceed further. The first difficulty was that it was difficult to differentiate "promoters" from other businessmen or salesmen, especially those with a history of varied enterprises. We could not easily locate a group whose promoting careers marked them as more like confidence men. Our second problem, made evident after the interviews, was that "legitimacy" itself was awkward to define. Promoters selected because they were legitimate (without known charges against them, well-reputed) sometimes told us of their criminal activities which were "white-collar" or "normal" crimes, such as income tax evasion, violation of regulatory practices and misrepresentation in advertising. On the other hand, several shady promoters denied wrongdoing of any sort and presented themselves as simply "sharp" businessmen. The degree of frankness obviously depended, at least in part, on the relationship of the interviewer, who was known to be identified with law enforcement. Confident friends and optimists spoke frankly; strangers did not. After these initial interviews, it was clear that the promoters we had found were, with one exception, well-educated, middle- or upper-class men who had not grown up in a delinquent setting (a criminal subculture) and who conceived of themselves as part of the normal "straight" community, regardless of their actual criminality. Our con men, on the other hand, were more often lower class, less well educated and black. Many were reared in delinquent environments and most perceived themselves as criminals (regardless of the fact that much of *their* behavior was normal and/or honest). Given these observations, it was likely that data on personality or on "sales" technique would be heavily contaminated by class, educational and self-identification factors, so that controls selected without careful matching would be valueless. We could not afford the latter.

CHARACTERISTICS OF CONFIDENCE MEN

Background

Among the 35 sample members, 27 were men and 8 were women. Seven of the women were Gypsies (Romany-speaking). Among the 27 non-Gypsies, there were 12 blacks; 1 half-black, half-Chinese; and 14 whites. (Among our smaller intensive sample, 8 out of 14 were black.) The age range was from 20 to 89, and most were in their thirties and forties. The block hustlers were a younger group, most in their twenties, as would be expected of those practicing a simple form of the bunco art before more complex skills and versatility are learned. No assumptions can be made about the distribution of sex, race and age among the total population of confidence men at large, for there is no known way to draw a representative sample.

Among those responding to the guided interview schedule, the education range reported was from grade school to college degree. Half of the group had some college education. Several had fathers in managerial-professional jobs; the remainder had fathers who had held white-collar clerical jobs, blue-collar laboring jobs or who were unskilled or in unemployed categories.

The confidence men themselves had held a variety of legitimate or straight jobs, although only two were legitimately employed at the time of interview. Both of these were simultaneously engaged in illicit occupations to a lesser extent. Sales jobs were most often reported, as 10 men had held such positions. No other single occupation had been engaged in by more than one reporting sample member; other jobs listed included banker, doorman, domestic, bartender, recreation leader, clerk, hotel manager, and stagehand. Three intensive sample members (3 of 12) said they had *never* held a straight job; only 4 had held more than 4 different straight jobs. Only 1 sample member had held the same legitimate job for more than a year.

Experience

Most had worked a variety of games,* although each preferred one or two as his favorites. The most often mentioned scams were short cons, the majority having worked Miss Murphy (also called Paddy Hustle, Write-Up, Carpet, etc.), half saying they used the Jamaican switch, the block hustle, the pigeon drop or another lost-and-found variant. Several (3 of 14) reporting engaged in card swindles. A number of other short cons were reported. About half of the sample had worked long cons, including the "payoff" (racetrack scam), marriage bunco, dragon's blood or voodoo scams, oil stock and/or mining swindles, counterfeit money scams and a variety of consumer frauds, some of which were complex financial swindles. The block hustlers reported an average "take" of 100 dollars a day, with a possible daily range from zero on a bad day to 300 to 400 dollars. Long cons netted more. The higher "scores" reported for these were in the 100,000 to 150,000 dollar range, which were, for several of the cons, once-in-a-lifetime events. One sample member, our most famous confidence man, had netted a score of 2,500,000 dollars—a figure verified by his rap sheet. This man had consistently scored in the 100,000 dollar range, although at the time of our interview, when he was 89, he appeared to be a poor man.

Preliminary Techniques

Locales for Operation

Locales for operation vary directly with the type of scam worked. Naturally, the place where the victim is found determines what bunco can be employed. Among the con men discussing their preferences, it was clear that all went where the people were; that is, they sought out victims in places where

---

* See Appendix for typical examples of games.

people congregate. They mentioned the following good locations: downtown streets near the larger stores (the preferred class of the victim determines whether "high-class" or "low-class" stores will be sites), in front of banks, grocery stores during leisurely shopping hours, bars in the evening, stock exchanges, hotel lobbies, airports, bus depots, race tracks, go-go and night-life entertainment spots, pool halls, expensive restaurants, tourist attractions and civic center parks and buildings.

Preferences in Victims

A con man's preference in victims varies widely, depending upon the social class, sex and race of the victim, all of which shape the reaction of victims to the confidence man. Preferences also vary with the game to be played and with the personal predilections of the bunco artist. Long cons require wealthier victims than short cons do. Members of the following groups were mentioned by our sample as being among their preferred victims: older men or senior citizens, well-dressed men who were drinking or are drunk, soldiers on travel orders and those returning from overseas, travelling salesmen or convention-goers, travelling pro athletes, Chinese, lower-class young men, Negroes, business and professional men, middle-aged men, lonely women and members of religious orders.

Finding, Selecting, Approaching and Qualifying Victims

Finding, selecting, approaching and qualifying victims are the steps which take the con from locating where an individual or a group of potential victims are to be found to confirming that the person will go for the game. Finding a victim may mean nothing more complicated than approaching every person on the street who fits a stereotype (as in block hustling) or it may require careful selection and long planning (as in banking schemes, playboy blackmail, etc.). Each locating method is geared to the scam itself. For short cons, an approach on the streets, in bars, parks, etc., to anyone who is a preferred target is routine. For consumer frauds, the use of mail-advertising lists, of telephones in boiler rooms (centers where many phones are manned by persons using a "canned" approach), of door-to-door salesmen or of "come-on" ads in papers or handbill flyers is employed. For specialty work, the con man concentrates on victims with appropriate interests, wealth, membership and sometimes with special personal characteristics. For example, one con specialized in defrauding nunneries; he used Catholic directories to find names, addresses and phone numbers. Another specialized in marriage bunco; he sought women at concerts, in fine restaurants and hotels, in expensive resorts, on shipboard, etc. Another specialized in high finance and worked the stock exchange, banks and financial district. Those working the Paddy Hustle frequent places where men go hoping to pick up prostitutes. In long cons, sample members described the use of a variety of ropers or steerers to identify victims, to begin the acquaintance and to prepare victims for "cleaning and dusting."

"Qualifying" victims is an important feature in any scam. It is the act of determining whether or not the person contacted is desirable as a victim and whether or not he is likely to respond to further overtures. In the short con, a mark is qualified if he (a) responds to the confidence man's overtures and begins conversation, (b) expresses interest in what the con man is selling and (c) indicates that he has money. Some more sophisticated con men also include a "control" test in their assessment; this will be discussed in detail later. In essence, it requires the victim to respond to an apparently irrelevant suggestion by the con man, so that the con man concludes that he can control the victim. Put another way, it is a test of suggestibility, deference or cooperativeness. Qualifying may also include the determination that the victim does indeed possess added features of importance, for example that he is a stranger in town with no local connections, that he knows no important people in town or that he is not a policeman (all designed to rule out unpleasant beefs).

Various qualifying tests are employed. Answers to direct questions are the most common. Requiring the mark to "flash," that is to show his wallet and his identification, is another successful device. Requiring the mark to appear for an appointment is another, as is directing the mark to some special location. Some use direct physical contact, as when a gypsy rubs a mans' genitals to evoke sexual excitement or when a "dragon's blood" salesman (a voodoo scam) rubs the forehead of the victim to induce a near-hypnotic trance. One common test is to regale the victim with a "success story," which is to hold the lure in front of him (promising wealth, telling of past success, speaking to third parties of fabulous deals, etc.) and to learn if the victim responds with interest and a request to be included. These latter devices are more likely to be employd in long rather than short cons.

For the short cons, qualifying takes, so our respondents said (confirmed by observation), no more than five minutes. "Middle cons" as some called them (a phrase not seen in the literature) might take several hours—this refers to the Jamaican switch and bank swindles. Long cons can take weeks or months to set up and may, in the cooling phase, go on for several years.

Illustrative Comments*

When a con is in tune with the world, there's something electric about it. He senses who he can beat. Any sale, for example, is just like getting laid. You don't choose something hopeless, you don't overstep your place—a guy with hobnailed boots doesn't chase ermine. Dress is a strong signal for "sight qualifying" or the quick qualify. It's a big world and there are lots of prospects. You don't take everything that comes along. You can afford to burn them off, since there'll always be plenty.

Go to a mediocre place and meet mediocre people. Travel first class and you go where the money is. Go where the people are and especially go where there are those who are looking for someone like me. Go where there are women who are bored and looking for excitement. Go where people are who are looking to find others with money, others who can give them pleasure and excitement. Don't be shy. Approach people easily and pleasantly. To rule people, you must not fear them. If you want them to do what you want, you must not show fear or weakness. In the animal kingdom, the weak get eaten. The moment you show any weakness, you are done.

The best qualifier is for the con man to be as near like the victim as possible. The same dress, the same speech, the same class—and the more alike in interests, the quicker the rapport. The qualifying comes naturally because the con man knows his victim already. Of course what you're qualifying him for matters a lot. It's got to be

---

* In these and other comments, we have tried to render exact quotes, but that has not always been possible because of interview and observation circumstances. The comments are thus, in some cases, approximations rather than exact.

something the guy wants or needs, like money, and he has to have responded to your first control efforts too. Of course it's more than that, too; there's got to be that intimacy—even if you have to bully or badger him into it.

The fact that I'm colored means I can never approach a young white woman on any scam—she'll think I want to rape her. Any colored or white men, or old women, are different. Of course a lot of cons work in a salt and pepper team (white and black) and that way the racial thing doesn't get in the way, fact is you can use race with a salt and pepper team.

(Marriage bunco). I find women who've been lied to. I like those who've been lied to and wronged many times. They don't believe the truth anymore. So if you lie they believe you.

In making a sale, look at them, look in their eyes. Be sure you know your subject. Speak frankly to them. If you're selling something, you can say, "even if you don't love your wife (and I assume most don't), you still have responsibility to your children"—appeal to their sense of duty. It takes guts to face them, use language at their level, adapt yourself to their situation. In the name of duty, help them do what they want. On a business deal or insurance, for example, they all want to beat the taxes.

One thing about this block hustling, half the people you hustle never learn they bought a block. Not unless they try to sell it or hock it they don't. But you've got to be careful with those burr-head hoods. Man, I don't sell them nothing. Never beat a bad guy is a rule. You do and they find out and they'll cut you up into little pieces. I don't even want to see those bad guys.

When you swap money, then you know he's really in. I'm always pulling the vic inconspicuously to see what way he'll go. I'm suspicious of a duke who's overeager, who plays along with anything. That duke may want to get me arrested.

It's not just who to sell, it's whom not to go near as well. I always look at hands and feet because the FBI and the cops wear class rings and black, plain-toe shoes.

I like to set up a mark. I like to work real estate men, contractors and others who do their business at other's houses. I call them up beforehand and make an appointment maybe a week ahead of time. I give them an address (a house where people are gone, a restaurant, etc.) and tell them I'm interested in buying whatever it is. Then I go there and hang around and when the guy shows up, I know who he is, I know he's out looking for money, and I know he's got time. After he's waited a while and is good and impatient, he's seen me pacing back and forth as though I'm waiting for someone too, he may come up to me—or me to him—and I end up asking if he's been stood up too. From there, it's routine—the Jamaican switch, the "bum," the "lemon" is real good (counterfeit money scam), whatever.

✗   Well, in finding a mark, you go where the kind of people already are who are ready to play the game. I work first-class commercial hotels a lot. It's no trouble striking up a conversation, everyone in such a hotel does that; I start with some safe but interesting common topic. You know, not a greeting, refer down to the sports page he's reading and ask, "Did you go to the ball game yesterday?" That gets you started. You can ask where he's from, how long he's been in town, whether he likes the town, what his work is, who he knows in town, things like that. Then I tell him about me, and I'm careful to choose a business as different as possible from his and a town that's a good ways away from his. I also want to find out about his experience, so if he's from a town where I know any of the rackets, I'll drop a few names of people or places to see if he responds. Then I'll test him for being con-wise and see whether he's been steered before; for example I'll say, "I had the strangest experience the other day, this fellow came up to me and asked if I were interested in racing . . ." I watch him to see how he reacts—if that sets him off on something that tells me if he's been steered or how he's gone when he's been conned before. If there's nothing there—neither interest or experience—I veer off, but I've learned what I need to know.

✱   It's not hard to get the dollar figures. Once you've been told what business he's in, you say, "Oh, yes, my son-in-law plans on going into that business once he's out of college. He's asked me for advice but I don't know anything about it. I'm real glad to meet you, since you know those things. For example, How much investment will my son-in-law have to make? What are the continuing expenses? How much can he expect to have put away after twenty years?—or how long the mark you're talking to has been at it—What are the profit margins?" etc. You then ask him about investments, say the son-in-law's learning about them at school but as an ignorant man you know nothing about it. Ask the mark what a fellow can expect to make investing, ask him if he doesn't think it's dangerous, that people will steal it, tell him you've been afraid yourself to invest. See how he responds, for that will tell you not only what he invests in and how much money he's made, it will tell you what kind of risks he's willing to take and what he's afraid of. You'll shape your game on that.

No one objects to direct, sensible questions if you don't mention the topic again. But you nibble at him (with inquiries) and he'll get suspicious. If he won't answer your questions, if he won't tell you about his money, he's not your egg. And not everyone's an egg. Some could be but it takes too long.

In your early contact with your egg, never let him walk away from you. Keep the initiative. You walk away from him. It shows him you're not after anything he's got. And when you're talking business, remember you've always got more than he has. If he owns ten acres of land, you own one hundred.

Take you (to interviewer), for example. I've sized you up by now. I'd clip you on gambling, girls and a shakedown where you'd pay off to avoid trouble with the police. The way I sum you up, you're used to getting tangled with females but you're not a big enough thief to go against a big gambling deal. If I get you in a compromising position, you'll bite in order to protect yourself. It would be easy. You like to make friends. You'd take a few drinks. You'd go for a sympathy story. Then I'd set you up for someone else to introduce a girl to you. Then she'd tell you some hard-luck story and you'd go for it, and after she had you, then I'd have you on a shake.

Sometimes you can play that one big. I've set up a girl playing a phony lady role. It takes months of planning. You set her up to visit some fancy house, playing the role of a niece or friend of some friends of their's who are in Europe—so they can't check back to see if she's legit—which of course she's not. When she's set up in that millionaire's family, she's got credentials that no one would challenge. And you do all that because you know that your mark is a rich playboy who knows that family. So he comes around and he meets that girl and he thinks he's doing real well when he finally gets her in the sack. So she gets him for 69 while somebody else is snapping pictures behind the curtain. And if he won't go for 69 where we can photograph it, the next time she gets him in the sack she's given him a knock-out drop in his drink before they hop in. That time he stays put for as many fine photographs as you'll ever need. It's a simple shake when we sell him his pictures back. Of course once she's in, if there's no playboy, she can introduce us to the family and we can take them on some other game entirely.

Generally, whatever the game, if you're using a good steerer who knows his business, you never miss more than one out of ten. And in all these years—I'm 67 now—I've only had one beef. That's the art. It helps to work a town where you've got the fix, then the police give no service to complaints. But when I'm on the sneak (no fix) I only play out-of-towners because even if they beef, they can only come to the fraud detail once, whereas the home guard (locals) can keep coming and coming to insist on service.

"Testing for catch" (qualifying) is it. But you can't mind if you miss a vic, downtown you've got 100,000 to insist on service.

The natural thing is to let the mark show you what he wants and then you just go along. I mean if you go to the races, you know everybody there wants to gamble, everybody there wants to win on a horse, so you go along and tell them how you'll make them sure-fire winners. That's the basis of any racing scam.

I look for jewelry, a thick wallet, behavior of the happy-go-lucky kind, maybe someone a little drunk, especially well-dressed people. Of course I like the foreigners—you can tell them by oddity of dress. In any event, in my business you need to know quality.

⼂ Play a person according to his mood. If he's resistant, it doesn't mean you leave, it means you've got to prime him, play him along, build him up a little.

You've got to dress and act according to where you work, according to the class of victim you have in mind. For "slumming" (also called "bumming," a block hustle elaborated with phony credentials in which seller pretends to be on his way out of town and needs to sell a stolen item), I dress up like the night-life people and sell there.

⼂ There's one con for every man. I'll approach anyone and it will take me just fifteen minutes to learn his interests and his weaknesses. Any good con has to have a background in the field of the pitch. He's got to know names of people, products, methods, horses, whatever it is. Once you've decided on the pitch, you've got to know what you're talking about. But as for finding out about someone, all you have to do is ask him. Ask him direct, ask him right away, and ask him only once. Ask twice and he'll get suspicious. Ask the first time and he's pleased you're interested in him. Take you for instance (to interviewer), wouldn't you like to help people? Don't you want to expose con games? I know you want to help your country, wouldn't you like to do that and make a lot of money too? Wouldn't you be interested in buying some land if you're positive it's going up in value? There, see?

General Technique

The references cited in Chapter II contain comprehensive descriptions of confidence games. As one reads confidence game descriptions or observes scams in action, one sees that there is a relatively consistent set of interchangeable elements. For most of the simplest hustles, these rest on an interpersonal approach which is friendly and attracts the attention of the victim in such a way as to arouse his interest rather than any sense of threat. The approach is usually informal or accidental-appearing; in better-engineered games it provides for the victim to seek out the con. The initial contact phase is separate from the money-extracting phase. In simpler games, the separation is by the simple device of the "switch;" that is, the initial topic which brings the victim and bunco artist together is adroitly abandoned and a new topic substituted. The switch serves to allay suspicion, since the new topic is presented in such a way that the con himself is not seen as having introduced it. Ideally, the switch allows the victim to sell himself rather than to detect that he is being sold. In more complex games, the switch—as well as preparation and processing—is accomplished by the use of a chain of accomplices, so that the victim does not see an underlying sequence in the events transpiring. Although many games require that the victim ostensibly "team up" with one con, purportedly to beat an "innocent" third party (or to cheat a system, institution or the like), it need not be so. All games do require, at some point in time, that the victim put up money as an investment, a purchase price, for a blessing, to show good faith, as a loan, etc. In simpler games, another "switch" occurs at that time, this one physical, in which "funny" money is substituted for the victim's cash. In more complex games, the invested money disappears through what appeared to be normal channels (betting on a horse, buying stock, contributing to charity, etc.) Once the money is taken, then the final phase occurs, the goal of which is to assure that there will be no complaint. This "cooling" technique is built into many aspects of the entire sequence and is not simply an append-age after the "dusting"; during the final period, however, more attention may be paid to it. Throughout the game, again exclud-ing the hustle, the cons ordinarily rely on teamwork, opportunism and a fast line of chatter which confuses the victim, as well as keeping his attention and appealing to his fantasies and interests. Other methods which are necessary to prevent complaints include the insulation of the victim from contact with others during the fleecing period and the judicious use of appeals, threats, flattery and persuasion. Throughout, leadership or "control" is deemed important, even during the long waits ("dragging") in the big con. Keeping the initiative is a fundamental principle in all cons.

Accomplices

We inquired especially about the use of accomplices, for most scams, except short cons such as the block hustle or specialized long cons such as the marriage bunco, require two or more men (or women) working as a team. Some of our sample preferred to work as loners and limited themselves to the one-man procedures. Most worked with one or more operators. Ordinarily, these partnerships were casual and lasted for the length of the long con or possibly for the period that a con man was working one city (presuming he moved from city to city as many did).

Their requirements for accomplices varied with their personal and professional preferences. The features mentioned as most desired included first and foremost the ability to appear square or straight (and thus impress the victim as being another citizen just like himself in contrast to appearing "kinky" or crooked), the ability to be a good talker (meaning to persuade, put at ease, impress), the ability to shift roles easily (the dramatic ability to play whatever role was required in the game) and competence in knowing the game (including its variants, necessary sign language, sensitivity to shifts in play, capability of ad-libbing, etc.). Accomplice roles often required by our sample members vary with the task at hand and include roping and steering, qualifying, holding the "mish" (bankroll, derived from "Michigan bankroll"), cooling the victim and a variety of other tasks. (See Appendix A.)

Illustrative Remarks

"The instruments of darkness to win us to our harm ply us with small truths to betray us in deepest consequences." I think that's from *Hamlet;* he knew how to play the con (quote from one bunco artist). [The actual line is from *Macbeth* and reads, "And oftentimes, to win us to our harm, the instruments of darkness tell us truths, win us with honest trifles, to betray's in deepest consequence." (Act I, Sc. 3, line 123)]

✴ The important thing is never to let the mark catch you lying. That means that everything not only has to ring true but that everything you tell him comes true, that's during the play, everything but the big thing, the delivery. ⸨That's the way you build his confidence, you get him to trust you, since what you say turns out that way.⸩ And by the time you take him, you want him in such a position that his hand reveals him as a culprit or co-conspirator. An revelation must indict him in the eyes of his neighbors and society. That's how you frame the deal.

Sometimes you can work without accomplices—either if there's no one around or you're a loner or maybe to avoid a conspiracy charge. One way to do it (long con) is to use the marks themselves, turning each one into a link in the chain. You bring him into the deal so he thinks and he brings in someone else and he brings in another and they play each other under your guidance. He thinks he's in, but he's holding the sack, each one a patsy for the other. I've used that (in consumer fraud, pyramid scams, franchise scams) just by sticking to local people with local references. Each thinks he's going to do real well, but each one gets it right in the ass.

➢ ⸨You've got to "bait" your promises with something real.⸩ You've got to show him what he wants. That's why you dress well, know the big names, put on a show. You flash for him and let him see real money so that you represent what he's after. Nobody goes along with a loser, everybody follows the winner. You're his winner and he'll follow you all the way. Sometimes of course it's easy, as in "stuff" (the short con). You don't do much there, just show him a block or a mish, that's all. Or with a junkie you don't even have to do that, you can take the money from a hype just by promising to score for him. They get burned (swindled) every day just like that.

Some cons just work the numbers. They know that ten exposures (contacts) net you three appointments net you one sale. They just work the probabilities. Take encyclopedia salesmen. See any top man in that business and you're facing one of the greatest unlocked thieves in the world.

The methods are all the same, basically. I specialize in commercial games and don't usually do the out-and-out bilk, although I've sold a few fight contracts; you know, you go into a town with a kid and put him in a gym and sell his fight contract and blow town with the kid and set up again in the next town. But lots of legit

enterprises are founded on scams, the ————— Furnace is one
of them. But it's hard to find a Yellow Kid Weil these days or the
old Doc D. W. who gave Ponzo his ideas—in and out politicos, the
clergy and the gamblers. He'd size up the factions in each town,
make a different phony company to deal with each faction, and no
matter which bunch, he'd have the town sewn up. He's one of the
great ones; why, when he was 80 he pulled a big stock swindle.
He also worked the yo-yo's with Duncan and he introduced parking
meters by installing one side of the street free and then when that
side would draw the customers he'd charge merchants on the other
side double to put the meters in on their side—that was after he'd
tied up the franchise for that town of course. Hell, even at 85 they
don't dare turn him loose. That's high-class grifting.

When you work you've got to have all the props so that every
little thing looks right to the egg. The whole show is for him and
the pieces have to fit. You need props to lend credibility, to set the
stage. The people you work with, telegrams, stationery, the store,
you need all that. You need a printer, first of all, because he's got
to make your identification, from cards and passes to driver's license
and what all.

Any two con men from anywhere in the country can work
together, once they talk a little and get the lingo. The important
thing is to put something together that works. There are different
names for the same set-ups, and you can add or take off a little on
any of them, but a good team can intermix elements easily and
quickly, depending on how things are developing. You've also got
to have your eye on trouble; never go in without knowing what your
exit is for each game, otherwise you'll get snapped sooner or later.

You've got to be working so that at whatever stage the accomplice enters he can join in. It's better if you're used to working
together, but everyone has to know his lines. You've got to be clear
about who's the cap man (fast talker), who's the lame (also "lamb,"
fool) and who's the straight man (takes the money).

Work their hatred. Everybody has hates. Just find out what it is
they hate and agree with them. When the heart takes over instead
of the brain, then the sucker is beat. If he's black and he hates
Jews, I tell him he can't trust those lousy Jew bankers and he's crazy
to have his money in their banks. I tell him those Jew bastards will
never let him withdraw it. You watch him hustle down there and
pull it out—half to prove me wrong and half because I've got him
scared.

The Jamaican switch is great on civil-rights types. They want to be good to colored. I give 'em a big chance to help this dumb black just off the boat. They want to be helpful.

I'm young and I've got a lot to learn. I always ask the fraud inspectors when I see them what's new. I learned the Jamaican switch from a fraud inspector, since no one I knew was doing it. I know a lot of bookies and sometimes I think maybe I'd like to be a bookie. You know something about they handle the juice, don't you (to interviewer)? You know about the tax business about bookies and IRS on federal beefs? Well listen, would you be willing to tell me what you know? Hell, I don't know anything even about taxes. I've never paid a cent of tax in my life.

You can't just go into this business on your own. Look around, the world is full of young punks who can't do anything but hustle rings. They've got no style, no finesse. You've got to take a long time learning the business.

Give them a chance to victimize you. They think they're stealing from me because I'm down on my luck and can't do anything about it. They're bargain seekers taking advantage of me, they think they're getting something for nothing. That's how it works.

In cultivating a mark, you must never lie; that is, you must never be caught lying—or you lose him.

The most important thing is control. Watch me, see how I make my voice softer so that you have to lean close to hear me? Now look at that painting——see how you do what I say? Let's have some wine with dinner, here would you look at the menu? See, if you do that, you're under my control. That's the way I test responsiveness. I can teach it. One time we were selling aluminum awnings. I had a couple of guys new to the game along in the car. The only qualifier I used was to drive along a lower middle class residential area looking for a man out watering his lawn. He was there and he cared about his place. Just to show them what can be done I drove right up the drive, damn near onto the lawn and took out my tape and went over to his windows and started measuring. I told him I was measuring for awnings. The man said he didn't want any, but I just asked him where his wife was and went on into the kitchen, bringing my boys with me. That man followed me in, repeating that he didn't want awnings. I hauled out the contract and sat down with his wife. He just sat there saying, "No, no, no." I pushed the contract into his hands, jammed the pen into his clenched fists and told him, "Sign that contract." I told him that maybe five times while I kept pounding that damned pen back into his hands. He signed out while he was still saying, "no."

Prevention of Complaints

The methods used were not only integrated into the development of the scam itself but reflected assumptions about the character and motivation of victims in general. Some of our con men said that a critical step which prevented complaints was that initial one which implicated the victim in some fraudulent or otherwise dishonest undertaking as, for example, being enticed into conspiring to beat the stock exchange, to buy a stolen ring, to encourage an ignorant Jamaican to put his money into one's own bank account and so forth. Once the victim became a co-conspirator, he was capable of being manipulated through his fear of arrest, blackmail, or shame upon exposure. The manipulation need not be necessarily explicit; often the victim needed no reminding.

Another method for preventing complaints emphasized that the victim need never find he had been fleeced. The goal of an artistic bunco was to prevent any such discovery. For example, the investment, if that was the scam, would be made to appear to have failed because of some chance factor unrelated to the con men selling the deal, e.g. refusal of a foreign nation to grant mining rights. Other variations on this theme of a quiet dusting include the reported death of a key figure (one never met) in the conspiracy, the illness of a fiance in the marriage bunco and so forth. Some con men relied on the length of the cooling period, combined with periodic promises or actual tastes of success to prevent discovery. One method was to return small amounts of stolen money disguised as initial profit, just as in famous stock-pyramid swindles, early dividends were taken from investments from newer purchases of securities.

Others (see Goffman, 1952) relied heavily on the self-concept of the mark of himself as a "good sport" who expects to "lose a few" in the course of taking risks and seizing opportunities. This was said to be particularly helpful among the "swinging" crowd who gambled, lived high and otherwise were fast and loose with their funds. Some respondents stressed the importance of reminding the mark what would happen if there was a complaint—he would be exposed in public, to his family and perhaps in court for his stupidity-cupidity. He would be ridiculed, embarrassed, divorced, etc. They would call to his attention how his reputation would suffer, for example, if he were exposed as having tried to buy counterfeit money (as one scam requires), as having tried to find a prostitute (as in "Miss Murphy") or in having fallen for the glib line of gab in a Mexican charity swindle. The advertised prospect of shame following complaint and subsequent exposure is deemed sufficient to silence most marks.

Some who work the long cons emphasize the role of the "square" accomplice who also appears to the mark to have lost in the swindle. The role of this chap is to emphasize the foolishness of complaining, to hold out hopes of eventual recovery through channels "known" to the covert accomplice and to focus the mark's attention (and sympathy) on the accomplice who is also represented to have lost far more than the mark. Thus the mark can feel sorry for the other fellow and can be glad he has not lost that much. Another device employed under pressure is the restitution of funds on the condition that no complaint is made.* One sophisticated fellow in our sample employed the device of intermediate brokers, an escrow account and a signed agreement by the mark under the terms of which there would be restitution only if his terms were met.

Two other devices are employed to prevent complaints, each one predicated on an assessment of the mark's response to being fleeced. One bunco artist said that complaints arose out of desperation when a mark was left completely broke, so that his anxiety over the need to recover his funds outweighed his anxiety over the results of exposing himself as a victim. The con man, therefore, never cleans out a victim but rather leaves him with sufficient funds to live and to continue his business or profession. He states that the mark who is optimistic about his chances to recoup his fortunes will forego complaining. Another approach was taken by one swindler. It was his technique to manipulate the desperation arising out of being completely cleaned out. His procedure calls for wiping the mark out completely, leaving

---

* The police may play the role of intermediary here, for they can threaten prosecution unless restitution is made. In some departments, it is more important to keep citizens happy than to "make cases"; when that occurs, a major activity of the police may be to secure that restitution.

him with no money and, if possible, no convertible reserves. In this state, the mark is approached by one of the accomplices, usually the straight man but possibly another intermediary, who rubs the plight in and then establishes a relationship which exploits the anxiety and dependency by providing enough funds on a week-to-week basis for the mark to survive (the funds are out of what has been taken, but the source may not be revealed) and by promising that if the mark does what his new friend requires, that the new friend (the accomplice) will get the money back. The requirement is, of course, that there be no complaint. It is rationalized as a device to prevent the "thief" from fleeing, from getting made or from being arrested and put in prison from where he would not be able or willing to make repayment.

Illustrative Remarks

One thing I do to cool the egg is to send him away with a beautiful story. Then I call him to reassure him and send him small amounts of money with a line of BS over the phone about how it's just beginning, just coming in, if we wait a while, it'll be a gold mine. I keep sending them telegrams, stories to warm their hearts, and in their hearts even if they suspect something, they know they're guilty as hell because all along the line your steerer managed to get them to sign a check with the wrong initials so they think they see prison bars whenever they look ahead. Another thing is to have the steerer make an error somewhere early in the game, let's say a forgery mistake which everyone—the egg and the steerers and all of us—catch but we go ahead anyway, but the mark thinks we're all in jeopardy of prison. So it comes out just at the end, as in the "payoff" (the race track scam) that if the egg wins, it means because of what the steerer has done, that "mistake" we all knew about, the egg will go to prison. So when another horse wins and the egg loses his shirt, the egg is grateful as hell since he's not caught up on that felony. That's a real con, a professional job, when the egg is grateful to you for taking his money.

That's the art. Anyone can take the money and get out, but blowing it off (cooling) is where the true con comes in.

Another method is to play the sympathy. I say I've got only a little bit of money but I'll share it. Then when they're taken, I promise to do what I can to help even though I've lost my shirt too. I tell him I'll keep his name and get him his money. I drag it on two or three years, maybe keeping him hoping the whole time.

Whenever you're cooling an egg, you've got to string them along. For example, I prefer to play men in their fifties or sixties who've done well. But by that age, they're beginning to slip a little. They can't think as fast as they used to, but they don't realize it—that makes them ideal suckers. Or if they do realize it, they hate the idea of slipping. That makes them feel old, so they deny mistakes—that helps keep them cool because they won't admit they've been had. These things work. The only peep I ever got on an egg on the payoff was an accident and I got pinched for it nine years later.

Brother Fisher's got a real thing going. He poses as a priest or Father Superior and he calls a Mother Superior and gives her the beautiful tale about how some Catholic Father's about to go up on a morals charge, but if they get the money they can keep it quiet. So he tells her he's sending one of his priests over and round he goes and picks up the boodle. The good sisters are innocents of course and they pay out and they never do find out, because just like the good Father said, the case is kept real quiet because they never hear anything more about it again. They think they've done their bit. On the other hand, if they do go to the police *they'll* keep it quiet. You know, most cops are Catholic and they'll be the last ones to want it out. Brother Fisher's got the cops over a barrel as much as the sisters.

After I beat somebody in tonk or bummy (card games) or the old three-card monte, I still instill a sense of sportsmanship in the vic, especially young, immature guys who you can do that with. I tell 'em "A real gentleman and a gambler never complains about losses." I also drop a little comment somewhere on how the cops in this town will jail anybody who's been gambling.

Anyone can rip it off, take money in a rough way. But that's nothing, that rayfield (Ray Field?) bit, because the victim knows what's happening and of course he'll complain, he'll screech his head off and you'll get busted. Rip it off only when you're really hungry, but it's no game. You always want to keep from being identified, keep the victim from knowing what's happening, keep from being arrested. And never carry a weapon; you do and they put you in the violence bag. You're unqualified as a hustler if you need to carry one of those (gun).

Dust your trick easy; get him so he's intimidated by his own duplicity; he thinks he's crooked too. Get him all confused so that's the way he believes it—only you're the one who told him he was crooked but things have been going so fast he doesn't remember anymore what really did happen. The best thing is to make him think it was all his fault, the whole thing; that way you clean him and leave him easy.

⤭ It's important to (take him to a killing ground) where there aren't any police; shake him off there where there's no one to nose around; turn him loose there.

Another way to beat the complaint problem is to work with the police as in the *fix*.

Anybody'd prefer to work under an umbrella—an umbrella 's when you split with the police. That's the way it was in New Orleans, Fort Worth and sometimes in Oakland too. (You want a tree if you can have one, a nice shade tree, that's your protection (from the heat)). For example, if you can get a burglary detail inspector to scout a target for you, or if you've got the beat cop to whistle when something goes wrong—or pick you up and take you off in the car if he has to and book you some nice, safe way so you can beat it with no trouble. Take ————— (Texas). There you call the bunco squad before you come to town; tell them where you want to work; if that's taken, they'll give you an area. But you've got to split every take. If the victim bothers the police with too strong a complaint then they'll lean on him, throw him in the can himself—unless of course he has juice. It takes money. Each cop has got to pay off his superiors. A shade tree can't prevent arrest, but it does stop the conviction.

What Are Marks Like?

Most confidence men in our sample said that the average man was greedy, trying to get something for nothing, a thief and on the con himself. In consequence, they deserved what they got, for they were punished both for their greed and for their stupidity by being taken. (From this perverse viewpoint, the con man may be seeing himself as a moral force punishing stupidity and avarice! More likely, the viewpoint serves as a justification so that the con man need not feel remorse—or suffer a loss of face vis-à-vis a straight citizen—because it levels the crime of the bunco artist to that of the mark.)

Some argued that confidence men were superior to marks by virtue of their cleverness or, by implication, in admitting their venality. Others admitted that they themselves were often victims so that no real differences dared to be claimed—every man had his weakness. A few bunco artists stressed that everyone was lured by hopes for fame and fortune, hopes that were fed by con men, hopes that led the victim to his fleecing. The desire for attention was also cited as common; this refers to attention which con men provide in the form of stimulaton, conversation, excitement and flattery. The parallel desire to be important was mentioned too. Some said that all men wanted to be proud of themselves and to be admired and that it was this fantasy that the con man fed by feeding the dreams of success by promises of easy money, remarkable cleverness and great glory. The marriage bunco artist emphasized the need for love and romance and noted how the con man joins with the victim in a fantasy shared by both. Both, he implied, knew it was not true and both, on another level, took it to be genuine.

When asked how people who fell for the con differed from those who did not, most men in the sample did not distinguish greatly between the two groups. They maintained their conviction of all-pervasive larceny. Merely because someone rejected an approach was no proof of honesty. Rather, the con men suggested that those who didn't "go" were "crybabies," "afraid of the police," "ashamed to admit they don't have any money," "gullible but just not stupid that time," "skeptical" or "immune because they have jobs" or "haven't time." Either directly or indirectly, all citizens were seen as greedy and thieves at heart; the difference was that the marks who did not go had not been approached with the right game and at the right time. Such confidence, of course, allows the confidence man, as a salesman, to continue to approach citizens without being concerned about rebuff, since all remain, in his eye, prospective customers.

Illustrative Comments

What are humans really like? I stand mute before that question. But if the trick is like me, if he is, then he's scheming. He wants money, he wants success, happiness, luxury, but he doesn't want to work for it. He wants no suffering in return. He wants to live without worry. Most of us have those rich dreams.

The difference between the vic and me is that I know *how* to fuck them. I know the tricks. But as long as I'm full of larceny, I can be beat by someone whose methods I don't know. And I've been beaten, believe me, I have.

It doesn't matter how many times a guy's been swindled, he'll go again on something. And if he's been beat and tells you off, so what, you've lost nothing. But you approach him right, get to his larceny, and you've got a game.

Humans take advantage of each other any chance they get.

You've got to realize that the victim *wants* to believe you. The other thing, once you've got him moving, is to listen, because everyone wants to talk.

It's true that all cons are based on sucker greed, but that includes unselfish greed too, as when a sucker goes for a con to do something kind for someone else.

I make the assumption that everyone I meet is a lying dirty son of a bitch not worth shit. Only once in a while am I disappointed —surprised—when they're not.

In any (long) con game, you have to show the victim your money. The victim is, after all, just another con man too—and it's your money he wants. What you're doing is jacking each other up and the first guy to get to the other's wallet is the winner. I remember once I was in a bar setting up a couple who said they were from some farm in the Midwest. I flashed for them and began to pitch about how I was a Texas oil man and I really had them going. The next thing I knew I was in the back alley stripped clean. They'd given me a Mickey and robbed me. They'd gotten to me first. But that's all part of the game.

TV has killed all the long cons. The public is more sophisticated. Of course the very sophisticated ones are overconfident, so they're as easy as setting ducks. That's one thing, you can never wise up the public because of the ego. No one thinks he can get beat. An egoist is the best mark in the world.

A con has got to take risks. It's like in business, if you minimize your losses you stand still and you pass up too much business. So you take risks and lose some, but you make enough to keep moving ahead.

Each one's different, but there's something (scam) for everyone. Take a woman going for the marriage bunco, for instance. Here she is with some guy wooing her like she's never been wooed before. Don't tell me that in her heart she doesn't know what's happening. She's buying her good times, the time of loving and losing. In her heart, she's fatalistic and in the meantime she doesn't want to be told (that it's bunco).

Take the safe citizen with the steady job and built-in security. He believes in reliability, children and a happy home life. Chances are he has money already, so you can't sell him a quick buck. All these things insulate him from being conned. But the same guy wants to buy things with that money and so he's a pushover for anybody with something respectable to sell. That's why consumer fraud is the big thing these days. Or take the same guy who wouldn't spend a nickel foolishly on himself. That guy has kids and has big dreams for them, or he wants to be a big man to them. So you don't sell him anything for himself but you take him where his dreams are and his dreams are for the kid. I beat a guy like that just because he wanted the kid to be what he himself wasn't. So I sold him a deal that would make him a million that he could put away for the kid. I took him to the cleaners.

These things that insulate people against fraud—having money and a family and wanting to hold on to their security by not taking risks—they don't really prevent fraud. In this country there are too many odds-takers, too much of a gambling spirit. Here everybody is greedy and if he's not that, he's rooting for the underdog or something. Just find out what his particular thing is and he'll go.

Comparing Themselves to Their Victims

The majority claimed no differences in motives or dreams, only in cleverness; con men at least knew the tricks. One mentioned as a critical difference that con men were acting a part, whereas victims were going "for real." Another suggested that cons differed by reason of their greater failure, that it was, in fact, the victims who had the money and were successful. Another proposed that confidence men lacked the respect of the public, whereas the average citizen, even though a mark and presumably open thereby to ridicule, was respected and actually more fortunate.

Illustrative Comments

Every con man has his own weaknesses. Most are gamblers. If I want to find a first-class sucker, I look in the glass (mirror). My biggest score for example was 115,000 dollars from an oil lease scam and I lost it all in one evening on roulette wheels in a joint I knew was crooked.

The younger generation coming up aren't con artists. They don't have either the principles or the brains. They're not learning the games. There's no class in these youngsters. They do the easy stuff, concentrating on babies(young soldiers). Half of being a con man is the challenge. When I score, I get more kick out of that than anything; to score is the biggest kick of my whole life.

The best day I ever had I took 150,000 dollars. I blew it all. Easy come, easy go. Parties, women, the best places, gambling and going back to the races.

There are so many people who are on the borderline between con and legit. Cons have only limited trades; they can't do everything. And you can't always trust a con either, not even if he's professional. For instance, Sam the Panic and I would work rings with girls. I'd go in a bar with a lovely girl and we'd size the barkeep up. Then depending on whether we'd figure the girl or me would take him, well, we'd have a mock fight and then one of us would leave and the barkeep would be over talking to the other and that one would sell the barkeep a whole set of phony rings. Then I'd either keep the money (if the girl had left) or take it from her when I saw her.

Cons want all the things our society affords and con games are the springboard to them. If I'm fat, I turn down games because I'm the type who worries about heat before and not after. If I'm fat I don't need to take a chance. Generally I only make one pitch a night, if it's a franchise scam, for example, because it wears me out. I may watch three suckers come in on an ad and I'll sit in the lobby and pick just one of them; I piece off the bellboy to get rid of the others.

A sucker is a projection of the con man himself. There's no line between a salesman and a con either. The calculating salesman gives himself the best of it by taking the best potential customer. A salesman identifies with a person he can reach, whether equal or inferior. But a con man on a long con will seldom go up against someone who's smarter than he is. It's not wise to do. That's the electric part again, knowing, it's in the air. It's always a love affair, just like a young man knowing with whom he can make out.

The best place to work is Chinatown. I hate those people, they're the cheapest. Chinese, southerners, I don't like 'em—any people I don't like I can hustle better.

I always use a partner when I work; of course you have trouble with partners too. One I'd known for twenty-five years ran out on me, but he only did that once. I've had partners snitch twice—once out of envy of me and once out of stupidity. That brings me to the two unforgivable sins. If I tear you off—if I end up taking something for myself which we've stolen together—that's one of them. If I do that, you're entitled to kill. And if I stool on you, you're entitled to kill. I've never used a gun except when I dropped my partner who'd stolen from me. But you won't find one out of a thousand partners who'll tear you off.

You've got to have partners, but a partner won't help you if you're no good in the first place. If I can't butcher a man up by myself why try to have help?

(Somebody who works the short gun (short con) has to be stupid. The reason is that in order to sell a deal, you have to believe in it yourself.) If you're going to sell a pigeon drop, you've got to believe it (the same) works. But the average citizen knows a pigeon drop is too idiotic to work and any smart con won't believe it'll work either and so he won't try to sell it. So someone who is less adroit comes along and believes it and, by God, he sells it.

You speak of a criminal con or a social con or a borderline type. I prefer to say "salesman." Now a good salesman has to be a good qualifier. He judges human nature based on his own experience. For myself, I don't know how I do it, it's undefinable. You have to have an outwardly sympathetic attitude and be able to put yourself in the other person's shoes. You've got to know what he's looking for. You've also got to be able to set the scene correctly. Any book on sales tells you that. There's one I read, *Sell the Sizzle and Not the Steak,* that's good. The only difference between a salesman and a con man is the opinion of the judge on the bench. But these cheap block hustlers are all kid stuff. Take Montana Dan or Sam the Panic, they just haven't given up kid stuff—they're not cons, just petty racketeers. There aren't any elaborate big cons left these days—you think of Ponzo or Jose ————— who was his bucket man here—those were artists.

(All kinds of people are in the game. You make a mistake to think that everyone is a criminal. I'm criminal of course but a lot of them aren't. A lot of respectable people are con men. Take some of the guys I've worked with or for, or some have worked with me. They don't have records, they don't even know criminals, but they're cons every inch of the way.

The marriage bunco artist is one of the strange ones. He'll never tell you the truth about himself because he doesn't know it himself. He goes through life making out on marriage bunco, making opportunities or falling into them, but he just thinks he's Lothario or someone and takes the ladies as they fall.

There's really no such thing as a con artist (from marriage bunco artist) because that distinguishes the con from the victim. But the victim is as guilty as the other. (We are all parasites who live on each other.) When the wind blows us together, we use each other. Now for myself, I love humans and want to help them but I've been conned by others so often that these experiences have changed me. Not that I've done anything wrong, at least I haven't done what anybody else wouldn't do, still. . . .

You see, the victim has the same responsibility as the victimizer. If the victim never wanted anything from you, he'd never go so far as to get in the condition to be conned. It's as with a whore, for without customers, she'd have to give up.

I believe in laws, in the police and in society. But the laws are straight up and down and not built for people. People invent ways to find their advantage. For example, when you came in, I'm over twenty-one, if something went wrong, it would be my fault for going along with you but it would be easier for me to blame you—and so I'd call you a con artist.

For myself, I love to make people do what I want them to. I love to command. I love to rule people. That's why I'm a con artist.

I'm very fond of women. I love sex. That's my weakness and that's where I'm always caught. I can never resist a woman. Women think I'm a good catch, but they treat me wrong. I'm hounded by women wanting to screw.

Let's take those two girls sitting over there in the lobby. They wouldn't be here, would they, unless they were looking for something. What they're looking for is right here (gestures to interviewer and himself). And if they say no—if they don't go with us, nobody is to blame. And if they do, there's no blame; they wanted it, whatever happens. No crime in asking them, is there, and if they accept, well, still no crime. It's always up to them when I offer them pleasure. And if they give me their love and their money that's no crime; am I not entitled to live, to existence? Am I not? If I say to you I'm broke and I need two thousand dollars and you give it to me . . . I never asked you, did I? There's no crime when I take it. Have I wronged you to take what you offer? When they do (give money), they are trying to impress you. At that moment, they want something from you which they get by giving you money. Only later do they wonder and after that they may blame you. But before they want to give it to you, you yourself must be a success. They give it to you because they think they'll gain from you from it.

As with a woman, she gives me money and hopes for love or an affair or marriage. No one gives anybody anything unless he expects dividends. The best is to show yourself as one who has great wealth but who has budgeted badly, so that you need the money only temporarily, since you expect to receive a great deal more very shortly. You are optimistic, and behind that is personal egotism which you must have. But to be overconfident, that is to be a sick man. To reach this level, you must actually have experience with that kind of money; otherwise they will see through you. A short con artist has no such experience, he is simply a thief. They are one-shot thieves who intend to defraud. But a con artist does it naturally; he does it without intention. Of course, even with him, things go wrong. A con artist differs from a swindler in that the swindler gives them something real. A man like Insul or Krueger, for example, gave them pieces of paper, stocks, ownerships, that sort of thing. The swindler has an idea and is selling an interest in it. If the idea fails, then it is fraud and he is a swindler. If it succeeds, it is business and he is a great man. To con, to be a con man, is, on the other hand, simply to meet your needs. It is not theft if I give you what you want. There are parallels with politicians. Reagan, for instance, conned the whole state by promising to lower taxes and of course he didn't. He met the taxpayers' needs to be told what they wanted to hear. He conned them all, but he's no criminal in the eyes of the law. That's why a con is different from a thief. For myself, I don't approve of thieves; on the other hand, I must admit I admire intelligence.

I gamble a lot. I like to go to the races and I blow a lot of money there. I like cards, but I don't play for fun. I cheat. Of course the guys I play with cheat too—they're none of them professional sharks—we just play for fun but we cheat and it can cost a lot of money. I expect everyone to cheat; it doesn't bother me. Anyone will cheat you on anything. Anybody will go for damn near anything too. I'm the same. It doesn't bother me when I get taken. I'll get even (recoup losses) the same day. Why be upset? That's why most people don't complain—because there's nothing to complain about. It's easy to be blown off (cooled) because you expect to cheat and you expect to be cheated. Everybody's trying to take everybody else. That's what I like about my girlfriend—she's a little different. She's not trying to take me right away. I can lend her money and she'll pay me back. She gives me a loan and I pay her back. I never knew a girl like that before. She's a hustling girl, but she's been to college and she's different. She don't use no pimp either. With her I can trust her—the loans prove it. I wouldn't

really want a girl who wouldn't con me at all. This girl she tries a
lot of little cons on me but I like that. It's interesting.

Interviewers Rate the Confidence Men

Each interviewer or observer rated the subject on an adjective
checklist upon completion of the contact. Instructions were to
estimate how the con man appeared to an average person in an
ordinary gathering. There was no reliability study on these
ratings.

The most often checked descriptive words and phrases were,
in order of frequency, as follows: pleasant, a good salesman,
polite and courteous, friendly, self-confident, knows his way
around, average intelligence, good appearance, thinks clearly,
a fast talker, easygoing and a swinger. Confidence men were
rarely rated as sly, shy, obvious liars, gullible, arrogant, generous
or unpleasant. They were *never* rated as a born mark or sucker,
looks like a crook, down and out, tightwad, or dangerous-looking.

Although in many cases poorly educated, raised in delinquent
environments and career criminals, nevertheless these men were
judged to make a good impression, that is to be friendly, safe,
courteous folk. What is more, their social graces were foremost
in spite of the fact that, as we shall see in the next section, almost
every one of them was severely malajusted, as measured by
conventional psychological tests.

Psychological Tests

MMPI

A composite MMPI profile based on the average score of the
twelve cases is presented in Figure 1 below. The average score
(a T score) for normal persons taking the test is 50. Each
increment of 10 represents one standard deviation from the mean.
That means that a score of 60 is one standard deviation from
the mean; beyond that point, one expects no more than 16
percent of the total cases to fall. Beyond T score 70 less than
3 percent of the total cases fall.

Assuming homogeneity of the group, the interpretation of a
composite test profile of this sort would suggest a remarkable
lack of lying and defensiveness on the test proper (considering

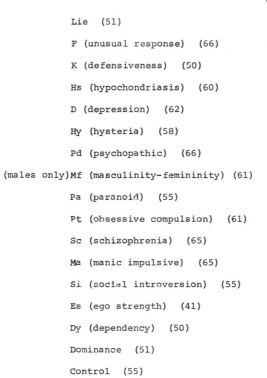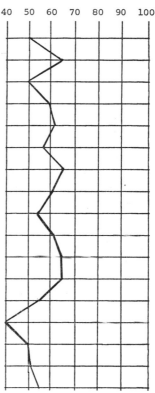

	40 50 60 70 80 90 100
Lie (51)	
F (unusual response) (66)	
K (defensiveness) (50)	
Hs (hypochondriasis) (60)	
D (depression) (62)	
Hy (hysteria) (58)	
Pd (psychopathic) (66)	
(males only)Mf (masculinity-femininity) (61)	
Pa (paranoid) (55)	
Pt (obsessive compulsion) (61)	
Sc (schizophrenia) (65)	
Ma (manic impulsive) (65)	
Si (social introversion) (55)	
Es (ego strength) (41)	
Dy (dependency) (50)	
Dominance (51)	
Control (55)	

FIGURE 1.

that (confidence men are liars by trade) and the presence of pervasive psychopathology. Paramount are the psychopathic deviate scales (T 66), the schizophrenic component (T 65), the manic or impulsive component (T 65) and the low ego strength (T 40). These features, supplemented by the high F for unusual or bizarre responses, lead to a picture of the group as impulsive, amoral, uncontrolled and detached from normal relationships and thinking processes. They are also depressed and compulsive.

A composite score conceals the individual differences in the group. Among the confidence men, we find one, for example, with a T score of 110 on bizarre responses (the highest we have ever encountered), another with a lie score of 76, another with pathologically low scores in the range of 12 (ego strength) through 30 (control) with only one trait score over 50 (manic at 53). Another yields an Ma score of 93, another as Sc of 105, another a Pd of 100, and so on. There can be no question that they are an unusually sick group in terms of mental health* and an unusually antisocial group in terms of lack of regard for others and the lack of control over their own impulses.

Strong VIB

The Strong Vocational Interest Blank scores indicate the extent to which one's interests correspond to those already in an occupation and by implication one's interest and suitability for the occupation itself. A correspondence in the A range means that the test-taker has the same interests as persons successfully in the occupation; scores in the B+ range indicate a lesser interest correspondence (about 15% of the successful men in an occupation are themselves in the B+ range. In considering scores, it is to be noted that a man may receive A or B+ scores in many, several, a few or no occupations. Table I below presents the A and B+ scores of 9 con men returning valid Strong VIB's.

TABLE I

A AND B+ STRONG SCORES

	Occupation	Number Receiving A Scores
A Scores:	Salesman, real estate	5
	Salesman, insurance	4
	Sales manager	3
	Advertising man	3
	President, manufacturing concern	2
	Other occupations: nine different, only one A score each	

	Occupation	Number Receiving B+ Scores
B+ Scores:	Sales manager	4
	Advertising man	3
	Salesman, real estate	3
	Lawyer	3
	Pharmacist	3
	Author-journalist	2
	Vocational counselor	2
	President, manufacturing concern	2
	Other occupations: six different, only one B+ score each	

------

* There was also a high percentage of illicit drug use (heroin, methedrine) and alcohol problems in the group.

Percent having A or B+ scores on one or more sales occupation: 89%.

It is evident that the great concentration of interests is in sales and sales-related occupations. The presumption is that the legitimate occupations most like the professional confidence man's are sales jobs and that the confidence rackets have drawn to them men with interests and skills in selling. It is to be noted that nearly half of the men (4 of 9) also have executive interests. It can be assumed that the organization and execution of some of the "long cons" or "big cons" which do require considerable planning and management skills are suited to the interests and talents of these men who, if not professional criminals, might have (given education and opportunity) done well as executives instead.

Observations on the Job

In the case of six con men in our intensive sample plus a number of noncooperative gypsies and hustlers, we were able to observe demonstrations of their skill. The police inspectors acting as research assistants had observed con men at work many times, of course, during investigation, but not in the role of companions. In six cases, the investigator became a companion on the job. During these periods, the con man served as teacher, giving his reasons for his choice of locale, target groups and individual victims. Because the rule we estabished was that contact with the victim was terminated once the victim was qualified, there were no later stages of the game to observe. Another opportunity for observation on the job arose as each cooperating con man attempted to victimize the investigator.

Within the limits of the operations watched, the observations confirm the reports given during the interview. Each con man in the intensive sample did act as a charming, self-confident-appearing, nonthreatening, socially adept fellow as he approached total strangers and, by one device or another, soon had them in conversation. The choice of persons to approach was made almost instantaneously once a locale for operations (restaurant, hotel lobby, street in front of a bank, bus station, store, etc.) had been selected. Selection was according to external cues—age, sex, clothing of the victim.

Of considerable importance was the close attention paid to

the presence and kind of companions and behavior in target groups. The apparent purpose was to exclude those who were protected by the presence of possibly critical or protective others, to exclude those whose ongoing activities would rule out a casual intruder and, conversely, to seek isolates, aimless groups open to distraction, those open or receptive to intrusion and those pairs where one would be vulnerable to show off to the other. For example, a group of three young soldiers were approached for a hustle but not a tired-looking sergeant; a young Negro swinger was approached but not two Negro hoods; two young women were approached by the marriage bunco artist but he took no interest in a self-contained middle-aged woman. A young couple dining were approached after it was determined they were not married (no ring, both intent on impressing each other, etc.), whereas a married couple of almost the same age were not approached; a middle-aged tourist couple were approached but couples not bearing the stigma of tourism (cameras, flowered shirts, bewilderment in this instance) were avoided. A plump, open-collared smiling hotel guest was a target but a grim-looking, fast-walking well-dressed chap in the same lobby was ignored. A Negro con man talked easily to an elderly white woman at a table in a cafeteria; he steered away from a table where two young white women were sitting.

The running remarks indicated a quick assessment based on a number of assumptions as to the significance of external cues, such as, "There, don't touch that fellow (the old sergeant), he's seen everything by now and there ain't nothing more you can sell him." "I never hit pipe smokers—they think too much." "He's not dressed well enough, won't have money." "That old fellow doesn't look like much but I've seen him in and out of the bank a lot, so he's for me." "See there—those are travel orders and that means he's got money with him." "Look at her coming off the bus, nobody to meet her and nowhere to go; she's ready for the first guy that gets to her." "She wouldn't be here unless she were looking for something." "The guys that hang around here are all track fans—they'll go for any racing scam."

The approach to victims was direct, polite, affable and conventional. It was, in each case, a bid to establish contact and, as such, had to be framed in an acceptable way. If one were to infer an intended "message" to be read by the receiving victim, it might be, "I'm an interesting, friendly fellow and if you are in any way curious, friendly, lonely or hopeful, it's worth your while to talk to me. I'll make it easy for you by taking the initiative, being absolutely proper and by not arousing either your suspicion or any response whereby convention would require you to reject me."

The con men enjoyed the contacts and the opportunity to demonstrate to themselves and to the observer how easily others could be manipulated. When rejections occurred, as they did often in the case of the young block hustlers, there was no evident embarrassment, sense of discouragement or anxious preoccupation with their own feelings. There was an impressive insensitivity to slight.

The frequency of rejection of hustlers by prospective customers and the large number of potential targets discarded by experienced cons prior to approach because of some undesirable feature point up something not evident from interviews. According to some interview data, all citizens are marks and most contacts are successful (although others did speak of playing the numbers and winning one out of ten), whereas it was evident that many citizens were never put to the test of their gullibility and that many who were proved recalcitrant. Our con men were like gamblers and tellers of fish stories who emphasize triumphs but fail to recount the daily fare of nonsuccess or disappointment.

In watching the con men at work, one was struck by their satisfaction in talking and in being with others. No friends to man, they were nevertheless stimulated by interpersonal exchange and dependent upon it. Their especial pleasures were interpersonal too, the victory of the score or blow off with its proof of cleverness, and mastery. The exuberance of the telling of triumphs, the choice of words used again and again to stress the theme—*beating* the vic, *butchering* him up, taking him to the *killing-ground*, taking him for the *kill, stripping* him and so forth. The victim, on the other hand, was a weak animal, portrayed in his complaints by *bleating, peeping or squawking*. These imply no small pleasures nor nonaggressive ones either. The term *get even* used to describe a successful day or month in terms of money-making suggests that additional satisfactions are vengeance and mastery.

The experience of being tested as a mark was enlightening. I was struck by the charming sociability (as in yesteryear's psychiatric descriptions of psychopaths) and seeming intense interest in oneself. There was the demand of courtesy to respond to polite overtures and to the casual probes as to one's interests, age, marital status and police experience. There were flattering appeals to be helpful, "I've just got this letter from this company back East in which I hold some stock; now I'm an old man, just an ignorant old fool you could say, whereas you're a well-educated man. Now I wonder if you'd do me the kindness of reading this letter and telling me what I ought to do about that stock thing they're talking about there." There were other inquiries, simultaneously subtle and blatant, "A guy can make a lot of money in this town if he's got a license but that takes juice. There's a lot of money if there's the juice . . ."* Or diffusely, "I'm pretty well-acquainted around town, I think I know a lot of people you'd be interested in—or a lot of places. We could work together . . ." And again flattering, "I could tell right away you were straight, straight as a string and I've tested you out now and it's true. Most got some larceny in 'em but you don't. Now look, I've been a criminal all my life but I'm getting tired of the gaff and I'm really serious about turning straight myself. Now my brother-in-law owns some land back in Colorado and it looks to me that there's an opportunity for me there, what's more it's a big opportunity because, you see, there's some oil under that ground and . . .!" There were threats that could lead to control as well, "There isn't anybody I work with that I can't get something on. You've gone for something sometime too and you know it and I'll know what it is, too, shortly now—and you're going to have to stand still for it if it comes to that . . ." "Look, this isn't a safe place to be around, you know that, why even the inspectors and patrolmen they don't come in here unless there are a couple

---

* An appeal to me to take a bribe and to set up others in the police department to do the same.

of them. I know my way around, you stick close by me and we won't have no trouble, you move out and man you can get a knife in you sooner than you'll know . . ." There were lighter invitations, as "Why not go out and have some fun? We been talking a lot here; hell, you work hard and you do all right for your family, why not break out a little? I know a girl . . ." And so it went, easy-going, probing, testing, pulling, tempting, challenging, flattering, and no matter how many times I said, "Sorry, no thanks" or "I'm not your man," the effort continued. Whether considered as an opportunity not to be missed, a challenge that could not be ignored or a compulsion to repeat again and again the ritual of seduction and destruction, the con man did not desist. In their eyes, the investigator, when not a cop,* was a mark.

Cop or mark, the investigator was also an employer, for each con man was paid—or offered pay—to induce his cooperation. Observations here proved most instructive. Although each was promised high pay (up to 10 dollars an hour), none took any note of hours spent. After the first pay, none asked for more, and when offered an opportunity to make more by other endeavors (recruiting other con men, etc.), none took it, even though I flashed hard cash. Some, asked to send a bill, did not. Others took checks, although they admitted they had never taken a check in their lives; one, through an accident in change-making, allowed himself to be shortchanged by 5 dollars without protest— even though he himself had played short-change scams. (I made restitution of funds!) Others, the noncooperative sample, refused to talk, regardless of offers of pay. There was not one person in the sample who took the money-making opportunities offered. Only one required pay for the later working periods after the initial fact was established that he was being well paid and after I confessed—as I did at the outset—to being a mark who could be taken easily. In these cases, the offer of high pay and the offer of easy money for small labors and the confession of one's being a mark were strategies adopted in advance in order to satisfy the con man that this mark had already been beaten, so that we

---

* The investigator is a consulting criminologist to a sheriff's department and it was in that capacity that he introduced himself to the sample.

could then concentrate on our business—the con man and his operations—rather than on his business of beating the investigator. I anticipated that lying would continue, perhaps as a series of petty conquests or simply because it was a lifestyle. I was surprised that obvious lying was minimal and that the lie score on the MMPI was not elevated over normal for the sample average at all. In any event, once initial token payments were made and an occasional dinner and drink purchased, the con men did not take the money they could get directly.

The conclusion, at least with the cooperating intensive sample, is that money itself is not as important as con men say it is. They did not take it or make it when they could. That money is necessary is not to be denied, but none in the sample would take all that was offered. They were willing to scheme and work at that, but they did not even present their bills or count the money paid to them. Obviously something more than money spurs them on; quite likely it is what one wise old grifter said, "Beating them, that's the thrill."

SUMMARY AND CONCLUSIONS

Observations and interviews were conducted with a sample of confidence men (and women). Approaches to and initial observations were conducted with 35; 14 became part of an intensive sample with whom a guided interview and psychological tests were employed. In addition, observations "at work" were conducted. Attempts to develop control samples of legitimate and shady promoters foundered on difficulties in definition, sampling, and costs.

Interviews, observations, and tests suggest the following impressions:

1. Confidence men come from a wide range of backgrounds. Although our sample was skewed in the direction of badly educated, lower-class-minority persons with delinquent backgrounds, some were well-educated with upper-class backgrounds.

2. Those confidence men who cooperated with us viewed themselves as professional criminals whose skill was acquired through training. Most worked with other confidence men to plan and execute the exploitative games which are their stock-in-

trade. All preferred particular con games but were experienced in others as well. Not all were experienced in long cons. All had engaged in other kinds of consistent criminality besides bunco.

3. Among legitimate jobs held, being a salesman was the most common. Their work in con games required skilled salesmanship and sometimes more elaborate executive abilities. On the Strong test, nearly all scored high as salesmen; executive interests ranked second.

4. Judged by others to be sociable, courteous, friendly and nonthreatening—and emphasizing these surface traits themselves as necessary—the test sample is revealed on psychological tests to be severely maladjusted. They average high on the psychopathic deviate, schizophrenic and impulsive scales and low on ego strength.

5. Given the severity of their psychopathy, contrasted with the excellence of their interpersonal skills in short-range encounters with the public (they do not fare as well in the long range, given arrests, drug use, etc.), one marvels at their social abilities. It is proposed that their choice of careers provides an opportunity to act out their hostility, their impulsivity and their lack of close relations to others, consistently to score aggressive interpersonal triumphs which may serve as endeavors at restitution as well as expressions of more primitive drives. It is likely that the nonviolent ethic of professional criminals provides control over their own impulses which are then expressed in "beating" the victim and, more generally, in other antisocial conduct. It is also likely that some portion of their test-revealed psychopathy reflects what they have learned in their delinquent environments. Personal predilections dovetail with the standards of the criminal community (the underworld).

6. It is also proposed that given the schizophrenic underlay in many of those con men we knew best, their grasp on reality— in the harsh, middle-class sense—is not, in fact, too strong. Consequently, the lies and fantasy may well become for the con man, as well as his victim, a temporary reality which, like drug-induced ecstasies, is "more real than the real." Should that be so, the lie of the confidence man, bold, blatant and exploitative as it is, may also be and become his world, at least for a moment, and suffice him as a sufficient reality. At this point, one is

reminded of Schlesinger's (1969) analysis of children's promises which he terms "propitiatory tales" and which can function as magical devices for warding off punishment, restoring the child to parental grace and so forth. Schlesinger points out that a promise that is intended to be kept implies considerable maturity; that is, the person must have self-control, a sense of time, anticipation of the future, a conception of interdependency and *quid pro quo* and so forth. If only mature people can offer trust that is genuine; that is, if only mature people—and by that is implied psychologically healthy ones—are capable of realizing what a promise means, then it is no surprise that our confidence men neither appreciate nor keep promises, nor maintain trust. It may well be that their promises have some of the same magical quality for themselves as they do for their victims.

7. The con men's attitudes toward the straight world are a mixed bag. They do assume the similarity of others to themselves as far as cupidity is concerned; this may be viewed as projection or as lack of discrimination in judgment. The view serves to justify their actions, allows them a confident base for approaches to others, and does allow them stereotype accuracy in interpersonal judgment. On the other hand, they also view themselves as clever and triumphant in the jungle world where the man-animals eat each other. Finally, some are aware of their inferior position with respect to status, security, income and jeopardy from authorities.

8. Their at-a-distance assessment of others is superficial but by no means inaccurate. (It is stereotype accuracy.) They rely heavily on external signs to indicate another's interests, status, group membership, wealth and vulnerability. In the long con, they may also investigate a potential mark by means of observation, reading of newspaper accounts, information from others and so forth.

9. Once contact is established, assessment proceeds by means of a variety of behavior tests which are, essentially, controlled stimuli, the responses to which are observed. In most games, several cons will participate (as ropers, "cap men," inside men, etc.), providing a variety of stimuli from different sources which become, as the con men communicate with one another (by sign

language or direct language) a set of pooled judgments and a reservoir of information. These tests, called "qualifying the victim," are probes of interests, background, wealth and susceptibility to control. Control in itself is an important feature and is attempted primarily through suggestion, although any question or command constitutes a "demand," which if acceded to, is evidence of control over the victim.

10. Assessment and qualifying are, in long cons, a set of steps rather than a one-shot process. Final qualifiers are those in which the victim becomes a co-conspirator or swaps money. At this point, the victim is committed. Assessment-qualifying does not occur independently of other procedures; rather the steps in the game have multiple functions so that, for example, an inquiry which is a qualifier can also establish the direction of the game; or a switch from roper to roper which provides a new testing opportunity also is a step in the game which tells more of the tale (i.e. gives the victim more false information) and serves as a "switch" to confuse issues and muddy the trail, etc.

11. A variety of techniques are used to con the victim. These do not differ from ordinary methods for persuading, selling or manipulating others. The competent con maintains an arsenal of devices which range from flattery and promises through threats and blackmail. One of his skills is his ability to try out a number of these devices without remorse, empathy or concern over rejection or disapproval. In this, his psychological traits of amorality, lack of closeness, exploitativeness, etc., serve him in good stead. It is also the case that his own personality and status influence which devices he can use effectively in any given situation; for example, a Negro con man inhibited by his race from approaching a young white woman can use his race to advantage in conning a "liberal" white male, or an older con man may exaggerate his age to appear more feeble than he is in order to appeal for help or to lull the victim.

12. The con man's own view of why he is effective, what humans are like or how often he scores cannot be accepted as valid on the surface. His assumption about the greed of his victim as a reason for his success (a claim readily accepted by many writers) may not account for much that occurs. Similarly,

the success stories play down what may be a considerable number of rejections. For a further understanding of the con game, it is necessary to examine the victim as well—and his interaction with the con and the nature of the culture in which the game is played. Features that deserve exploring include the role of the con as an antidepressant, i.e. to provide stimulation to sad, bored people; and as a fantasy machine, that is, a device whereby the victim and the con both act out a fantasy. At these times, the con man and victim are engaged in a *folie a doux*. The insights of a few cons into these possibilities at times approach the poetic.

13. (An important feature in the con is the ability to prevent the victim from complaining. For professionals this is the mark of artistry.) Various devices are employed to prevent or squelch complaints. They range from the ideal—which is to prevent the victim from ever realizing that he has been swindled—to the guaranteed—which is to operate under police protection.

Chapter IV

FRAUD VICTIMS

To UNDERSTAND THE operation of confidence games requires that one consider both of the participants—the con man and his victim—and their interaction. What does each put into the game and what does each get out of it? From a criminological standpoint, the answers may be useful in planning programs of crime prevention; from a psychological standpoint, they may reveal points of interest about trust violation and deception, gullibility and shared fantasy.

COMPLAINING VICTIMS

Method of Analysis

We sought a sample of victims who had complained to the police by reviewing the records of a major city police fraud detail. Those complainants reporting cases of bunco and swindles during the prior twelve-month period were identified. There were 44 cases.* Contact with each was attempted; 4 refused to be seen, 4 had not been city residents, and 12 could not be reached. Twenty-four were interviewed. A guided interview schedule was employed and from one to three hours were spent with each victim.

---

* Forty-four cases in a city of nearly a million people suggests either that confidence games are rare or that con men are correct in saying that most victims do not complain. In view of the fact that we ourselves had found nearly half a hundred con men, only one of whom was retired, in that same city and had watched some at work—indeed, could observe 44 cases being initiated by our noncooperative (observed but not interviewed) sample in any six-hour period (most of these hustlers)—the magnitude of the noncomplaining sample can be imagined.

61

Characteristics

Background

There were 10 men and 14 women in the interview sample.* Three-fifths (15 of 24) were white, one-fourth (6 of 24) were Negro and 2 were Oriental. Most had at least some high school education, 3 had some college! 3 had not reached high school. Some high school was the median educational category. [The sample ranged in age from 21 to 89 with a median age in the 60 to 69 bracket.] Yearly incomes were low for families and unrelated individuals; 4 received less than 1,200 dollars per year; about three-fifths (15 of 24) received between 2,400 and 6,000 dollars, with an estimated median of 4,800 dollars; five earned more than 6,000 dollars per year.

Family backgrounds were working or lower middle class; only 3 respondents had fathers in business or professional work; most had been farmers or tradesmen. Reflecting the high average age of the sample, half of them were retired; of those not retired, several were tradesmen; there was 1 professional person. The majority were not married at the time of the fraud; 8 were widowed, 4 single, 3 divorced, and 1 separated. Of those 20 who had ever been married, 6 had been married two or more times. The women in the sample were dependent entirely on retirement incomes in half of the cases. Among the women, only 4 had children. More than half reported themselves to be deepy religious ("near fanatics" some were termed). Most, from their language and demeanor, appeared to be lower or lower-middle class.

Comparing our small sample with 1960 census data for the city may be instructive. In 1960, the average income for families and unrelated individuals was 4,757 dollars, a figure most certainly increased by 1967. Median education in the city is a high school diploma; 80 per cent of the population was white; about two-thirds were married, males and females about equal in number and the median age was in the 50-54 bracket. On its face, our sample contains more minority-group citizens (although

---

* The total sample of identified complainants had included 13 men and 31 women.

the city now has more blacks than in 1960), receives less income, is somewhat less well educated, is much less often living with a spouse and is considerably older.

Our inference from these face differences, assuming that census data for city population characteristics has moved in the direction indicated, is that complaining bona fide fraud victims willing to cooperate in a study are more likely to be female, older, less educated and less wealthy than the city average. The sample of all complaining victims (44) is more heavily female than the population at large. Quite likely the sex, old age, widowhood, education and income features are part of a constellation of vulnerability and complaint. We suspect, but cannot here prove, that the women who are conned and do complain less often have children than the population at large and that they are more emotionally religious. Be this so, it implies loneliness, lack of family nearby on whom to test ideas or who could control foolish ventures and perhaps a self image as "good" or charitable with possible ensuing naiveté.

Experience as a Victim

The con game experience which led to the complaint was most often the pigeon drop (see Appendix A), accounting for 11 cases. Seven were victims of the Jamaican switch, 3 of gypsy bunco, 1 was a card scam, 1 a bank swindle and 1 a real estate swindle. The gypsy games are long cons of a simple nature; the others are short cons. Most victims said they had only been victims once; only 2 reported that they had been victimized more than once in their lives. None appeared to be "professional victims" in the sense that they fell again and again. The most experienced victim was a Catholic priest, a three-time loser.

After the victimization, the police were said by most (17) to have been the first persons told about the event; 3 had told friends first, 2 of the 8 married victims had told the spouse first; the other 2 victims had first told relatives or a business acquaintance. Men more often than women had gone to the police first (9 of 10 versus 8 of 14). It is noteworthy that an official rather than a relative or friend was first to receive the news of the bunco.

Victims said in one-third of the cases (8 of 24) that they had been reluctant to complain because of pride and shame. Eight told the interviewer they wished the fact of their complaint kept secret. One man said he was afraid of retaliation. Most men (8 of 10) and a minority of the women (3 of 14) contended they had felt no reluctance to complain. When asked why other fraud victims might be reluctant to complain, pride and shame were the factors cited.

Most victims reported that they had first met the con man, a stranger to them in each case, on the street (14 of 24). Store meetings ranked second (5 of 24); restaurants, bars, churches and parking lots had 1 contact each, and in 1 case contact was by a telephone solicitation.

Other Crime Experience

Victims had suffered from other crimes; thefts had been experienced by 10 of 24 subjects, burglaries by 6 of 10, and 4 had been physically assaulted. Eight said they also had been victims of offenses by others leading to traffic accidents. Men more often than women reported some criminal victimization (7 of 10 men, 6 of 14 women). In addition to statutory crimes, a minority of victims (7 of 24) reported instances of being defrauded where it had not been certain that laws had been violated, as in being cheated or lied to. High-pressure salesmanship was ranked first (3 of 7); faulty merchandise, 2; mechanical-electrical repair fraud, 2; and insurance fraud, 1. Consistent with their inexperience in prior bunco, most of the sample are not aware of earlier nonbunco victimization.

Regarding their own criminality, most victims (19 of 24) denied any record of arrests. Four men had been arrested (1 each for a juvenile offense, an alcohol offense, battery and non-support); 1 woman had been arrested for peddling without a license. Only 2 victims had spent time in jail, both men who had served less than a year.

Victims were asked if they themselves had conned or swindled anyone during the last year. Four men said they had; all other subjects denied it. They were also asked if they believed that most people did con one another as part of being human. All of the men believed they did, as did 8 of 14 women. Asked how they themselves acted to protect themselves from being cheated or swindled, only 1 person said she had no such defenses. All others felt they took defensive steps which included most often staying clear of strangers (12 of 24), avoiding involvment with other people (7 of 24), being alert (4 of 24) and so forth. It is to be noted that each had nevertheless been victimized by a stranger who had involved them in a scam. Asked what general advice they had for preventing swindles, the most often-proposed step (11 of 24) was public education through publicity about fraud. Other suggestions included intervention by bank personnel to question any large withdrawals (7 of 24) and avoiding strangers (9 of 24). One sensitive woman suggested the prevention of loneliness.

Spending Habits

Most did not budget expenditures; a minority (10 of 24) said they spent according to a budget. Asked about major money commitments, the majority indicated that most of their income went for food and rent. Among men, major expenditures were also reported (1 for each of the following) for gifts, auto payments, alcohol, travel, child support and supporting a brother's education. Two men said they had heavy installment payments to make (other than auto). Only 2 women reported extra expenses—1 on insurance and 1 on medical costs. On the other hand, in response to a budget analysis, 1 woman did report installment payments taking more than 25 per cent of her income. Asked about the most recent credit purchase, half had made 1 or more. All women who had made credit purchases (9 of 14) said they knew what interest they paid; 4 of the men did not. Three men and 1 woman reported outstanding personal debts. Most women said they had never made loans to anyone, whereas most men had (7 of 10). The 2 women making loans had given only to relatives; that was not the case with men.

Fantasies

MONEY. Six of the 10 men admitted to daydreaming about the lucky day when they would come into a lot of money. No women admitted to such fantasies. Asked how they would handle a sudden fortune of 100,000 dollars, the men said they would invest it (5 of 10), give it away to friends and family (2 of 10), spend it on pleasure (2 of 10), give it to organized charity (1 of 10). One didn't know. Six women would give it to charity, 2 would give it away to friends, 3 would spend it on pleasure, 2 would bank it, 1 would pay medical bills, and 2 didn't know.

Asked how multimillionaires made their money, men said they got it through shady deals (5 of 10), hard work (3 of 10), investments (1 to 10) or luck (1 of 10).

WAY OF LIFE. Only a minority would keep to the life they were living if their dreams were to come true (5 women, 2 men). The dreams of the rest were diverse. The men would be professionals (3 of 14), be an artist (1 of 10), enjoy financial security (1 of 10), enjoy a happy family life (1 of 10) or travel (2 of 10). The women would be (1 in each case) a professional person, a nun, a missionary, a charity worker or a traveller. One wanted to die; 2 did not know what they would do. Many would continue to live in the city in which they were now residing (5 of 10 men, 6 of 14 women). The choices of the others were diverse.

In the "dream" life, given a choice of friends, old friends would be the people they would spend their time with (4 of 10 men, 4 of 14 women), followed by those who needed help (3 women), intelligent people (2 women) and others. Two men would seek minority race friends. Only 1 man gave evidence of status striving, saying he would be with people who had money. Three persons said they would want to be with people they would trust.

In the dream life, asked what they would want others to think of them, none spoke of wealth or power. Seven persons said they did not care what others thought; most wanted to be well thought of.

MAGICAL BELIEFS. We were interested in unusual habits which might reflect gullibility or exposure to exploitation. Asked about horoscope readings, 5 women and 3 men admitted to currently following their horoscopes. Two men and 1 woman had recently gone to an astrologer, 4 men and 3 women had visited a gypsy fortune teller, 2 men and 2 women believed in witchcraft, and

6 men and 1 woman entertained a possible belief in flying saucers. All denied answering "personals" advertisements.

SOCIAL PATTERNS. Most women (12 of 14) did not belong to any club, society or organization; most men (7 of 10) did. Most who were working (N=14) had stable job histories; only 5 held 2 or more jobs in the last 5 years. Half (12 of 24) had stable residence patterns; only 3 had moved 3 or more times in the last 5 years. Most (5 of 10 men, 9 of 14 women) said they had many close friends, only 3 (2 men, 1 woman) had no close friends. Most close friends had been known for more than 10 years. Nine women were regular attenders at church, as were 4 men; 5 women did not attend. Asked about their alcohol consumption, 11 women and 5 men had not consumed any alcohol the prior month; only the men had consumed more than 2 glasses in any 1 day; only 1 man drank more than 2 drinks, doing so most days of each week.

Psychological Test Results

Thirteen of the complaining victims (7 men, 6 women) completed the California Psychological Inventory which all had been asked to take. Table II below gives the normalized scores (T scores) obtained. A score of 50 is average; 10 points higher or lower represents a deviation from the mean equal to 1 standard deviation.

TABLE II
RESULTS OF THE CALIFORNIA PSYCHOLOGICAL INVENTORY

Characteristic Tested	Average Score for Victims
Dominance	43
Capacity for status	37
Sociability	39
Social presence	31
Self acceptance	37
Sense of well being	40
Responsibility	44
Socialization	43
Self control	51
Tolerance	34
Good impression	52
Communality	44
Achievement via conformance	39
Achievement via independence	37
Psychological mindedness	40
Flexibility	33
Femininity (males only)	59

The usual interpretation of a profile of test scores requires that one consider patterns and correlates; however, in presenting averaged scores for a group, no such interpretation may be offered, since the scores represent a range of individual values expressed only as a central tendency. We will limit our remarks, then, to a comment on the discrete values.

What is most apparent is that the group of test-completing victims score consistently below normal; some of the averaged scores approach 2 full sigmas below normal. The most extreme scores—below 40—are social presence, intellectual efficiency, flexibility, tolerance, self acceptance, capacity for status, achievement via independence, and achievement via conformance. Individuals—and by implication, a group of persons—with such scores would be described as remarkably uncertain, unoriginal, cautious, confused, conventional, lacking in self-discipline, worrying, rigid traditional, retiring, suspicious, intolerant, self-abasing, passive, narrow, conventional, dull, uneasy in new situations, compliant before authority, submissive, lacking in self-understanding, easily disorganized under pressure, insecure and opinionated. These are hardly complimentary attributes, and they strongly imply a collection of persons with difficulties in social adjustment and limited personal resources. There are, for the group, few redeeming features suggestive of strength or good sense; at best, the men may be blunt and impatient, and the whole sample concerned with what others think of them and not overly impulsive. These characteristics are not surprising in a group characterized, as earlier noted, by old age, low education, social isolation, naiveté and possible religious preoccupation.

Comment

Neither interviewer impression, replies to question nor test characteristics suggest that the sample fits the picture of victims painted by many confidence men. Rather than a group of larcenous, shrewd, competitive conspirators, one finds a group of simple and narrow-minded lonely folk unable to cope with others, anxious for approval and seeking human contact; they are passive pople trying hard to be nice and possibly sensible without being able to examine what they are doing, what others are proposing or what the consequences of their compliance with the bunco proposition will mean. As the interview data show, they can also be innocent and indiscreet in money-handling. Currently unhappy for the most part, they do dream dreams of a life satisfying and respectable and beyond their reach; some use outright magic trying to find it. Far from being dishonest, most lead stable upright lives; unfortunately their "uprightness" involves both rigidity and narrowness which has ill-fitted them to assess fraud when it comes their way. That they do complain to the police is not surprising; by their standards they have been victims of a pure and simple wrong. Embarrassed perhaps, they nevertheless do not feel that they have been at fault, at least not by harboring criminal designs.

These general statements do not reveal the tragic conponents present. Several of the old ladies were obviously depressed. Without friends or family, they were lonely to the point of desperation. Out seeking someone to talk to, it is likely that they were willing to pay a high price—even to be a victim—in return for the stimulation of the bunco artist and his momentary opportunity. Careful not to talk to "strangers," the confidence man ceases to be a stranger simply by an approach which is proper and conventional in the extreme. For the several women in the sample, whose assets consisted of insurance benefits from their recently deceased husbands, the money itself was tainted, revolting, a reminder of the death of their last tie to life and joy. Their remarks indicate quite clearly that to be bilked out of "death money" was no loss; to the contrary, they wanted riddance, riddance in the old Greek sense of *apotropia*. To give money away was already a virtue, to rid themselves of death money, of cruel ghosts, was a compulsion. There is another tragic aspect to that loss. Several spoke of dying soon; several wanted to die. To rid themselves of their money was part of a broader clearing-the-decks; it was, at the least, a jettisoning of an encumbrance, perhaps even a symbolic suicide on the order of the Armageddon syndrome which may be stated, "Let the catastrophe be total!" Without insight, these women would not admit to seeking riddance nor to welcoming victimization, but at a deeper level, we must offer the interpretation that they were not unaware. As the confidence men said, they met a need in their victims. What the bunco artist may not have realized was that this need was one of riddance and a step much closer to death.

NONCOMPLAINING VICTIMS RESPONDING TO A "PERSONALS" AD

Method of Analysis

It is evident that a sample of 44, comprising all of the available bunco victims complaining to a metropolitan police department in one year, is not an adequate sample of all victims. One must ask, "What is the majority like who do not complain?" We undertook to gather a sample of those noncomplaining victims by putting an advertisement in the "personals" column of the city's morning newspaper. The ad ran for 2 weeks and 2 weekends. A confidence man who himself used newspaper advertisements to secure victims wrote the copy for us. It read as follows:

> BUNCO AND CON GAME VICTIMS: Sheriff's Dept. research team seeks victims of swindle or fraud. It is imperative that we interview victims who have not reported their losses to police. All interviews in strictest confidence. Your experience will help in crime prevention. Please call.............

Following the advice of our confidence man "consultant," we employed an answering service. The service was so arranged that victims calling in would (a) "commit themselves" by giving name, address, phone number and (b) "hand over the initiative," that is, they would be told that we would call them back. During the period of the ad, a number of calls were received from persons unwilling to commit themselves, by cranks and by curious nonvictims. Each person who left a name and phone number was contacted, and in an initial telephone interview, it was determined whether or not he appeared to be a bona fide victim.

Of those responding, 15 persons, 6 women and 9 men, who had been fraud victims were interviewed. A revised interview form was used, with the revision based on expectations derived from interviews with the earlier group of complaining victims.

In evaluating the ad-answering sample, it is well to keep in mind that they were not only victims in terms of their having experienced past fraud or bunco, but that they were exposing themselves to possible bunco simply by coming forward in response to the "personals" advertisement. That most remained vulnerable may be inferred from the initial fact that only 2 of the 15 asked for interviewer credentials. We do not assume that this small sample is representative of all noncomplaining victims, since we cannot know the characteristics of those who did not come forward in response to the advertisement or who did not see it. The sample consists of presently vulnerable victims of bunco, most of whom have not before gone to the police. We would be wise in assuming, however, that they were ambivalent about complaining, for they did come forward to cooperate with a police agency in response to our advertisement, and as it turned out, several had been to the authorities about their cases.

Characteristics

Background Data

The age range was from 20 to over 60, with a median age in the 40 to 49 bracket. Nine were men, 6 were women. About half were church-attenders. Most men were in skilled trades or business; 3 women were housewives, 3 were employed. Husbands of women in the sample were in skilled trades. Ten were married and living with a spouse, 3 were divorced; most (12 of 15) had children. Educational level ranged from some high school to college degree; the median was a high school diploma. All were white.

Confidence Game and Fraud Experience

All but 3 of the victims had been involved in consumer fraud or long cons which included illegal adoption, investment schemes, franchises, new car sales, real estate fraud, loan fraud, welfare fraud, home construction fraud, camera fraud and city permit kickback fraud. Among the short cons, there had been 1 carnival bunco, 1 gypsy bunco and 1 marriage-and-blackmail scheme. One victim reported multiple fraud experience; she had been victimized repeatedly.

Asked whom they told about their experiences, 5 had consulted an attorney, 3 had told friends, 2 had told family members, 1 had complained to the product manufacturer and 4 said they had approached law authorities (by letter or in person)—2 to the district attorney, 1 to police, 1 to postal authorities. In each of these latter cases, their complaint had been rebuffed.

Those who had not gone to authorities were asked why not. Three expressly challenged the competence of law enforcement, 2 others indicated pessimism over the outcome if they had complained, 1 was afraid the gypsy would seek revenge, 1 confessed his own involvement had been illicit, 2 others wished to avoid public exposure. They were willing to respond to our advertisement, they said, because they were hoping for help (7 of 15 cases), since our advertisement promised anonymity and no official record. Four said they wished to perform a public service, 1 came under pressure from his wife; in 1 case, an emotionally distressed woman came whose motivation was not clear.

Personal Habits, Feelings and Interests

Our inquiries on the second round of interviewing reflected our expectations, based on the first-round interviews, that at least a portion of the sample of bunco victims would be bored, depressed, deferent, nonaggressive "good" people who did not see nastiness even when it faced them head-on. We suspected that this portion of the victim population would be naive, nonaggressive, socially isolated, in need of social stimulation and dependent upon the approval of others, even strangers. We also expected that some victims would fit the con man's own notions of sharpsters out looking for something for nothing and not above being a bit crooked themselves while they were at it. The following data reflect our inquiries into these propensities. (The categories are overlapping.)

HABITS AND ACTIVITIES. Most (14 of 15) reported they did have hobbies and enjoyed leisure-time activities. But 6 of 15 did find themselves with time on their hands, and 9 of 15 admitted they were sometimes or often bored. Six often or sometimes went "shopping" without intending to make a purchase. One-third sat in parks or public places. Six recalled chattting with strangers when on a walk within the last month. Two-thirds had seen friends within the week. Seven did not have relatives in the same town and most (11) had not seen a relative within the week. Nine did not belong to any clubs, associations or other groups; only 3 had been to any group meeting within the last month. About half (7) spend more than 11 hours a week watching TV; favorite shows were those we judged to be excitement-adventure (mystery, westerns, war) in most (9) cases. Only 3 had any interest in news or documentaries.

PERSONAL FEELINGS AND SELF-DESCRIPTIONS. Eleven were sometimes or often depressed. Although only 3 admitted to thinking of death as a relief or a solution to their problems, 10 were unable or unwilling to reply to the question. (This is the largest "no answer" item.) Nine often felt they wanted adventure or excitement. Eleven reported they would like to be hypnotized if it could be done safely. Most had not been formally hypnotized, but when asked if the con man had done so, if there was an element of "hypnosis" in what had happened, 11 said "yes." Recalling their childhoods, 5 said they had been very obedient, 4 said they had been ordinarily obedient, 6 felt they had been disobedient children. Asked how they had been on the whole as children, 7 said they had been very good, 6 ordinarily good and 2 felt they had been bad children. Asked who would remember them after they died, the majority (11 of 15) said it would be family members; only 2 said no one would remember them. Asked for what they would be remembered, the most often given reply (5 cases) was for "good deeds," 4 others spoke of their admired personal traits. Asked what they enjoyed about their dealings with other people (a multiple coded item based on a set of checklist phrases), most of the sample ("most" defined here as 12 of 15 or greater) said they enjoyed the following:

1. Being liked.
2. Being helpful.
3. Being a good sport.
4. Being honest.
5. Being practical, expedient.

Fewer, but still a majority (between 8 and 11 Ss out of 15) said they enjoyed the following:

1. Being a winner (mostly men).
2. Beating them in a game of wits (mostly men).
3. Having many close friends.

Some (3 of 7 persons) enjoyed the following:

1. Showing who's boss.
2. Playing practical jokes.
3. Getting back at them if they hurt you.
4. Not getting close to anyone (more women than men).

Only a few (1 or 2) enjoyed the following:

1. Being feared.
2. Putting them on (lying).
3. Fooling them.

Asked what we should know about each person and his life so as to understand how it was that they became involved in a swindle, the following explanations were offered:

1. Subject wanted money (2).
2. Subject said she had an emotional-psychiatric problem (2).
3. Subject describes self as
   a. Egotistical (1).
   b. Too trusting (1).
   c. Naive (1).
   d. Having prior business risk experience which influenced decision (1).
   e. Being a stranger in town (1).
   f. Having watched too much television (1).
   g. Having insufficient education (2).
4. Two could not tell us why.

INTERPERSONAL MECHANISMS, EXPECTATIONS. Few had ever looked after pets of friends or neighbors, but about half (8) had helped them out with repairs or yard work. Of those driving a car, half (7 of 14) had helped by pushing strangers' autos with their own. However, most drivers (10 of 14) had not picked up a hitchhiker within the year. Among those witnessing a crime or traffic accident, all but 1 (1 of 11) had reported stepping forward to volunteer as a witness. Of those going to bars, about half (5 of 11) said they had bought drinks for a stranger met in the bar (those admitting buying were men, 4 of 5, whereas women did not, 4 of 5). Most (9) said they did not worry about the possibility of their being a victim of a criminal assault or robbery; on the other hand, most (11) said they felt citizens have much to fear from criminal elements. Conversely, most (9) said that they considered most people to be decent and honest, and nearly all (13 of 15) said that if they acted kindly towards others, others would act kindly towards them. Of those giving a direct answer, the majority (8 of 13) said they felt it was the best policy to look for the good in people rather than looking at the good and the bad. Most answering directly (8 of 13) said that people who led a good and honest life were more likely to be successful than unkind or dishonest people. Similarly, the majority answering the question (8 of 14) said they felt that people who did good deeds would be rewarded for them. Most (10 of 15) said they felt that crime did not pay. One said it did pay but not for Negroes. Asked whether to influence human behavior by reward or by punishment, there were only 3 who advocated punishment primarily; 6 advocated both, and 6 said reward was to be preferred. About half of those giving a direct reply (6 of 13) said that people obey laws which prohibit a given behavior. Asked about problem-handling, the majority (9) said they preferred to talk their problems over with others, and, on direct questioning about instances, two-thirds (10 of 15) had spoken to someone (family, friend, professional) about a problem within the last month. Five (3 men, 2 women) admitted to a record of arrest for other than traffic offenses (vice, fishing without a license, nonsupport, drunkenness, city ordinance violation). Two had been arrested twice and 3 had spent time in jail. Of those answering a question about how friends view a bunco victim, the majority (8 of 13) said he loses the respect of friends if they learn of his victimization.

MONEY HABITS, ATTITUDES AND FANTASIES. (All said they trusted banks as a place to keep money.) One-third had withdrawn money from a bank without having prior discussions with anyone about their intentions. One-third often or sometimes carried more than 50 dollars on their person. (None had more than 25 dollars on them at the time the question was asked, and only 1 "flashed"—showing the interviewer his funds.) Only 3 had gambled in the last month. All but 1 considered themselves as (bargain hunters when shopping, and all but 3 felt they were "sharp" in getting their money's worth.) About half (8) reported they had swung deals whereby they had gotten something for nothing or almost nothing. Most (9) had been approached by non-family members for loans within the last year. Of all those recalling any loan approach in the past, about half (7 of 15) had given the requested money. Most (12 of 15) said people admired a person who had lots of money; one-third (5 of 15) felt that money would make it easier for them to be liked. Two-thirds (10 of 14) said they dreamed about what it would be like to have lots of money. Asked about money-making methods they would employ, 8 said they were willing to take risks in a new business, but all denied willingness to engage in "corner-cutting sharp business practices" or "to steal if you had to." Only 1 said he would engage in shady operations if he were positive he would not be caught. The rest (6 of 15) denied willingness to take any risks.

Comment

The noncomplaining (ambivalently so, to be sure) advertisement-answering-still-ready-for-more fraud victims are, on the face of it, different from the complaining ones. The former are more often male, slightly better educated and better off financially, very much more part of the community—married, involved in organizations, having children, working and so forth, and are less emotional about religion.

In the complaining group, the women were essentially lonely, simple, old and tragic, whereas the men were dull, foolish, seeking stimulation, hopeful and unintegrated into a protective or interesting social life. In the new group, the "personals ad" responders, a different pattern—indeed several patterns—suggest themselves. Instead of short cons on the street, nearly all persons were victims of more complex and, in a sense, conventional, "business" fraud. These included consumer swindles, long cons and the like. Not quite so sure of their own grounds, whether because of complicity, embarrassment or the finer artistry of the con man, most had made discreet inquiries into means of recovery other than the simple expedient of the police. Unlike the complaining sample, some of the new group admitted to serious doubts as to police competence. As it turned out, these doubts did not preclude a request to us for assistance, so that finally 14 out of 15 asked that we give them help. We explained that ours was a cooperative relationship with the state attorney general, and 14 out of 15 asked that we bring their cases to the attention of that office. On the other hand, when given a name of an official to call, only five made such a call. It is obvious that the group sought as noncomplaining were all willing to complain to us, almost all were willing to have their case come to official attention, but only a few were willing to take the initiative and make a further effort.

Some members of the "personals ad" group had characteristics mindful of the earlier sample. We see them seeking social stimulation, exposing themselves to overtures by strangers, trying hard to be liked, being bored, being passive and, importantly, being depressed. Here, too, the reported good citizenship, neighborliness, denial of evil in other humans, trust that if they acted well toward others it would be returned in kind, confidence in law-abiding by others and hoping to be remembered for their "good deeds" (or being conscientiously regretful about having been "bad") are presumed correlates.

On the other hand, there were, in a small portion of the sample, quite a different set of features. At best, there was aggressiveness and competitiveness or, seen in a more unkind light, predilections in the direction of which the con men spoke. Consider those who admitted that they enjoyed lying, being feared, fooling others, showing who's boss, hoaxing, getting revenge, besting others and being a winner. Consider the higher proportion (5 of 15 here, versus 3 of 34 earlier) admitting adult crimes. Consider those who said they were out seeking excitement and adventure, the many asking for hypnosis, those going to bars and buying drinks for strangers, those who did look for the bad in people and those who believed that the good guys lost. There are those, too, who do carry large amounts of money on their person, those who gamble and those who dream the big dreams about money. We have not tested these items for interrelationships, but on their face, we take them to represent something quite different from the little old ladies in the first sample; something different, too, from some of the more innocent men in that sample.

The second sample, best characterized as ambivalent about complaining to authorities rather than noncomplaining, contained a large number of trusting, neighborly souls who needed excitement, quite possibly to counteract their depression. Some were pursuing their hopes for bargains or victories, others their fantasies of big money or big adventure through a device quite acceptable to them—responding accommodatingly, indeed "hypnotically" in most cases (just as Norfleet said!), to the proposals of strangers who were welcomed wearing conventional masks as purveyors of business opportunity.

It was not, of course, just business. For a few, there were other offerings, such as healing by a gypsy, an illegal adoption, the fun of a carnival and in one case, an apparent (but not necessarily real) fraud by a welfare agency. We assume that even the business offers involved more than things material, given the unmet interpersonal needs of the victims for approval, for deference, for excitement, for palliatives for melancholy and for the need to affirm the goodness of themselves and others. The kindly con is there to cater to their wants. Yet the con man himself is mistaken if he thinks that all that compels his marks is material greed, just as the con man simplifies himself if he thinks that his larceny is only for money. The con man has the thrill of the beating, the substitute pleasure of the killing, the repetitive assurance of his cleverness. The victim, so it seems from what we have observed, occasionally gets his pleasure from similar games but much more often, at least among victims we have met, from pursuing conventional goals with an added fillip of gratification for deeper needs, needs for the most part indicative of sadness, passivity, isolation, naiveté and frustration.

NONCOMPLAINING VICTIMS: "STRAIGHTFORWARD" CONSUMER FRAUD

The foregoing inferences are limited to the samples investigated and must be recognized as speculative, at least in part. That not all fraud is so complex or "psychological" in nature must also be acknowledged. One would anticipate that the more conventional the fraud, the closer it is related to an ordinary business practice, and the less aggressive the victim is in seeking it out, the fewer "depth" aspects will be found. To demonstrate, it will be instructive to consider a study conducted in 1965 by Herschel Elkins of the office of the Attorney General of the state of California. Responding to a television commercial which appeared to be misrepresenting a home remodeling offer, the investigator reviewed newly filed second mortgages which specified the advertising company as the mortgage holder. Householders having signed these deeds of trust were approached by letter and asked how they had fared in their dealings with the home remodeling (stone siding) representative. Of 40 approached, 38 replied and 32 said they had been cheated. None had complained. The 38 were interviewed. Most often, embarrassment over having been cheated was said to have often, embarrassment over having been cheated was said to have restrained them from complaint. Some were punishing themselves for having been stupid—"It will teach me a lesson." Some did not know the channels for complaint—"I thought since I signed a contract that there was nothing I could do about it." These consumers did not know that criminal action was possible because of misrepresentation. Some thought only civil action was possible and did not wish to pay lawyers' fees, since they were not optimistic about winning. Others had complained to the company but were soothed and persuaded they had received a "good deal." A few were fatalistic—"Chalk it up to experience."

In some consumer frauds, the primary technique is door-to-door selling in which the consumer is, essentially, trapped in his own home, and because he is too polite to throw out the salesman, he becomes a victim of the ethic of courteous hospitality. Commonly, calls are made at eight or nine in the evening and the sales pitch continues relentlessly for four or five hours until the exhausted citizen signs. "A professional salesman versus an amateur buyer" can have only one outcome. It is the inability of the citizen to be aggressive to a "guest in the home" which is the critical point.

In one case of Elkins' (1965), in order to demonstrate the

pattern of misrepresentation in the pitches by all salesmen of that particular company, a homeowner was asked to record by means of a concealed tape recorder the proceedings after inviting a salesman to his home. The citizen was told what to expect, the nature of the misrepresentation was explained to him, and his role in the prosecution was outlined. He was to reject the salesman after the pitch was on tape. The willing citizen invited the salesman to his home and, after listening to the entire pitch, signed the offered contract! The Attorney General's investigator, dumbfounded, asked the victim how he could possibly have signed the contract after being forewarned that the pitch was fraudulent. All the citizen could shamefacedly say was, "Well, I dunno, it sounded like such a good deal."

Chapter V

TRAITORS: HISTORICAL CONSIDERATIONS

INTRODUCTION

"TRAITOR" IS AN emotionally loaded word. More moderate is the term "defector," embracing as it does a greater variety of political and criminal behavior. Either as traitor or defector, the individual whose violation of trust involves a crime against the state is of interest in a study of deceivers and betrayal.

Before turning to the analysis of cases, it is essential that attention be drawn to the complexity which surrounds the classification of conduct as treasonous, a complexity which not only pervades the law and leads to consideration of the relationship between crime and political power, but which raises issues of social and moral philosophy as one examines the relationship, changing over the centuries, of the individual to the state. Unlike the confidence men of the preceding section whose actions and intentions are relatively simple in regard to the criminal codes, the traitor—or better, the concept of the defector as criminal or of man in a relationship of obligatory trust vis-à-vis the state—can be described with an historical process in mind. For that reason, our consideration of the defector begins with an history of treason.

A defector is ordinarily considered anyone who secedes, rebels or deserts; a traitor betrays and politically is one who betrays his allegiance to his government. The defector need not violate trust, for his renunciation of a cause or country may be frank, as with an immigrant who sails away or a rebel who first announces his secession without violating the confidence of those against whom he rebels. A traitor does violate a confidence, although it must be marked at the outset that the confidence so violated may be one that is imposed, obligatory or assumed rather than one that is a function of trust given and received between individuals. A citizen or subject to the state or sovereign may not have tendered any promise of loyalty, may not have acted in such a way as to generate any such expectations and may have entered into no reciprocal relationships involving trust but yet may be—indeed was and is—required by authority to act in certain ways, any deviation of which is challenged as a betrayal. Although such unilateral requirements are most easily envisioned in men's relationships to political authority, the same possibility of an obligation assumed by one but not acknowledged by another can exist interpersonally and can also lead to charges of betrayal. In either case, such charges carry a great weight of emotion, as can be inferred from the popular conceptions in Chapter XII.

TRAITORS IN ANCIENT TIMES

Alcibiades is one of the best known early political figures to be characterized as a traitor (Poole & Poole, 1968). Brilliant, debauched and unscrupulous, he utilized his talents to the advantage and to the disadvantage of Athens, his home city for which he served on several occasions as general. After intrigue and counterintrigue in Athens during its war with Sparta, he was ordered to stand trial on charges of religious desecration. Instead, he escaped to Sparta where he gave Spartans advice which helped them defeat Athens. He then stirred revolts against Athens in Asia Minor and arranged an alliance between the Persians there and Sparta. Soon losing the confidence of the Spartans (among other things he seduced the wife of the Spartan king), he turned about to undermine Sparta with the Persians and simultaneously conspired with dissident Athenians to bring about a revolution at home. The revolution successful, he was appointed an Athenian sea commander and was victorious over the Spartans. Once condemned to death by Athenians, it was the Spartans who managed his assassination.

As a youth, Alcibiades was selfish, charming, vain and cruel; he did not hesitate to insult and embarrass his uncle, Pericles, who had, without interest or affection, reared him. At age 15, Alcibiades had fallen out with this surrogate father and established his own household. As an adult, his traits were the same, although his love of power and his great competence encompassed city-states and nations, whereas as a youth his interests had been limited to show, pride, sport and lovers. Because of his impact, his reputation for perfidy and triumph both were great. Alcibiades has his modern counterparts who, although playing less magnificent parts, show flagrant vanity, opportunism, a history of difficulty with authority figures and a personal history of self-indulgence and delinquencies which become linked to treason. As one examines the data on modern defectors, one shall see the same syndrome reappearing.

Alcibiades was neither the first nor the last of Greeks to be considered traitors. Epialtes is well known (See Herodotus, Book VII, para, 213) for his betrayal to Xerxes of the Spartans defending the pass at Thermopylae, an act done "in the hopes of great reward" but one resulting in the Amphictyonic League's putting a price on his head with heralds sent through Greece to announce that fact. Thucydides also offers accounts of betrayal in his history of the Peloponnesian War. For example, Pausanius, the Regent of Sparta, deserting the struggle against Persia, instead connived with Xerxes. Flattered by that king, Pausanius became so identified with Persian ways that he revealed his intentions. The Spartans, whose general he had been, recalled him on pain of being declared a public enemy. Confident that he could clear himself through bribery, Pausanius returned. The Spartans lacked hard evidence until an homosexual partner of Pausanius, asked by the latter to serve as his messenger to the Persians, became afraid and then vengeful and turned informer. His action arose from his observation that no earlier messengers sent to the Persians had ever returned; suspecting Pausanius' treachery, he opened the letter and found it did contain instructions that the messenger be put to death. Upon seeing that, he went to the Spartan magistrates and connived with them to arrange a conversation in which Pausanius would be overheard admitting his intrigues. The proof in, the magistrates planned his arrest, but Pausanius was warned by one of the magistrates and took refuge in a temple where the Spartans starved him to death. Not all treason was dealt with so harshly, though. Demosthenes (740:14), in his case against Tomocrates, remarks that the latter had once paid a fine of three talents (about 1,800 dollars) on conviction of treason.

What is apparent is that political betrayal was common in ancient Greece, where shifting loyalties, opportunism, pride in cleverness, intercity warfare and expanding wealth were the substance of the times. The Greek conceptions of treason were several. The verb for betrayal (*prodidomi*) also meant to give away, to forsake or abandon, to play false or to desert. Herodotus (Book III, para. 45), for example, describes the caution of Polycrates, ruler of Samos, who when faced with an attack from rebels he had exiled, shut up in sheds the wives and children of his loyal troops, for these hostages were to be burned alive if his troops deserted. Aeschylus, in *The Libation Bearers* (line 271), has Orestes speak of his hope that the Delphic oracle will not betray him; that is, it will prove correct. The same word also meant to adulterate wine or to be thankless, and described a useless defensive fortification. Another verb, *prodosis*, which meant to advance money, also meant to betray. The noun *prodotis* meant betrayer and included the idea of one who abandons another at a time of danger. Herodotus (Book VIII, para. 30) observes that, when given an ultimatum by the Thessalians aligned with the Medes to pay tribute or be laid waste, the Phocians (in any event enemies of the Thessalians) replied they would not be traitors to Greece if they could help it. In the same way, in chiding the Spartans for fearing they would accept a treaty proffered by the Persians, which they rejected outright, the Athenians said they would fight rather than come to terms and betray the Greek manner of life. Another noun, *prodosia*, also meant traitor or one who gave up. Herodotus (Book 6, para. 88) speaks of a man of Aegina who, when the Greeks were at war with that island, because he had a grudge arising from his being exiled from Aegina, offered to betray the island by capturing, with his men, a portion of it and holding until the Athenians landed there. In another instance, Herodotus (Book 8, para. 128) describes how Timoxeinus, the commander of a contingent of men from Scione allied in beseiged Potidaea, contrived treachery with the Persians outside the walls. Discovered in communication with them, the other commanders "decided not to deal drastically with Timoxeinus for his attempt at betrayal for the sake of Scione, lest the people of that city should be called traitors from that time on."

Plato (*Republic*, 443A) speaks of *prodosia* in relation to the conduct of a just man, one who has self-mastery, is in harmony with himself and whose birth and breeding assure a balance (harmony) among reason, will and passion, which, as his internal components, must be coordinated into a whole. Such a man would not be expected to betray his comrades or the state, nor would he be expected to perpetrate the crimes of embezzlement, sacrilege or the breaking of his vows, a constellation of violations of trust which Plato linked as the acts of those who might be, in modern times, termed "maladjusted" or "sociopathic." And Plato's propositions are certainly sophisticated in terms of modern psychology. As we shall see in the data on modern traitors, Plato's implication of correlated misbehaviors, derived from personal intrapsychic conflict or incompatibility with moral codes foreshadows future events, just as Alcibiades' personality as a constellation of intellectual gifts and social vices is an early mirror of certain modern defectors.

Under the Romans, the concept of crimes against the state was fully developed (Schisas, 1926; Lear, 1965). Under the Republic, the first such category of offenses were *perduellio*, meaning at first a bad war or warrior but later coming to designate an inner enemy and applied to any act inimical to Rome and every violation of allegiance thereto. A second concept, that of *maiestas*, embraced violations of the principle of respect owed to the eminent and by implication set off the powerful against the less powerful. A magistrate, for example, could define any attack against his person as *crimen maiestas*. Noteworthy under the Roman law was the fact that a community as well as an individual could be guilty of *perduellio or crimen maiestas*. Thus applied, peoples in subordinate (occupied) or allied lands could be charged with crimes against the Roman state, Roman magistrates or Roman citizens. Revolt was so classified. Also in that category would be assassination of a magistrate or emperor, providing the assassin or those who hired him did not in turn become emperor, for the emperor, as with magistrates, had the power to decide what constituted treason and what its punishment should be. The emperor Domitian, for example, killed a historian because he did not like the parallels the man had drawn (MacMullen, 1966). He also decreed capital punishment for reading aloud speeches praising tyrannicides, Greek or Roman. Nero prosecuted poets for treason. Wiser writers, Seneca, for example, censored their own works, for as MacMullen affirms, terror does suppress subversion, driving it underground. So it was in Rome. The responses of the emperors were to become more fearful and terrible and the charges of treason looser, broader and encompassing guilt by association. Even so, the philosophers who came to lead the opposition (MacMullen says that ethics gave them strength for defiance and the vision of the moral ugliness of repression) acknowledged the rights of the emperor to be above the law of the state as long as he remains reasonable, allowing private morality, and adheres to the natural law, the latter a conception requiring further comment shortly. In any event, the writers and thinkers were persecuted because they "supplied dangerous ideas and stories to dangerous men" (MacMullen, p. 70). Thus Philostratus could write, "wisdom has become a crime" (Philostratus, *Life of Apollonius*, 7:11). Very important in the development of the Roman opposition were the Greek ideals that philosophers knew; the themes were the tyrannicide, splendid statements upon the martyr's interrogation, his suicide leading to martrydom (or his torture and death) and then, as MacMullen notes, his elevation through cult and literature. These concepts are both Greek and Roman themes, as well as Jewish and early Christian ideas, but they are also contemporary, for treason, assassination and the propagation of martrydom are joined through Western history. Another of MacMullen's themes also bears modern watching. That is that the treasonous opposition in Rome was not composed of the deviant or down-and-out but rather of the elite itself. It was the combat of persons of similar social and cultural backgrounds, although in the history of Rome, these backgrounds were not the same over the centuries, being first the elite and then involving peasants and finally barbarians as each shared in and opposed the ruling power. Protest, or treason, originated within the dominant groups and classes. "Any ruling culture," MacMullen writes, "arouses an internal nonconformity . . . the foes . . . arise from friends." Compare this assertion with that of Metternich in 1820, "The governments, having lost their balance, are frightened, intimidated and thrown into confusion by the cries of the intermediate class of society which, placed between the kings and their subjects, breaks the scepter of the monarchs and usurps the cry of the people" (cited by Waelder, 1967, p. 223).

Jaszi and Lewis (1957), considering the development of political opposition in classical times, focus on tyrannacide and stress the differences between ancient and modern viewpoints. In Greece, the tyrant was also the usurper (which is not to say that his rise necessarily offended the mood of the city), so that it was honorable for the citizen to remove him. There the tyrannicide was called father-killer, a clear association to the family-clan-political power constellation. The Greek concept of political honor, like Plato's view of the ideal statesman, derived from an assumption that regardless of the affairs of politics or whatever laws might be written, there was a higher code known and knowable to man, which formed the basis for proper conduct. Aristotle and Cicero likewise subscribed to the assumption of principles based on harmony in the natural order, sometimes stated in terms of divine order or human reason, against which laws, as well as conduct, could be judged. That concept and its brethren are referred to as the natural law. It is that concept which may be identified in much that is treasonable. Cicero, in *De Republica* (cited by Jaszi and Lewis), wrote,

> There is . . . a true law, namely, right reason—which is in accordance with nature, applies to all men and is unchangeable and eternal. By its commands, this law summons men to the performance of their duties; by its prohibitions, it restrains them from doing wrong. . . . To invalidate this law by human legislation is never morally right, nor is it permissible ever to restrict its operation, . . . God who is the author of this law, its interpreter and its sponsor.

Given the assumption of the natural law and that a tyrant was abhorrent to it then man had not just the right but the obligation to restore the natural order. Seneca is quoted as saying, "No offering is more acceptable to God than the blood of a tyrant" (cited in Jaszi and Lewis, p. 11). Plutarch, too, said of tyrannacide that it was a "remarkable act of virtue." Through the Roman law, which had from early times through the right of *provocatio* (appeal) sought to control the exercise of magistral power (capable of being set aside by martial law) over citizens sentenced to death (as in *perduellio*) and which in Civil Code states ". . . the prince profess himself bound by the laws, since our authority depends on the authority of the law," the possibility of the natural law as superior to the laws of kings or states contributed to medieval and thence to modern thinking.

MEDIEVAL TIMES

In north Europe after the fall of Rome, the German peoples evolved conceptions of treason which, although they had the foundation of the law of *perduello,* emphasized bilateral contracts and pledged agreements, rather than obligatory ones, upon the lesser folk in the hierarchy in which they had no chance to concur. Supreme treason to the Germans, according to Lear (1965), involved the breach of faith which had been pledged. Families and clans, as well as individuals, could be involved in such troths, so that there arose a set of crimes describing various forms of lack of fidelity. As the structure of government grew, chiefs and kings played a greater role as principals in allegiance, but families, tribes, village corporate groups and others continued to expect individuals to enter into and to maintain their pledges, subject to charges of breach of faith. Over time, treason came to be applied generally to bad faith arising between leaders and followers. Traitors were those who could not be expected to live up to their voluntary pledges and obligations. The Visigoths also set up legal codes by which to govern their Roman subjects and in these, the *maisestas* provisions included revolt against the Emperor or public authority, waging of war without the Emperor's consent and creating disturbances in the military. Under the Code of 642, treason was the denial and destruction of the symbolic authority of the realm, allegiance was the acceptance of that authority. The latter was binding only so long as the king himself obeyed that law which recognized the customary rights of the land and people. High treason against the king (plotting his death or injury) was much narrower than treason against the fatherland itself, which was defined as fomenting disorder or scandal, acting disrespectfully or rebelliously toward the country, conspiring with hostile nations, failing to heed summons to battle, deserting or being insubordinate.

Some of these same Visigoth principles entered into Anglo-Saxon law, but by the eleventh century (Dooms of Cnat), the royal power abrogated to itself many of the former offenses against the land and people, so that public order and general welfare were subject to the king's peace, and it was the king who decided their violation. Contempt for the king's orders became subject to the laws of treason. Among the Franks, a different code evolved, one in which the families and clans retained a less powerful place than among Visigoths, and offenses against the king and his apparatus, the state, constituted treason. Among the Alamannic peoples (north Rhine), special provisions for offenses against the church were entered; there, too, the duke, as holder of authority in lieu of the king, when plotted against or harmed invoked the high-treason law. The Visigothic fatherland laws of treason (*landesverrat*) were also in effect. In Bavaria, slightly different codes emerged, so that a merging of the offenses of high treason against the duke and those offenses against the fatherland occurred. Thus any crime subversive to the people's welfare became treason against the duke (as was also true in the Alamannic law), for it was under his jurisdiction that the land and folk were kept, as was the ducal peace. In general, says Lear, the Germanic law evolved so that the king, his ducal authority and the church all became special interests capable of receiving allegiance and capable of defining its violation in many offenses that simply challenged the general peace or public order. The element of contract remained in the feudal agreements, as between king and vassal, but the obligatory allegiance, as between king and subject, appears to emerge (although Lear does not label it as such) in such form as to allow the authorities a very broad range of prosecution for treason; this range extended well beyond attacks against either the king or his deputies or the conventional adhering to enemies of the state or interfering with the military. One sees in twentieth-century prosecutions in the fascist and Soviet countries what seem to be derivations of these broader applications of the law of treason.

Another set of themes, separate from those derived from Roman law or evolving out of the folk and fatherland Germanic laws of breach of pledged faith and offenses against the public order, were derived from Hellenic and Christian sources. Jaszi and Lewis discuss the notions of authority and obedience as set forth by New Testament sources. Paul is an important writer. He believed, they hold, that the depravity of man made government necessary so that the ruler became God's own instrument, or as Peter said, "Submit yourself to every ordinance of man for the Lord's sake . . ." (I Peter 2:13-14). Augustine, carrying this idea onward, saw even in tyrants God's wish and hand, citing Proverbs 8:15-16 "Through me kings reign, and tyrants through me hold the earth." Jaszi and Lewis say that the doctrine of the divine right of kings and its corollary requirement of the Christian duty of obedience to temporal authority grew out of this. Pope Gregory made the concept clear, "Those who murmur against the rulers set over them speak not against a human being but against Him who disposes of all things by divine order." Early and later Christians argued against this dictate, saying that God might ordain the office of king but man need not accept the kingship of one who abused the office. Isidore of Seville found a semantic solution which was that those would be called king only who ruled rightly.

In the eleventh century, Manegold of Lautenbach proposed that there was between king and subjects an implicit contract. Therefore, an evil rule constituted a breach of contract out of which authority grew, and so subjects were then freed of their obligation of obedience. Thomas Aquinas, in the thirteenth century, expounded on the obligations of the king to provide a flourishing environment for the soul. If that were not provided, then the citizen had no obligation of obedience. A further step was taken by Lucas de Penna, who argued that tyrannicide was justified because it removed a public enemy who himself endangered society. Aquinas disputed the propriety of killing a tyrant with rightful title but acknowledged—in the Greek tradition—that one who was a usurper might properly be assassinated.

As the structure of social, religious and political institutions changed with the ending of the Middle Ages, it was inevitable that the intensity and complexity of issues surrounding relations between sovereign and subjects would be magnified. For instance, Pope Innocent IV in 1245 in his conflict with Frederick II proclaimed that God had deposed the king, and he forbade Frederick's subjects giving him aid or loyalty. In this act, there is evidence not only of the to-be-expanded struggle between papal and secular authority and what Jaszi and Lewis see as the exercise of institutional (papal) restraint upon the sovereign but of the conflict between the religious-moral sense of righteousness (albeit also papal-political) and the law of the sovereign (i.e. of decrees, later to become the body of state law as sovereigns were removed, albeit this had strong moral components). Thus the issue of the natural law of God, as posed either by Cicero in favor of subjects or by Paul in favor of kings, and the positive law, as that written by men—whether kings or parliaments—had become central by the fourteenth century. It is also evident that the terms themselves, natural versus positive law, embrace concepts and arguments that are not exclusive so that the definition of either may be arbitrary (see Mannheim, 1965).

Ullmann (1966) presents a careful and edifying analysis of the position of man as subject and constituent element in society in medieval times. He also shows man's slow emergence, with the breakdown of the Middle Ages, as an individual with rights of his own. This development is intimately linked with those relations between man and state which bear on the doctrine of treason. The medieval Christian, as a member of the Church, accepted the law as given to him. His faithfulness consisted in his obedience to the law derived from God and, as Paul required, to the authority of princes in which it was vested. Man had neither rights nor autonomy, nor was law linked to consent; rather faithfulness and obedience were one. Pope Gregory the Great in the ninth century sanctioned inequality and established the principle that no inferior could accuse a superior nor did he have the right of resistance against authority. The king, on the other hand, had the duty of guardianship and caring for his subjects, but the subjects could not enforce its exercise. When the king was tyrant, the subject could only pray for his improvement—or kill him, since there was no other mechanism for change nor did any higher body exist which could declare the king a tyrant. Thus any act against the king became high treason, as Ullmann says "high" because it was against the majesty (Latin, *maiestas*), an act which challenged the divine power itself. Petty treason was defined as murder of the master by the servant, of the bishop by clerk or layman, or of husband by wife. Medieval treason was a crime of inferior against superior. This relationship of treason to authority, evident in Rome and in Europe during the Middle Ages, deserves further analysis as a psychological phenomenon, one linked in modern times to inner as well as external conflicts with authority.

Treason was also heresy, according to Ullmann, because its expression demonstrated not just a challenge to the king and his divinely granted status but a symptom of corrosion which threatened society itself, that society being founded on faith and obedience. The traitor-heretic showed that he preferred his opinions to those of his betters—including God and the king. In so doing, he jeopardized the whole fabric of the medieval world.

The rule of law in the Middle Ages which defined these obligations was so strong because, given the cohesive nature of a society as a community of the faithful, the law was seen as the soul of the social body, as Ullmann says, "the norm of the right order of living. The law, as the soul, ruled the corporate entity" (Ullman, 1966, p. 47) and the king was the embodiment of that law.

This view, more compatible with the interests of the ruler than the ruled, was less prevalent among the lower classes. Ullmann states that the lower reaches of the community nevertheless assumed they had the rights which the religious-political thesis denied them. At the village level and in commerce, an informal social structure existed in which "original power resided in the members of the community" (Ullmann, 1966, p. 56). Village self-government implied equality among persons and consent of the governed. Since it worked, these assumptions which operated as custom became customary law and formed an element in a modified conception of the natural law. Because it was functional at the village level, that law posed a threat to the divine right. Thus one sees the potential conflict between custom derived from practice and law derived from linked power and ideology. The former is more useful to individuals; the latter, to elites.

In the Middle Ages, only subjects of the king and not his vassals (land-holding tenents under a contract of homage and aid) could commit treason. Ullmann points out that a feudal lord, king included, who was tyrannical might produce in his vassals the simple and lawful act of repudiation, which was the withdrawal of loyalty from one person by another.* As with village functioning, the feudal functioning required such contracts among individuals based on personal feelings and obligations which, when failing as in the case of tyrants, deprived the tyrant of resources and gave him potential enemies. In such matters, reality mattered, as did individual responsibility, and higher dogma meant little. Subjects, however, could not repudiate their relationships, and insofar as the modern law of states denies citizens the right of renunciation and the withdrawal of loyalty, one finds a continuation of the medieval dogma earlier described. Constitutional law, on the other hand, with its emphasis on individual rights, was drawn in part from feudal law. Ullmann points out that the Magna Carta takes some of its substance from a German feudal code of 1037, namely the provision of trial by peers under charges based on the law of the land. He terms this the first instance of the English common law which barred the Roman and canon law from further English inroads. This was the beginning of parliaments and the requirement of consent; it was the doctrine which held the ruler to the law and, more broadly, held rulers bound by the natural law. In contrast, Ullmann suggests that on the Continent, the thesis of the descending law (from God to ruler controlling those below

---

* These vassals were usually local chieftains with their own armies whom the king could not easily challenge. Only with the development of modern armaments which the monarch and state could afford but which lesser local leaders could not did monarchs consistently affirm their power and expand the sovereignty of the state itself.

through faith and obligation) extended past the Middle Ages as governments became bureacratized, a royal bureaucracy. The bureaucrats had reserved for them the high status of authority and civil servants exempted by the *droit administrativ* from protest; they were immune to the complaints of citizens and inflexible compared to the English system of citizen contract and consent. This is a very important point to bear in mind as we compare the kinds of traitors who defect from the Soviet Union to the West with those who defect from England and the United States to the Iron Curtain. Ullmann contends that it is due to the feudal contract and functional village customary law that the revolutionary young United States, bequeathed the English common law, resisted the power of monarchs and elaborated the rights of individuals. In parts of Europe lagging far behind England, this resistance to tyranny was less vital, and the institutions of a powerful bureaucracy immune to protest provided a broader base of power for traditional forces. Revolution was the necessary device for challenging those forces, although as we can see from modern European states, it was not a device which necessarily replaced the tyranny, only the holders of office.

MODERN TIMES

While in England there was enacted in the fourteenth century the Treason Act, in Italy a sequence of great events was occurring which was the Renaissance. In a very different way, contributions were being made to concepts and laws, shaping man's relationship to the state. In the thirteenth century, the people of Italian cities had already enunciated rights and duties and the nature of their sovereignty (Jones, 1965). Their citizenship was a heritage of Rome. Subsequent events mirrored earlier events in Rome and Greece when in the fourteenth and fifteenth centuries new tyrants appeared within the north Italian city-states. Their emergence under the new social and economic conditions, intercity rivalry and a heterogenous ideology was also connected with changes in morality, considered by some to be moral degeneration. Certainly it was a period rife with the violation of trust. Jaszi and Lewis quote an Italian historian,

Sismondi, who said, "Spies watched and denounced . . . insinuated themselves into families to betray them; they abused the sacred ties of kindred, home and neighborhood to convert them into snares . . ." Against the intrigue, suspicion, assassination and poisoning which were the methods of rulers, the reaction was to use these same devices as counterweapons. Boccaccio (cited by Jaszi and Lewis, p. 39) wrote, "Against (the tyrant) I may use arms, conspiracies, spies, ambushes and fraud; to do so is a sacred and necessary work." Machiavelli, aware that the knife cuts in two directions, counselled princes to safety through winning the respect of the subject. He also held that the multitude would never rise against the tyrant; by implication, it must be the elite who do so. And so in Italy, as in Rome of the Caesars, the elite, who were taught philosophy and an admiration for earlier tyrannicides, Brutus himself most gloriously, were the active opposition. Thus Lorenzio de' Medici assassinated Alessandro de' Medici, and Galeazzo Sforza was stabbed by Milanese nobles. Given the atmosphere, the professionalization of intrigue was inevitable, a development primarily supported by the despots themselves. In Venice, the Council received bids for poisoners and kept a special register of assassins, as well as a poison cabinet. Later, schools for assassins taught use of the daggar. The professional assassins were outcasts and criminals. That development is an important one, for it marks the simultaneous presence of two types of political assassins (traitors). The first was on the model of Brutus, an elite idealist invoking right custom or the natural law in opposition to the tyrant. The other was the criminal or deviant who, without ideals or normal ties to the community, pursued his self-interest, whether that be money, vengeance or some cruel or idiosyncratic pleasures. The idealistic tyrannicide, according to Jaszi and Lewis, was the rarer form, for it was based on principle and courage among an educated elite. The simple pursuit of power which spawned the widespread conspiracy, betrayal and assassination—and of course warfare—was a much more common human commodity. As we shall see, this distinction applied to modern traitors remains vital.

During the same period in England the first of its laws on

treason was passed, one derived from Roman law. This was the Treason Act of 1352, which encompassed the crimes of plotting against or killing the king or his family, violating the king's female companions or family members; warring against the king, adhering to his enemies or giving them aid or comfort; or slaying the king's chancellor or judges. The Act, later altered in this regard, also cited forgery of the seal and counterfeiting coinage. Otherwise the Act remains essentially in force, supplemented by clauses dealing with interference with the succession. The law in the United States, about which we shall have more to say shortly, derives from this Act.

Elsewhere in Europe, except in England, royal centralization proved effective and absoluteness was not diminished. Even Luther, distrustful as he was of fools and scoundrels in office, did not acknowledge the right of resistance, for his rulers were also his agents for change. "Therefore, let everyone who can strike, slay and stab secretly or openly remember that nothing can be more poisonous, dangerous or devilish than a rebel" (cited by Jaszi and Lewis, p. 45). Calvinists, on the other hand (but not Calvin), were a "Christian despotism" in power, as Jaszi and Lewis term it, but when out of office were a determined force for opposition. Thus John Knox "maintained it was the duty of subjects to establish the true religion by force if necessary," a doctrine applied by the Puritans in the Bay Colonies (Erikson, 1966) and one which, as practiced, leads to comparison of the fanatic ideology of New England to that of more modern times, with evangelical Communism as a strong example. In Scotland, too, and in France, Protestant thought developed to declare that believers had a right and a duty to resist any attempt to subvert the true religion. From this, one foresees a new development of the natural law, the ideology of the true believer who pits himself against the state. That the believer and his fellow ideologists may ally themselves in common cause or united fronts with others of differing sentiments for the pursuit of power, done under the guise of compelling morality, is apparent. It was out of such a development that Protestant England judged its Catholic minority dangerous during the conflict with Spain after the Pope in 1570 excommunicated Queen Elizabeth and forbade obedience to her by her subjects. The papal Secretary also supported proposals to assassinate her, a support followed by assassination attempts against her.

In such instances, it is hard to say what portion of an intrigue rests on political grounds and what rests on a consensus as to the dictates of the natural law. It is apparent that the justification of treason or assassination by appeals to any form of tradition, custom, morality, divine sanction or righteousness is open to any whose ideals or interests are served by opposition to the ruler or the state. It is also clear that one must expect several levels of motivation or instigation to treason within persons and groups and among groups united in such a cause. These levels are likely to be ennobled by ideals and convenient interpretations of the natural law but may very well also embrace crass power seeking, resistance to interference, conflicts of value or response to oppression. As one examines the modern traitor, it will be well to bear in mind the probability of complexity, inconsistency and the abrogation to one's own conscience of the privilege of interpreting what is righteous.

By the end of the eighteenth century, according to Jaszi and Lewis, arguments and concerns shifted from tyrannicide, for the ruler had evolved into a state, whether a royal bureacracy or otherwise, and opposition thereto was focused on a system as well as a man. It had been a limited and conservative doctrine to think only of deposing a man in office; as men were individualized and came to evaluate governments as such, programs turned toward radical change. The revolutions of the American colonies, of France and of Russia are examples of an attempt to overthrow the larger authority of monarchy—or as with Communists to eliminate the economic causes of which the despot was the symptom—and to institute an innovative regime instead. Thus treason came to be associated with revolution and efforts to overthrow the state, rather than tyrannicide, although assassination, as of the Czar, would still be a part. The optimism about revolution was part of the romantic tradition carrying through the nineteenth and twentieth centuries. However, that romanticism was countered by pessimism, following very shortly after, as the outcomes of French and Russian revolutions made themselves painfully apparent. For as part of these movements there arose what Jaszi and Lewis call "distorted tyrannicide," which is the programs of conspiratorial violence, anarchic disruption, mass terrorism and other techniques whereby a minority, invoking ideals, could become despots themselves. Lenin's brother, Ulyanov (Jaszi and Lewis, p. 139), justified it in the following: "Terror is the sole form of defense left to a minority that is strong only in spiritual force and in the consciousness that it is right, against the physical force of the majority." For those who could not succeed in overthrow, anarchistic destruction was still a necessary symbolic act. Nechaev (Jaszi and Lewis, p. 136) said, "The Revolutionary knows only one science—destruction . . ." and Sorel (Jaszi and Lewis, p. 14) argued that violent crimes were a heroic act. In these beliefs, one finds conduct and issues applying to the traitors of today, such as the symbolic function of acts even when futile, the glorification of destruction even if the object is not clearly related to the enemy, and the association between crime and political heroism as viewed from the standpoint of perpetrator, just as there is an association between acts that are defined as criminal and the political status of the offender or offending group vis-à-vis those passing the law.*

------

* Quinney (1964), in considering crime in political perspective, considers criminal law to be an aspect of politics, that interest groups formulate laws favorable to themselves, and that criminal laws are passed (citing the Espionage Act of 1918) to control political crises and dissenters. He states that Americans are particularly intolerant of political and social differences compared to other democracies and that our criminal law reflects disapproval of the values and beliefs held by groups that are simply different, not necessarily rebellious or oppositional. Marx, of course, had earlier discussed the use of law to protect capitalism, and others have been concerned with the use of law in our democracy simultaneously to protect and suppress dissent and pluralism.

Matza (1964) argues that the criminal law is fundamentally a criminal matter, since "it has been one major focus of the ongoing conflict between authorized officials of the state and the citizenry" (p. 153). When conceived of as an excuse for intervention by the state on the customs of citizens, it also represents a conflict of value system. The law also adjusts itself to changing political power. George Washington would have been hung for treason if the Colonies had lost the War of Revolution; he was President and patriot for these same acts by virtue of winning. Matza indicates that whenever a large group of citizens disagree with a prohibition, then the state is viewed as unjust in enforcement. It would follow (as with the Whiskey Rebellion) that the state may face opposition and insurrection if enforcement endeavors are pushed. Mannheim

A further development, as conceived by Jaszi and Lewis, is the systematization of political murder well outside the justifications of custom or morals of the society within which it occurs. These are murders that the homicides themselves may not bother to excuse on any ideological grounds. History is full of these, although it becomes difficult to separate them from acts of brigandage, revolt, warfare or suppressive rule. Jaszi and Lewis contend that political murder reached its peak in pre-Nazi and Nazi Germany. They cite evidence to the effect that more than 400 political murders were committed in the years 1918-1922. Most of these were attributed to secret societies* acting on

---

* The presence of the secret society is a social phenomenon of considerable importance, although one rarely commented upon and, until now, not subject to social analysis except as a subordinate aspect of political inquiry. An example is the operation of Communist cells, terrorist units and the like. George Simmel (1950 trans.) wrote a pioneering sociological essay in 1908 in which he proposed that such societies arose during transitional periods when the substance of their beliefs (confidences) were new and required protection from the disapproval of more traditional society. He cites the rise of liberalism in Germany which in the eighteenth century was associated with secret societies. On the other hand, he notes that decaying as well as emerging values may be deposited in such groups, an event which he sees as prodromal to the end of these value epochs. Their presence is a counterpart of despotisms, for without oppression they would not be necessary. Their presence implies a moral solidarity in which trust and

---

(1965) examines related issues more thoroughly and asks how many persons adjudged criminal do in fact commit their crimes for moral reasons or out of a sense of injustice. He calls attention to the irrelevance of most crime (excepting tyrannicide, treason and revolution) as contributing to political change and cites Friedrich Engles to the effect that crime is a primitive and individual action which cannot hope to solve social problems.

One should also remark in response to the fashionable contentions that crime is political, with its implication that the positive law is but a weapon in the hands of the powerful (implying the virtue of the critic as the true keeper of the natural law), that the probability is that for most of the offenses charged, the offender, as well as the accuser, will agree that the act is wrong. They disagree more often on whether it was committed by the accused. Finally, when persons argue that the criminal law is only a political device, they extend the word political to include much of social process, including morality, for the legislative process in democracies which leads to criminal law can hardly be conceived as a simple act exercising the crass interests of the powerful. Even so, it is to be recognized that legislative action can represent the powerful minority, or the majority, in ways that severely punish conduct and interests a minority conceives as legitimate, as for example when Indians of the northwest are arrested for salmon fishing.

behalf of the embryonic Nazi movement; their victims were persons labeled by them as a "social pest." It was only a step to the mass exterminations practiced in concentration camps. The Stalanist purges, conducted by trial rather than secret society proceedings, produced the same effect and were shortly followed by the mass deaths of prisoners in Soviet work camps. Against such state operations, the individual in opposition is nearly helpless. Not only does he lack power but he also lacks, as Jaszi and Lewis point out, the opportunity to assess public opinion to learn whether his revulsion is idiosyncratic or widespread, since the totalitarian society is closed to any airing of opinions about the propriety of the rulers. If he sets out to assassinate, revolt or betray, he may therefore have to act without knowledge of a larger consensus. He may appear to himself, or a small group of conspirators may appear to themselves, as deviant or criminal in fact and without the support of current custom or visible morality. Thus Penkovskiy, defecting to the West from the USSR, was a lonely man. That this lonely status and the fact of no consensus may lead to the interpretation of conscience as madness is also possible. Indeed the individual may be mad, a viewpoint given government sanction now in the USSR where large numbers of political dissidents are sent to mental hospitals rather than Siberia (Tarsis, 1965).

In the West, those who oppose the state may assess their position openly, comparing it to the national consensus and

confidence are prime interpersonal components which take on a compulsory power. As to confidence itself, Simmel sees it as a basic synthetic force in society, one intermediate between knowledge and ignorance of other men. Simmel's analysis of secret societies ignores the psychological aspect of shared fantasies, of the possibility of their existence as means of intensifying relationships even when protection is not necessary, of their role not in transitional phases of values but as permanent repositories of disapproved but functional conduct (as for example the Chinese Triad societies) or their existence as ways of demarking status roles within societies, as, for example, the fraternities of tribal societies marked by exclusion of others from secret rights. In any event, the secret society with its social and psychological functions deserves thorough study as an element in the lives of those opposing governments. It is quite possible that the membership in a secret society is so attractive to some who become defectors that their ideological content is secondary; thus individuals might well act in treasonous ways simply to maintain membership but without having either specific oppositional intents or ideologies except as these are embraced as a prerequisite for acceptance.

weighing it against the various revelations of natural law which groups abrogate to themselves. In such situations, the opposition which resorts to terror and subversion can rarely claim moral support, although they may, as with Calvinists or Communists, claim superior revelations. In the democratic Western world, one would then expect traitors to be of two sorts, with neither one being lonely men of conscience carrying with them the higher principles of a subverted culture. The first are the well-known subscribers to fanatic and righteous dogma, such as militant Communists or anarchists, whose various methods are well-documented. (See, for example, Selznick, 1960). The other traitors, not members of a revolutionary cadre, are social deviants without a group purpose. These would be expected to be delinquents, neurotics and others, whose acts, while given social-political significance by the state which brings the charges, are likely to be much more personal in origin and also expressive of prior as well as current maladjustment.* We shall see that our sample defectors to the Iron Curtain are of both types. The latter are much more often represented than the former, simply because the former are usually identified by security procedures as dissident politically and so not allowed the kind of access to secrets which is required to meet the criteria we employed for identifying traitors.

One can see that the evolution of treason has been slow and reasonably consistent, yet necessarily made complex by changing times which include altering conceptions of man, society, government and divinity. The development of our own law in the United States also reflects these events, partly because of events in the Colonies and partly because of the historical developments in England since the fourteenth century. By the sixteenth century in England, treason was deeply implicated, as we have noted, with the fear of subversion of Protestantism by Catholicism. According to Simon (1961), it was also associated with antintellectual impulses, perhaps not inappropriately in the

---

* David Rothestein is reported by Joyce Brothers (1967) to have studied persons attempting to assassinate presidents. He describes them as sharing a constellation of neurotic features which include emotional disturbance, masculinity doubts, failure in military service and a brooding hatred for authority.

sense that teachers and philosophers throughout Roman, Renaissance and Reformation periods had taken a leading role in
formulating "dangerous" ideas and "giving ideas to dangerous
people." By implication, conspiracies—and later, revolution—
were believed to require the leadership of an intellectual elite.
In England it was also the case, according to Simon, that as
political parties developed, they were not beneath accusing their
opponents of treason. This more desperate charge was linked to
crises of desperation within parties threatened with defeat or
extinction. It was especially the case that conservatives rallied
support by accusing their more change-oriented rivals with
treason, i.e. Catholic royalists so charging Protestants, Tories so
accusing Whigs. Simon feels that it was this predilection on the
part of politicians to use the charge in defaming their opponents
that had made the definition of treason so difficult and so subject
to abuse. These factors led the English judiciary often to reject
charges of treason, whereas the public, aroused by the emotion
connected with the "ultimate" crime, demanded action against
those politically if not judicially charged.

A very important feature contributing to inconsistency in
the history of changes and events associated with treason has
been the fact that, as Simon says, the concept of treason has
depended on what the crises of the times have been. It is
interesting that Mannheim (citing Welzel), argues that the
idea of the natural law itself could originate only in a time of
crisis. What is implied is that political crises represent a period
of strain in which two or more sectors disagree on the moral
bases of society and at least one of them disputes the propriety,
however sanctioned (whether by custom, positive law, the
assumed divine right, the prevailing religion or whatever) of
what those governing do and, further, denies them authority,
that is, contradicts them the right to rule. Such denial must be
legitimated, and indeed may have to arise, from a countervailing
set of ideals which necessarily must be perceived by the dissidents
as superior in an absolute sense. Thus the events complained
about in the charge of treason will reflect, on the part of authority,
the kind of acts and arguments which characterize the opposition
at any given time. But the countervailing cry of immorality,

irreligiousness or whatever else constitutes the basis of accusation for those adhering to the natural law will also reflect the ideological (and political) content of their morality at that moment. What they see as good defines what it is that is evil in authority and justifies their opposition—which that authority, in turn, defines as treason. The conflict between the natural law (of the dissidents, tyrannicides, or traitors) and the positive law of the rulers occurs only when groups seek to derive justifications for charges or actions from morality, from a source in custom or from ideology or heroic tradition (e.g. Brutus, Castro). It is a very different situation when an individual acting out of accident, impulse, greed, or power-seeking apart from an ideology and sociopolitical crisis commits violations of trust which constitute treason. Both styles of conduct characterize traitors of our own time.

In English history, as in Rome and later elsewhere, the focus of disputes invoking charges of treason and its countercharge of tyranny was on elites who shared, as MacMullen showed with Rome and Jaszi and Lewis with Renaissance Italy, cultural and class similarities. In that sense, the rulers and the treasonous or tyrannicidal opposition were the few acting against the backdrop of an almost irrelevant citizenry. Simon suggests that it was not until the English Treason Acts of 1795 and 1800 that public conformity began to be a feature of that governmental concern which expressed itself in law. Such concern can be understood against the events of the American Revolution of 1776 and the French Revolution of 1787, in which citizens, not just elites, acted in large numbers to overthrow what they said to be tyrannies. That is the same development which Jaszi and Lewis described as the transition between individuals and small elites acting as tyrannicides and the active intelligent opposition of large groups or whole peoples which constitutes revolution. That change is associated not only with the development of the state into bureaucratic and colonial monoliths but with the rise of education and political competence in citizens as a function of the growth of commerce, the industrial revolution and its correlated middle class and expanded intellectual leadership. It was during this period, according to Simon, that English mon-

archs continued to enlarge their efforts at control and added to
the law of treason a number of "quasi-treason" statutes just as
reformers sought limitations and procedural safeguards. Then
in the seventeenth century, treason was broadened by judicial
declaration, and in the eighteenth century the supplemental
laws were enacted. The latter reflected the important participation of the common people in politics. For example, there had
been in 1661 an act against "tumultuous petitioning" which sought
to control the use of mobs as had occurred in the Long Parlia-
ment and by means of which the King had been blackmailed
into accepting legislation. In 1714, the Riot Act included capital
punishment for some forms of rioting, and following mutinies
of 1797, the inciting of soldiers and sailors to mutiny was included among the quasi-treason statutes.

In 1795, the Seditious Meetings Act was passed, which introduced the sedition laws requiring that all meetings held for the
purpose of criticizing or petitioning the government (or church)
for change must be registered and held subject to official approval; failure to disperse became a capital felony. Another act
made it felonious to stir up people to the hatred or contempt
of the King or the government. Simon finds that these efforts
to separate treason from sedition were irrelevant, for both
provided heavy penalties for political crimes and, while attempting to fashion degrees of treason, did not systematize the body
of political crimes. ". . . to the Anglo-American mind all political
crimes fall into the category of treason" and further, "as a consequence of this classification of political crime by degree rather
than type, . . . narrow definitions of treason serve not so much
as protector of the accused but as a license to the prosecution
to describe under the vague term of treason all manner of what
properly might be described as quasi-treason or minor political
offenses. Further, they provide license of any number of un-
official agencies to use the term treason" (Simon, p. 703).

Tyranny has become one of the attributes or options of
modern nation-states. Because of that, Comfort (1950) can
claim, "The individual today is far less menaced by local gangster-
ism than by the aggression, tyranny or suppression of rights
which he anticipates from the governments of other countries

or of his own" (p. 72). Comfort refers not to Britain but to invaded or dominated countries, a modern interpretation which parallels earlier justification of tyrannicide against usurpers. In any event, the modern citizen will recognize both the device of mass demonstrations and the counter response not only of government but of traditional citizens, which considers these forms of civil disobedience, sit-ins and the like as political crimes.

The peculiar development of the law in the United States arises from our own special history. During colonial times, individual liberties were the lesser concern, whereas with the advent of Revolution, the distrust generated by experience with England was directed toward the use of treason laws to intimidate the citizenry. Nevertheless, the crime of betrayal of the state was recognized, and as Hurst (1945 a, b) points out, the thrust was to safeguard the state. In some states, treason was defined during the revolutionary period as conveying information or supplies to the enemy without the need to show an intent to betray; in others, intent was required. Adhering to the enemy and levying war against the state were included. Constitutional deliberations emphasized the importance of limiting the scope of treason, there being a special effort to prevent the application of treason laws to penalize struggles for power within domestic politics or to allow its misuse by governmental authority. The aim was to focus only on the intent to betray allegiance. Hurst comments that since the adoption of the Constitution, neither executive nor legislative branches have used the treason charge as a primary device for the maintenance of the security of the state against citizen efforts against it. He notes that there have been fewer than 40 federal prosecutions under it during that period and no executions, perhaps in part because the law does require, among its many limits and protections, that intent and an overt act be shown and the clear and present danger to the state be demonstrated. On the other hand, under the Alien and Sedition Acts, the Espionage Act of 1917, the Smith Act of 1940, and various other acts such as one prohibiting trading with the enemy, charges have been, and can be, brought against those alleged to have committed political crimes. It is also the case that the conventional criminal law is brought to bear when other statutes fail; Alger Hess, for example, was convicted of perjury.

TWENTIETH CENTURY

We are now led to treason in our own times. Our analysis will not seek to duplicate the thoughtful reviews already available in the works of Boveri (1963), West (1964) and Grodzins (1956), nor the related commentaries on organized intelligence operations as such (Dulles, 1963; Wise and Ross, 1964; Wilensky, 1967). We shall allude to the analytic works. Boveri, for example, calls attention to the magnitude of treason, citing (undocumented) figures to the effect that during the purge of collaborators in France, more than 500,000 persons were arrested on suspicion and 160,000 brought to trial for treason; in Belgium, there were 60,000 cases and in Holland 130,000.*

Boveri's thesis that modern treason is a mass phenomenon may be exaggerated, but it is consistent with the historical trends. Recall the shift from individual and elite opposition which is coincidental wth the rise of industrialism and the modern state to opposition via revolution involving large numbers of people. Think, too, of the repeated conquests and subversions in which the victors, fascists or Communist, have faced resistance movements and have, under new laws, been able to label resistance as treason. And consider how modern authoritarian regimes or revolutionary causes have sought to establish their ideologies in the minds of masses, thus making men's minds a battleground for conflicting beliefs, a situation which can readily produce a definition of treason either as governments shift or as minds are changed. Boveri makes a special case for shifts in government policies or in public fashion which make charges of treason a function of whether the citizen is in or out of phase with shifting beliefs. She also complains that circumstances which artifically

---

* Compare these figures for persons charged with the larger population of defectors as such. Dulles (1963) estimates eleven and one-half million "volunteers" from Communist lands to the West from 1945 to 1962. His figure includes refugees from Communist China, North Korea, East Germany, Hungary, etc. Since then, one would have to add North Vietnamese, Tibetan, and Czechoslavakian emigrants to the list. Few of these are likely to have been involved in treasonous acts.

divide people, such as the division of Germany into East and West and of Korea into North and South, can suddenly create impossible requirements for allegiance among citizens suddenly divided and asked to have new beliefs. Boveri does not restrict her cases to persons actually charged with treason, but encompasses any person who for reasons of state security is not hired, is fired, is banished or suffers any criminal penalty because of his real or presumed opposition to the state. She also considers as cases propagandists such as Joyce, Tokyo Rose or Ezra Pound, collaborators such as Laval and the entire French administrative apparatus under him which operated under the *droit administrativ* and plotters of the sort who sought Hitler's life. Thus the mass phenomenon of which she speaks exists largely because she extends her classification well beyond the law itself. Yet in doing that, she does call attention to the ease with which all political crimes or even dissident ideologies may be called treasonous. Insofar as a state or citizens do require conformity in ideas and enthusiastic allegiance and do consider deviation to be a violation of trust (their demand that all citizens should believe as expected), then the attitude which underlies popular conceptions of betrayal is indeed relevant to sociopsychological considerations, if not legal definitions, of treason.

There are several other themes of Boveri's which are worthy of note here. One is her distinction between collaborators and resistance fighters, on the one hand, and espionage agents on the other. The first group have essentially political goals to which they are personally committed and for whom acts of treachery may be necessary but subsidiary activities—steps on the way to better things. The latter, differentiated from professional or intelligence officers who are citizens of an opposition nation (e.g. Colonel Abel sent to the United States, and who do not usually become citizens engaging in that treason that subjects or citizens commit by violation of allegiance), are citizens in the service of another power (usually but not necessarily hostile) whose treachery is, says Boveri, the primary set of duties. For these agents, there may be no sense of involvement, no political dedication, no larger ideological framework; they may not even know the reasons behind their spying assignments nor are they likely to maintain the kind of social relations with their co-conspirators that characterize the group commitments of those others whom she classes as traitors. The implication is that there exists a set of traitors who operate devoid of ordinary human emotion and interchange, as loners without commitment. Contrasted to these are the involved, politically aware individuals who work closely with others who are in opposition to a contrary set of values and laws but who act from more easily understandable motives. Her distinction reminds one of the difference in Renaissance Italy between the criminal assassins and the noble tyrannicides. Some such distinction is in order.

Boveri's final point arises from her thesis that contemporary political phenomena arise from the current conceptions that nationalism is a good, that each man comes to his ideals out of his own reason, that the people are the state, that religion provides no community among men and that supranational structures based on interpersonal loyalty exist. The result has been, she contends, a middle-class rule based on materialism, the suppression of individuality, technological progress and reason which has fostered almost all that is treason in the twentieth century. She argues that each traitor, whether he strove to return to earlier political forms or achieve new ones, sought to return power to individuals. The century's greatest traitors, she indicates, revolted against reason and sought to come in touch with their own wellsprings of instinct, creativity, love and religious feeling. Denying the desirability of smooth social machinery or of happy human products, they accepted suffering, sacrifice and insecurity for sentiments that were essentially religious, although expressed in political terms and acted out through ways that others called betrayals. Her view, somewhat akin to Simmel (see footnote, p. 99) and that of Rosenstock-Huessy whom she quotes (p. 4), implies that the secret ideals of traitors are germinal ideals which, while currently opposed, represent the first transitional stages which, should they succeed in their endeavors, would bring about innovations that might well revolutionize a world whose sociopolitical structures are not only unsatisfactory but grotesque. Her view also suggests an existential component. By acting, regardless of which direction his actions take him, the rebel makes himself whole. Through betrayal he finds a deeper self, just as others have argued that through using LSD (another illegal act) they suffer but in suffering find a deeper man and more profound relationships. It is also anarchic, since the present order, wherever it is found, is deemed unacceptable, and its opponent need not have a better order in mind nor need he achieve its overthrow yet to achieve the passion—and it may well be self-sacrifice—which he requires. Martyrdom is part of the constellation. The *Urmensch* of Boveri is Germanic and mystical, and her protest (if we infer correctly) is that of the mystic against the machine. It is also the romantic against the alienated. She would presumably dispute any imputation of existentialism, for she cites Martin Buber's criticism (p. 42) of "existentialist" distrust, which is the assumption on the part of all modern men that one's neighbor will and must be a deceiver. Buber's thesis is that the modern world itself generates betrayal and thus makes human relationships ugly. Boveri, accepting this, proposes that the resistance, called treason by states and systems which are bad regardless of their political colors, will return the world to trust. Yet it is ironical that they must do so through treachery, for as Simmel said, it is confidence which is the glue cementing the social order. Shall the world then be regained by destruction's tools?

Dame Rebecca West's analysis, of a very different sort and more likely to be known to the reader, grants Boveri's point. A man's desire for liberty must, she says, test the limits imposed by the state; a man's desire for change must challenge traditions which, because they are just that, may no longer fit. If there are no challenges, then no new traditions can be born. "All men," West writes, "should have a drop of treason in their veins" (p. 361). Unlike Boveri, West advances stronger counterarguments. She feels that treason and espionage are wasteful, since both the security effort and the treason it combats mine energies and monies that could well be used constructively. She further proposes, on the basis of her analysis of defectors who fled from West to East, that ideals and morality have played no role. The modern traitors' goals, she says, have been selfish ones, such as money, power or security. She observes that such a base man is not just a political criminal but likely is delinquent in other ways as well. Further, his own corruption taints others and in doing so undermines confidence in society as a whole. Thus despair arises and the public degrades the compelling worth of its own morality. She further comments that the very security organizations which arise to protect the state pose a danger for that state because of invasions of privacy, restrictions on freedom, incompetence never revealed and the promotion of theft and deceit which make it public policy to encourage that which is tawdry simply because it is felt to be expedient. For the traitor himself, she recommends neither hate nor sentiment, only the recognition that he is, she feels, a thief and a liar. Her recommendations are few but strong. Security is one, the screening out of obviously maladjusted persons from sensitive position is another, and limits on infringement of liberty is a third. As for her case analyses, these are also provocative, but we leave them to the reader to pursue on his own. Her comments on intellectuals and scientists, as well as the "silly" delinquencies of many of the spies she reviews, show insight.

Grodzins (1956), a political scientist well-versed in social psychology, offers a different thesis based in part upon his earlier work with displaced Japanese-Americans during World War II. His feeling is that disloyalty, out of which charges of treason arise, can be accounted for primarily in terms of overlapping or conflicting loyalties; that is, individuals are simultaneously members of diverse groups, each of which demand different kinds of conduct and each of which may impart differing beliefs. When conflicts occur in demands or beliefs and when the individual remains in both groups by virtue of group pressures, situational requirement or personal predilection, one route of adjustment to the incompatible is to conceal deviation to one group as the demands of the other are apparently met. Grodzins suggests that disloyalty is, in fact, a highly specific phenomenon, one defined by the members of a particular group at a given moment in time but not one to be envisioned by an observer in terms of a general form of conduct or an enduring one. As a good example take the definition offered by Dulles (1965), former Director of the Central Intelligence Agency (CIA), of Westerners going over to Communist countries as "defectors," whereas Communists deserting to the West are praised as "volunteers." As we shall see, there is a difference between the two groups, yet one must be aware that the classification is relative, depending on one's own position. Grodzin's view is situational; he does not deal in terms of cases, delinquencies and defects such as West does, nor does he seek a world view and an embracing theory as does Boveri. His point of view should be kept in mind, especially in those cases where it can be shown that simultaneous loyalties have been present and that treachery is an accommodating reaction. That betrayal often serves such purposes is demonstrated in the analysis of ordinary lying presented in Chapter XII.

There are other modern writers and investigators whose work or comments bear on the understanding of defection and treason. For the most part, these are analyses of selected case histories, more theoretical examinations of systems, or typologies based on experience. As previously noted, Dame West emphasizes the professionalization of treason, discounts the ideological component and offers a career analog to criminals based on evidence of selfishness, immorality and delinquency. Gabriel Almond (1954) studied American Communists, persons whose legal status varies not only with their acts but with the passage of laws and interpretation of those laws by the higher courts. His findings as to the presence of neurosis, i.e. psychopathology, should apply to some Western defectors. Selznick (1960), studying communist operations rather than individual cases, emphasizes the vulnerability of institutions and persons. He views any decline in social participation, the weakening of personal ties to groups with moral values, as critical. Marx first noted this "alienation" in modern man and both Marx and later scholars see it as the essence of the "mass man." Accordingly, the "mass man's" lack of firm commitments and meaningful relations make him discontent, open to new appeals and rebellions, and vulnerable to exploitation.

Selznick describes the mass man's mobilization by a communist elite, his openness to extreme behavior because of the loss of traditional primary group ties and of mediating controls exercised by such groups integrated into a societal fabric. Vulnerability increases, he says, when a man values himself because he no longer esteems values held by traditional groups and dissociates himself from them. This may be, of course, the result of a neurotic as well as social process, a point documented by Almond (1954). An "activism" results, in which lack of personal commitment is the key, along with reliance on stereo-types and on radical "pragmatism" to achieve new ends not yet tested and found worthy but sought nevertheless and with fewer constraints limiting the means employed to their end.

These activists, themselves without any but superficial beliefs, are in turn exploitable by others. "Under conditions of political combat, those who have no firm values of their own become the instruments of the values of others" (Selznick, 1960, p. 308). If this is so, one would expect that persons with a history of social despair or rejection, of alienation from traditional beliefs, of personal neurotic distress, of self-doubt accompanied by the rejection of traditional group relationships, persons searching for new symbols and superficial affiliations, may be more likely to be exploited for defection.

Thus we expect that the choice of deviant political behavior is associated with prior dissatisfaction, whether this is attributed to personality or seen as a function of group relationships. Insofar as "choice" may imply only personal determinism, one should add that others may do the choosing.

Defection is not necessarily a spontaneous activity; rather the recruitment of the defector can be managed by others who utilize his sociopsychological state to exploit him. As we shall see in the study of police informants, the recruitment process is critical.

The available literature on political defectors tells us too little about how their recruitment was managed; on the other hand, it will be seen to suggest important things about what kinds of people are recruited in what situations.

Penkovskiy (1965) remarked, "Spotting is considered a very important, if not the most difficult, part of agent recruitment" and once spotted, the management process remains critical. Penkovskiy quotes Lt. Col. Prikhodo (of the GRU), as saying, "success in performing intelligence tasks in the United States depends on agent handling." Handling is the business of maintaining a relationship which utilizes those motives, values and emotions of the defector in such a way that he stays in the business without reneging or revealing it. The literature tells us nothing further about this mechanism.

Another provocative work is that of Waelder (1967), whose analysis is not only of the style of treason within the context of revolution, but of the inconsistencies by its practitioners. As with others, he calls attention to the immense difference in the context of treason in this age of relativism and revolt, compared to earlier centuries. He attends to the "secret religion" of modern liberal man, a Manichean view of progress which assumes a struggle between progress and reaction. The furtherance of progress takes on the rigor of a natural law allowing a variety of challenges to positive law and the state. His concern is with the vulnerability of intellectuals* who devise ideologies which can be correct in any argument and which, therefore, can sustain a hidden ambition for political conquest.

These ideologies, developing during a period of considerable liberty in which authority is undermined and moral relativism is hailed, can be associated with social creativity (he cites Pericles) or irrationality, treason and disaster (Waelder refers to Alcibiades) as the ethos of community is destroyed. One of Waelder's points is that the conviction of political equality leads easily to an assumption of equality in ideas and morality, thus providing each individual with an irrefutable base for esteeming his opinions as the best. Thus each person can regard himself as the minister of Gospel, for the natural law and the positive law is deemed irrelevant. In such a circumstance, conflicting moralities (or egotism) may go to war and the state itself is the

---

* H. Stuart Hughes (Farber and Wilson, 1961) emphasizes the free-floating guilt which he believes characterizes most intellectuals and which makes them manipulatable by authorities who seek to manufacture assent. What is done—and he cites Lifton's 1961 study of Chinese brainwashing—is to intensify that guilt and then to provide escape and forgiveness via the new ideology. He quotes the closing lines of Orwell's *1984*, "He *loved* Big Brother." Harold Lasswell (Farber and Wilson, 1961) conceives of the same manipulation in terms of the anxieties of every man which make him weak and dependent. Political strategists exploit the anxiety to "maim" men, making them mass believers in political myths.

object of the newest form of war, the guerilla war; that is, internal war waged by highly developed political organizations of the kind Selznick has described in *The Organizational Weapon.* The guerilla fighters become terrorists who, as Betrand de Jouvenal described (cited by Waelder, 1967, p. 270), combine "the manners of gangsters with the moral benefits of martyrdom." In their rhetoric, it is the state which is guilty of treason while they themselves are deserving of the power which they seek. Given such a rhetoric and the conditions of combat (read Mao Tse Tung or Regis Debray, 1967), the uncertain social milieu (as Waelder and other sociopolitical commentators describe the West) and the various heroes (a la Boveri), neurotics (as Almond found), egotists and delinquents (as West found them), and empty men (a la Selznick) who become defectors, it is no wonder that the notion of treason and the classification of traitors is difficult, at least within the free (or at least more free) world.

Behind the Soviet Curtain, it is a different ball game. Although one may assume forces of ferment and liberalization, the power of the state is absolute, the Hegelian-Marxist doctrine of history and ideology is binding, and the seeds of relativism have not flowered. China, itself subject to a revolution within a revolution, provides myriad examples of the charge of treason used as a weapon and symptomatic of intense political conflict as factions within the Party struggle for supremacy.

The foregoing discussion and review cannot raise all of the points pertinent to a study of political defection in our time, let alone the past. It cannot hope to provide an adequate review of the literature of politics, ideology and personality bearing on defection. We hope it provides a notion of the development and complexity of the issue and allows the preliminary identification of components which may be expected to be found in the acts and careers of contemporary traitors.

One expects these acts and careers to depend on (a) personality factors, (b) situational contexts, including the relationship of the individual to important groups around him and in the governing structure, (c) the contingencies of the moment, including shifts of power or the nature of elites within a country, the opportunities for defection, and the existing definitions of what constitutes treason and (d) accidents and opportunities which put persons in touch with aliens or agents who recruit and manage them as defectors.

One must not expect all traitors to show similar traits; instead, individuals must be expected to act for a variety of reasons, although the significance of treason is great enough to assume that it is not a casual matter and that as an act it signifies a whole set of meanings on the relationship between the individual and those about him.

One would not wish to construct anything as formidable as a theory of treason out of the data at hand. One can affirm the obvious, which is that the kind of trust violation which occurs and the form it takes depends very much on the larger political circumstances in which the individual lives. It also depends on the stresses and strains of life in a given society and the means available for their resolution by individuals.

A PREVIEW OF FINDINGS

We shall see in the next chapter that with the United States and England, the central feature seems to be in the inadequate development or nurturing of individuals beginning early in life and extending through their careers, so that a variety of maladaptive or undesirable forms of personality and conduct emerge. The final act of defection is simply the end of the chain. In the USSR it is not to psychopathology that one looks but to the harshness of the political environments, the frustration and danger in the work situation, and the conflict between institutional (state) demands and either personal hopes, interests or morality. In Europe, especially Germany (whether Iron Curtain or NATO) the differences are less clear, whereas China appears to produce defection out of circumstances closer to those in the USSR. However, the Chinese pattern is unique, for the typical styles of conduct which are the culture's are imposed upon the unusual act which is treason.

In identifying preliminary and situational stresses as necessary for an action so remarkable as treason, there is clear implication of trust violation as a conceived solution via escape and/or need. Yet it seems clear that the individual and the situation do not generate the idea of the solution. That, along with the mechanics of defecting, must be learned. It can be taught, as in the usual Western case when a Communist agent recruits someone to the cause or to the mechanics of theft. The recruiter, as Soviet intelligence personnel have been quoted as saying, must be a good psychologist or criminologist, for he must identify those whose problems and desires are great enough and whose moral or social barriers are weak enough to allow him to entertain a solution so drastic.

The solution, as a culmination of the events leading to disaffection and radical restructuring, as we shall see described among Soviet and Chinese personnel, is much more often the individual's own enterprise. That is the case in large part because in those societies, there is far less opportunity for exploration and admission of unconventional or disapproved sentiments among acquaintances. Therefore, one who is disaffected may never know his colleagues feel the same way and his solution must be arrived at on his own. Yet the idea is not generally invented. It is borrowed, for we shall see in Chapter VI that the Communist defector often follows the lead of someone who has gone before, either a family member, a friend or a colleague who has fought the regime and/or escaped from it.

Neither disaffection nor the idea of the solution are sufficient for treason; there must also be an opportunity which means access to state security data and access to representatives of opposing powers as well. For agents-in-place, there need not be an escape route out; for others there must be. The escape route is not only a physical one but social and psychological as well, for it is a map in the mind which conceives of people and places, and it mirrors expectations which give confidence as to the escape. The data suggest that the map for Communists reads more clearly and more confidently if the individual has foreign language skills, especially English. One can posit that these skills not only help in making mental maps of what will be but that the very learning of English has been an exposure to the idea of a different place. Thus the Soviets, in teaching English to their civil and military servants, also place in their hands a means for deflating the image of the hostile capitalist bogie man and a means for establishing covert liason with the West. In contrast, the Western defector need not do his own map making. It is his recruiter who knows the potential defector's language, guides him to his espionage and his escape, and generally appears to act in the dominant—and sometimes coercive—role. That is in keeping with the general personal inadequacy (be it vanity, greed, poor judgment, delinquency, or what-have-you) of the United States and NATO defector who must be guided, as well as is more easily manipulated, than the Soviet or Chinese defectors in whose hands the initiative generally remains. At least this is the picture which our limited data offers.

It is tempting to derive from all of this a set of recommendations for the prevention of treason, assuming that is a bad thing deserving prevention. Dame West's recommendations would then be strongly affirmed from our data. For the United States and other NATO countries, the problem is primarily one of personal security, the careful checking of backgrounds and the careful supervision of individuals at work in sensitive positions. It would mean attention to the individual who develops an alcohol problem, who gambles, who shows other signs of a personal difficulty which is being acted out in ways that are simultaneously harmful to self and others. Fundamentally, security needs get linked to mental health needs and require general improvements in childrearing and mental health, the elimination of alcohoic fathers and other features of the sociopathic family environment so well described by Robins (1966). In terms of supervision, it means sensitivity to the morale and circumstances of employees and the careful training of supervisors who understand human frailty and can build confidence and loyalty in others rather than negating these. Prevention of treason in the West, and we stress here that we are limited only to classical espionage and not to the much more widespread contemporary phenomena of terrorism and internal warfare, also requires that one attend to the ideological commitments of civil servants demonstrated over time, including those of their families, for that is how ideologies are conveyed (see Blum and Associates, 1969). It means, too, that the associates of persons in sensitive positions are important, for there is generally a recruiting agent who is the necessary catalyst. These, of course, are all security principles well known to security managers, although ones not always practiced. Their affirmation will be displeasing to citizens who prefer that the state not scrutinize the beliefs, actions, qualifications and associations of persons who desire to become or who do become confidential civil servants. As Dame West remarks, such procedures are unsightly in the eyes of individualists and freedom-loving people. Yet the cost of an uncompromising commitment to freedom from any investigation or constraint on persons holding state security trust would inevitably be an increased rate of violation of trust. Perhaps that cost is an acceptable one; certainly one accepts the risk of some treason under present procedures over the reduction of risk by means of totalitarian imposition. Again, Dame West's arguments are cogent and need not be repeated here.

It would be less than fair not to make recommendations for the Communist security personnel as well. Their tasks are the harder ones, since the social system under which they operate appears to be at risk of continual strain between individualist desires and ideals versus the demands of the state and of the Hegelian-Marxist dogma. It seems also to be the case that their civil servants and their families are more likely to suffer at the hands of the state, e.g. arrest, and to experience frustrations and stress in their organizational posts. That being the case, the recommendation would have to be that modern management be applied, which means the sensitivity of supervisors to the individual needs of personnel, sometimes giving these priority over the needs and dogma of the state. It would also require, for security's sake, that personnel be chosen who have not received any broadening education (i.e., exposure in university to Western ideas or language), that personnel never be assigned abroad, that they never have a chance to meet Westerners, and that they never be trained in deception or concealment, since those tools can be used to deceive the state as well as to confound the West.

These modest recommendations do seem to pose something of a challenge. For fundamental prevention, the West must eliminate its sociopaths, which means eliminating families and peer groups which produce selfish, unkind and short-sighted individuals. Short of that, it must maintain security measures which are unpalatable to the spirit of democracy. The USSR and China, on the other hand, must alter the state and its organizations so that they are benevolent, must provide opportunities for individual expression and satisfaction, and must reduce power struggles between elites of the sort which pose dangers to the lives or careers of those competing.

Short of these measures, Communist security personnel might recruit from the least well educated and maintain these workers in a splendid isolation that would, for the most part, make it impossible for them to accomplish any of the tasks required of management-level personnel in science, the military, intelligence or diplomatic activities. These are all, of course, impossible tasks. Each side can only exploit its current assets; for the West, these are the relatively benign conditions of work, including skilled management and human relations programs, which means that there are few acute work stresses which would precipitate such drastic solutions as treason. The West also has the advantage of advanced methods for personnel evaluation and a number of forms of benign intervention for employees who show increasing personal distress, e.g. treatment for alcoholics. The Communist nations have the advantage of great knowledge of individual histories prior to job placement and the advantage of a highly coercive system to maintain supervision and control, restrict opportunities and prevent education which would lead to relativistic (international-political) views. For neither side does treason, in its classical espionage form, occur very often. Thus the risks are low and present methods will probably be deemed adequate.

For both East and West, what is so often construed as treason in its newer forms—that is, organized intentional efforts to overthrow the state as part of the expression of marked social change throughout the technologically advanced world—will be an expanding challenge. The statuatory means for combating classical violations of trust are ill-tailored as a response either to the rise of anarchy and violent dissent in the West or to rising liberalism and relativism behind the Iron Curtain. How nations will respond to these challenges, ones which are not at all individual violations of trust but may be, rather, large-scale rejections of the assumptions upon which the states in question are founded, remains to be seen. If we anticipate outcomes, one will be that modern states will not thrive if dissidents are regarded as subversives or traitors. As a corollary, the criminal law (as applied to treason) will be found not to be an effective means either for reducing widespread discontent nor for securing the state from the threat of change demanded by significant groups of dissatisfied citizens.

Chapter VI

DEFECTORS: COMMUNISTS TO THE WEST AND WESTERNERS TO THE IRON CURTAIN

INTRODUCTION

Our study goals required (a) the identification of political defectors (traitors), (b) finding open literature descriptions of their histories and person, (c) reading all available documents to determine whether or not the person had characteristics which we expected to be associated with defection, those expectations having been set forth on a checklist of behavior descriptions and (d) complementing the original checklist with additional data, including names of defectors, and deriving new or modified expectations from an initial round of study. On the basis of this latter step, a second round of inquiry was undertaken, one using a modified and expanded checklist and a new sample of defectors. This latter sample constituted a partial cross-validation of findings from the first round and was as near as we could come to any methodological control. The style we have selected for presentation of findings is designed to facilitate readability. To present the data itself for both the initial and second samples is incompatible with any level of patience.

The sample of political defectors is limited to persons whose switch in national service, residence and stated loyalties occurred since World War II. It has been restricted to persons coming to North Atlantic Treaty Organization (NATO) countries (including the United States) from Communist lands and from NATO countries to Iron Curtain countries. Each person selected has met our definition of violation of trust in that he has conveyed classified information to which he was privy to an acknowledged opposing or hostile power, information which he had agreed not to communicate. It is evident that defectors so defined differ from immigrants or refugees who have crossed a border in order to take up a new residence but have not ordinarily been privy to classified information and have not undertaken to convey such information to an opposing power. It is true that immigrants and refugees may be used by a host country for intelligence purposes, in the sense that they may be interviewed upon arrival; nevertheless it is presumed that the intent of the immigrant is not to betray a specific trust which is to conceal state security material entrusted to him in what is, essentially, a contractual relationship with his homeland government. For the most part, this definition escapes the problems of ambiguity raised in the preceding chapter's discussion, although there are cases which are difficult because one does not know what may have been intentions or acts concealed under the guise of immigration. The definition also escapes the problems posed by the revolutionary participating in internal warfare, terrorism, subversion, tyrannicide and assassination, or other efforts to topple governments. It is recognized that such acts may be treasonous and may involve conspiracy and exchange of information and/or weapons with a hostile power, and so forth, yet we have not included such cases. Instead, our study sought to limit itself to classical cases of espionage where highly confidential military, intelligence or scientific information was transmitted. Soldiers captured in warfare or those electing to remain behind after capture, as for example, Korean repatriation refusals, are thus excluded. During the first round, these criteria for inclusion in the sample sufficed.

During the second round, i.e. the "cross validation" sample, it proved helpful to distinguish two groups within the defector category. The Grade A level continued to be the witting and intentional violation of state secrets held in trust through an understanding and communicated to an opposing power. The Grade B level were persons holding positions of responsibility in closed societies or in charge of facilities or equipment considered secret by a society. These men, while not directly involved in military or intelligence operations, were privy to information of a variety of sorts that was not public and which when transmitted was considered a trust violation by that nation. Government officials or military pilots defecting with their aircraft were Grade B defectors; all were from East to West, for in an open society, administrators or others in nonsensitive posts deal with generally public information so that if they should migrate to a Communist land they would nevertheless not convey data labeled secret. As for pilots, we did not identify any Western military pilots defecting in the years 1945 to 1968.

Trust violation, that is, deception or betrayal as we have conceived it here, implies theft, the embezzlement of data at least, if not of physical plans or equipment. Our definition did not require that the theft or information transmittal be successful, only that the attempt was made and documented. Thus one defector who delivered his stolen data to the wrong Embassy met our criterion, even if he did not meet his own! We did not require that the trust violation be of a great order of magnitude; any transmission of secret data sufficed to include the person in the sample. Sometimes in reading the literature there was a question about whether a person defecting from a sensitive post did in fact turn over to his new host country the information in his possession. We have made the assumption that a violation of trust did occur if he did defect, even if the host country did not announce that sensitive information was received. Espionage intentions were not always ascertainable in persons who did not migrate and who denied, when charged, the theft of classified materials. If the open literature contained evidence of materials found and aduced evidence of intentions or transactions, we classified the person as a defector even if, in his legal defense, he denied espionage.

It is necessary to distinguish between defectors, who are persons who shift service or presumed loyalties, and professional intelligence officers who are assigned the task of procuring intelligence information in a foreign country and who, in so doing, take on false identities and false "loyalties." These professionals do not shift loyalties unless they shift to reveal confidential information about their homeland to the nation to which they are assigned. When they do that, they become defectors, or if they continue to provide information to both countries, they become "double agents." The double agent can be hard to classify, since his role may be known to and acknowledged by both nations employing him, each assuming the double role is a necessary feature for his work for them. In point of fact, it may never be known whose side benefitted the most or whether any real defection, defined as unauthorized information conveyence, occurred. Another problem in terminology arises here, since the word "agent" is usually limited to defectors, frequently ones operating "in place"; yet in the case of intelligence officers working undercover, the word "agent" is sometimes found in the literature. Double agent (or double-dealing intelligence officers) are described in the open literature, but we have not included them in our sample. Professional intelligence officers, informers, defectors—all are included under the popular rubric of "spy," a term we avoid.

There is also a problem in evaluation and classification which arises when an individual is naturalized and then is found to be a defector. With United States citizens, the problem is most pressing, since for those who were naturalized, one may not be able to say (at least on the basis of open literature information) whether individuals came on undercover assignment to be naturalized and to operate as intelligence personnel or whether they were at one time "loyal" and then altered course to become "disloyal." Only in the latter case would they be defectors in our sense. It is a sticky wicket, since so many persons identified as intelligence operators have lived and worked in several lands and have had several nationalities. William Joyce is an excellent example; executed by Great Britain as a traitor, he never was an Englishman, a matter about which attorneys and thoughtful citizens are still arguing (see Williams, 1948). Dr. Z is a different example; naturalized as an American, the allegation found in the reports is that he had begun an espionage career for Russia in the 1930's (chasing down Sedov, Trotsky's son) and that he came here as a professional intelligence officer. Mr. H., a native American, apparently long worked as a Soviet agent but not in the United States. The Krogers were recruited in the United States but operated in England. Each presents a problem of definition; we included the Krogers but excluded Messrs. Z and H.

Our requirement for the demonstration of intent was that

state security material be carried or otherwise sent across a border. For many cases, there was also autobiographical or observer data illuminating intent. This requirement of intent, as in the laws of treason, does not require one to establish the antecedent circumstances of inferred intent; that is, the reasons why (the motives) need not be known in order to classify a person as one who betrays state trust. Yet motives are important as one speaks of conduct, and insofar as possible in the analysis of documents we sought to identify motives. The assessment of motives is often difficult, not just for this study but for any observers (including self-observers) of the human drama. However valuable in popular psychology, the construct of motive as an explanatory or determining factor in a study of this sort proved to be open to much question. What a defector says about himself in his own defense or justification or how he evaluates his actions months after they occurred can produce reports which overlook much that may have been happening during the periods prior to and at the moment of defection. The accounts of interviews, journalists, interrogators and others are also colored by assumptions, if not outright distortion. Biographers also take a point of view; some saw Commander Crabbe as hero and others as traitor. Barwich wanted peace, he was an idealist, and he acted courageously in smuggling Djilas' books into East Germany for his friends to read. Yet when his testimony is reviewed, one finds a scientist with personal interests emerging; for example, he dickered for the best in scientific facilities for himself. He left two children behind the curtain who were jailed after his defection. He says he planned for them to come West with him and that he does not know what went wrong. Does he know? Does anyone? Consequently, our approach has attempted to rely on items of fact about the person's life, his circumstances at the time of defection, the forces pushing and pulling him from family, work and the like, so that we need to rely as little as possible on what the man himself says about his reasons. Characteristically, people cloak their actions in ideological language. What they do tends to be specific and personal more often than compelled by ideas and causes. That does not rule out the important role of beliefs and morals; it simply points out that we should go slowly in accepting what a person says were his reasons for actions that themselves are matters of censure and guilt—as defection in either direction is likely to be.

One must also be slow in accepting simplistic accusations that abound after a person has defected. As Margaret Boveri (1963) wrote, "In the last analysis, it is the highest form of insanity when a man who happens to have been born in Leipsig is a traitor if he sympathizes with the capitalist system and the man born in Heidelberg is a traitor if he spreads Communist ideas. Surely this is the quintessence of political schizophrenia."*

She was referring to Otto John, who was an unusual case, defecting in both directions on different occasions. Yet John, as the chief of an intelligence agency, however torn he may have been by the plight of the two Germanies and granting his own disappointments over the rise of Nazis of the West German Republic, did in fact agree to protect information and to hold a position of trust. He could have resigned, but in defecting he violated his contract and the trust of others.

The ideals and motives of individuals are only a part of the problem encountered in the study of persons through documents. For many persons identified as defectors, there was no information of any kind available; for others, the open literature was grossly inadequate. There is no format which biographers, autobiographers, newspaper reporters, Congressional hearings or trial courts all adhere to in order to provide comprehensive personal data, even assuming the accuracy of observation and reporting.

----

* It is here that we may have stumbled badly, for even though we all recognize that humans tend to enoble their own actions—and delinquents to justify their's—we nevertheless conclude on the basis of the descriptions available in the open literature that Iron Curtain defectors more often acted for ideological reasons than did Westerners defecting to the East. Consequently, we do end up with a kinder portrait of those who join the West than of those deserting it. This smacks of bias of the worst sort and yet, on the basis of all that is written, is the conclusion that offers itself. An alternative deduction is that since the evidence is so self-favoring for the West, it must *ipso facto* be proof of bias. We reject the latter as even less evidential than the former. In the absence of an opportunity to directly examine a sample of defectors from both East and West, we are all well advised to remain skeptical until some fine day when the CIA and KGB join hands to conduct an objective and direct evaluation.

For us, this means that most of our tables are partial tables; it also means that Mr. X, who constituted an entry in one table disappears in the next table. One had no choice but to record "don't know" for these (majority) cases. Sometimes estimates were possible. For example, Drummond was under security observation due to a misdemeanor which became known when he was serving abroad. We therefore made the assumption that he was under surveillance from the time he had his first encounter (after the misdemeanor) with a Soviet agent. On the basis of that assumption, we entered in the table dealing with lapsed time between trust violation and discovery an estimate based on our inference. Insofar as possible, estimates or qualifications to our data include direct quotes from the defector or paraphrases from his writing or statements to support our inferences.

There is another limitation which is denied correction. We could not obtain controls for the samples involved. That is to say when we conclude that, as in the case of Iron Curtain defectors, acquaintance with someone who had earlier defected appeared to play a role in the defection decision, we cannot compare defectors with non-defectors in the same situation and having the same life history and personal characteristics to see if this really is a differentiating feature. The only comparisons are between Western and Communist defectors and, to a smaller extent, among Soviet, non United States NATO, eastern European non-Soviet and Chinese defectors. As we compiled the data, we came to assume differences, some no doubt based on faulty estimates as to the cultures, organizations, peer groups and persons of which the defector was a part. The American or English reader will use his own yardstick in deciding what other civil servants might be like in comparison to Philby or what other Army sergeants might be like compared to Dunlap; the reader has less personal experience to serve as an anchor when comparing Col. Penkovskiy with other Soviet army intelligence types. As a general source of information on the Soviets, with special reference to the work situation and work satisfactions which come to loom large in the career of Soviet defectors, reference is made to Bauer, Inkeles and Kluckhohn, 1956; Granick, 1961;

Bauer, 1955; Inkeles and Bauer, 1961; Inkeles and Geiger, 1961; Milosz, 1953; Leonhard, 1958 and similar works.

There is, of course, a wealth of additional work on the Soviet Union, but little of it can be converted into reliable estimates by which a control sample of Soviet scientists in sensitive work, and of military and intelligence personnel could be constructed. The foregoing citations are relevant and, it will be seen, lend background to one looking at political defector's careers and characteristics and trying to judge (unscientifically as it must be in this case) whether one has identified factors which do indeed contribute to their trust violations.

In the first-round study, by dint of reading commentaries and histories and pursuing secondary sources listed therein, 150 cases were identified.* Out of these, there remained only 44 who met our criteria and about whom some information was available. Twenty were Iron Curtain defectors and 24 were from NATO countries (plus Wennerstrom from Sweden). In this first study, we referred to the Iron Curtain defectors as Communist volunteers (CV) and the NATO people as democratic defectors (DD). In the second round (cross validating), 62 CV's were identified, upon whom there was data on 28; for 97 newly identified DD's, there was some information available on 39. All told, from among 309 names from which, after deducting double agents and professional intelligence officers, facts were tabulated on 111. One longs to know what the other 200 were like, let alone hundreds more never identified!

For the first round, a checklist of 212 items was developed. Items were armchair creations drawn from criminological studies predictive (or more often after-the-fact) of criminal or delinquent behavior, from typical personnel security background check files

---

* The search for information relied upon sources such as the *Guide to Periodical Literature,* PAIS index; newspaper indices, including *New York Times, Christian Science Monitor, London Times, Wall Street Journal, Washington Post;* Library of Congress catalogued data from the Senate Internal Security Subcommittee, hearings of the House Un-American Activities Subcommittee, Annual Report of the Attorney General, Department of Justice press releases, data from Bureau of Social Science Research, and as many biographies and autobiographies as could be found. Most of these were used during round two, since round one was a more limited enterprise.

(see Blum 1964), and from psychological and sociological theory and research dealing with maladjustment, conversion and the like. The checklist is the same one used in the informant study of Chapter VIII. When data was contradictory, a decision on a behavior item was made, conforming to the majority of sources. For round one there was no subject on whom it was possible to complete the checklist. Only one item could be completed for every sample member; for most items, the "don't know" category was predominant. For round two, a revised checklist was employed in which items were clarified, reordered and expanded. Again there was lack of data. This fact, when considered in the light of the larger sampling problem—300 identified defectors out of an unknown N of actual ones from 1945 to 1968, with data on only one third, and none of it complete on any one individual— suggests that we would do well not to guarantee any of our conclusions. It would be pretentious to try statistical testing on hypotheses—if we admit our check list as a set of expectations, which they were—so incapable of crucial testing. We think the cross-validation method, testing one's findings against a new sample in round two, was the second best course available.

Given the consistency that was found between the two rounds (itself subject to an error bias if there is a constant unidirectional bias in reports about all defectors) and given further the harmony among the items published, which serves to make an understandable history of trust violation in each setting (West or Iron Curtain), we are not adverse to accepting the picture which emerges until a more adequate method of exploration is found. The more adequate means for exploring backgrounds and personality through inspection of institutional records and direct interviews and testing of the people involved is hardly available to the university researcher interested in traitors.

Our findings, stated in the following pages as tentative propositions, must be recognized as being based both on soft methods and small numbers. Since statistical testing would be at best pretentious, we have avoided it. Since the repetition of numbers makes for dull reading, we have followed a simple convention in presentation: "all" means all cases on which we had data, even if there were only ten. "Most" means between

three quarters and all; "many" and "the majority" signified over
half of the cases, "some" refers to between one fourth and one
half of the cases, "a few" is either less than one fourth or when
very few cases were available for analysis, it simply expresses
that fact. Having made do with that which was available and
having found that that which emerged makes sense, we trust we
are one step closer to identifying events, situations and personality features which influence political trust violation.

FINDINGS

The following tentative statements can be made about the
twenty defectors from Communist countries to the West, based
on the data brought forth in round one.

Communist Defectors

1. Communist defectors were likely to come from backgrounds in which relatives or friends had been hostile
   to the Communist system.
2. Some showed early dissatisfaction with Communist youth
   groups; in general their childhood and teen-age relations
   with peers and family were normal, and as children they
   were judged as normal.
3. Dissatisfaction with the regime was contrasted with
   expressed affection for the homeland itself. Regime and
   country were always viewed as separate.
4. Precipitating events associated with defection were in the
   work and career situations. Work frustrations and anger
   were important.*

---

* By way of comment on the control problem, that is, of like-placed men
not defecting, Bauer, Inkeles and Kluckhohn (1961) report that Soviet émigrés
through 1945 who were not peasants or manual workers were "satisfied with
virtually every aspect of their work situation" (p. 122) that most co-workers
were friendly and that friendly personal relations were a rewarding feature of
Soviet life. They also found that "the most desirable jobs were . . . the most
dangerous" (p. 121), that there was a great deal of mistrust, that younger persons
were more likely to accept the system unless one of their family was harmed by
it, that exposure to the West was associated with defection but that there was
little disaffection and disloyalty. They write further, "There is . . . no direct . . .
line leading from dissatisfaction with the conditions of life and hostility toward

5. Relations with work colleagues were often unsatisfactory; competitiveness, uncongeniality, cliquishness and selfishness were imputed to colleagues; colleagues, in turn, were likely to consider the defector an outsider.*

6. Defector evaluations of their own status and power tended to be lower than others' evaluation of his role; relatively, defectors had higher aspirations with subsequent dissatisfaction over present status and career progress.

7. Frequently, defectors worked for organizations which had been responsible for the harsh treatment (death, imprisonment, firing, etc.) of their own friends or family.

8. Relationships with immediate work supervisors were often poor.

9. Just prior to defection, there had often been a particular work event productive of distress—disciplinary action, humiliation, loss of support, etc. Changes in the organization which threatened the defector's position also occurred.

10. Defectors were familiar with earlier routes of defection and knew persons who had earlier defected.

11. For some, defection was an "anniversary" or "holiday" syndrome, taking place on days of special personal importance (birthdays, Christmas, etc.).

---

* Leonhard (1958) gives a picture of the Soviet party and intelligence organizations which appear to be tense occupational situations which are less friendly than the ordinary work settings reported above.

---

the regime to active disaffection . . ." (p. 262). "We are struck by the long and involved path which most people trod before they came to feel genuinely disaffected from the Soviet system . . . many refugees (from the USSR) have never reached it" (p. 262). Bauer, in another paper (1955), suggested that for the younger people (young in 1940-1945), ideological opposition was rare (compared to those with pre-Revolutionary memories) and that disaffection required a specific and personal conflict with the system—being hurt, threatened or rejected by it or losing faith in it through personal experience; as time passes, individuals rather than the system as such are blamed for faults. In a more recent study (remember that our sample all defected after the Harvard Project interviews of Bauer *et al.* had been finished), Granick (1961) examined defectors in *The Red Executive* (most sample defectors occupied executive positions) and observed an atmosphere of continuous strain, a very high probability of job failure (pre-World War II data), frustration among ambitious men and an estimate that junior and middle managers are more dissatisfied with promotion than their American counterparts would be.

12. Most Communist defectors were described as independent, self-reliant, hard-working, ambitious, intelligent and successful persons.
13. Work dissatisfactions over career progress, supervision, work content, colleagues and the organization were expressed by blaming not only supervisors but the system and the Communist regime.
14. Most were careful not to show any changes in mood or conduct prior to defection, but some did indicate increased anger or tension; others developed new interests or friends or were away from home more often.
15. Defectors were rarely recruited by Western intelligence agencies; most decided for themselves to defect and then sought out Westerners.
16. Defection was facilitated by knowledge of a Western language and by knowledge of, and direct access to, routes out. When these were lacking, defection success was sorely hindered.
17. Self-reported motives for defection stressed escape from career dissatisfactions or from personal threat or danger coming from the organization or regime. Revenge was also noted. Positive ideological reasons were secondary to situational pains and pressures, although ideological components were present and important.

The results from the second round study, N=28, of Communist defector biographies suggest the following:

As Children

1. Defectors come from stable families and their childhoods appear to be reasonably healthy and well adjusted.
2. There is a hint of poor relationships with fathers and of unkind behavior on the part of the father; there is also reason to suspect that defectors lost their fathers at an earlier age than one would expect on a morbidity basis for a western European country.
3. By late adolescence, there is evidence of an interest in and an opportunity to learn a Western language, usually English.

4. There is evidence of relatives or acquaintances having been opposed to the Communist regime.
5. A few became informers or "spies" during early teen years.
6. A few had adolescent experience with false identities.

As Adults

7. Most were described as competent and successful, stable and practical. They were also intellectual and idealistic.
8. Among Eastern European defectors, as distinguished from USSR proper (most from Germany and Hungary), there is evidence of less stablity and of occasional profound conversion experiences, either political or religious.
9. Very few undesirable personality traits are found. Most prominent are anger and bitterness, described most often among eastern European (non-USSR) defectors; these appear to be a response to life and not pathological features derived from childhood. Among the Red Chinese, there is emphasis on impatience which, while not necessarily a flaw, may be a critical trait for Chinese defectors, given the emphasis in that culture on patience as a virtue.
10. None are flamboyant persons, yet most are noticeable in their own right. It is not likely that any personal feature would have been identifiable by casual acquaintances as predictive of trust violation.

Careers

11. Most were skilled men with stable job histories and successful careers or ones holding considerable promise. Since most had come from lower-class origins, there is strong evidence for ambition, status strivings and competence.
12. Most had jobs frustrating in many ways; especially were the Red Chinese in frustrating job situations; this was least so for eastern European defectors.
13. Almost all were distressed about their work, even though there were satisfactions from high status and high pay. What bothered them were daily problems, work procedures and the philosophy of the organization and the regime it represented, that philosophy expressed in day-to-

day handling of people and problems. Dissatisfactions over pay and status occurred only among those lower on the ladder.

14. There is strong evidence that job frustrations, pressures and unpleasantness were accumulating for long periods of time and were resulting in increasingly intense dissatisfaction with most aspects or work.

15. Frequently there were poor relationships with supervisors on the job; supervisors' failure to appreciate or support played an important role in intensifying work distress. It also contributed to what we infer—although it is not clearly stated—to be anger toward supervisors which could have been expressed through defection as retaliation or revenge. There is general implication of poor-quality supervision especially among eastern European organizations.

16. The organization for which the defector worked often employed harsh and coercive techniques on its employees and quite often the organization had visited harm on the family or friends of defectors.

17. Colleagues, especially in eastern European (non USSR) countries, were generally described as unpleasant and untrustworthy. Unlike the findings from the earlier study, we do not find clear evidence for these colleagues disliking the defector nor of his having gotten along badly with them. Given the undesirable nature of many of the colleagues as seen by the defector, we must presume relationships were not always smooth.

18. No defector was proud of the organization he worked for. Work morale was uniformly low for defectors.

19. For the Red Chinese, there were almost no satisfactions from the work; for the USSR there were some, for eastern European defectors there were many—especially pay, status, respect, good assignments and the like. Most common dissatisfactions were dislike of work itself—including its immoral side—its progress and career-futures. Organizational changes ongoing were posing threats or introducing unpleasant new procedures or persons—or

sometimes danger to the individual. Although most defectors were of high status, some, especially eastern European, measured themselves against others within the organization, felt relatively inferior and were unhappy about it.

20. Important difference in policy, ideology and doctrine occurred which, while part of personal conflicts with others, were also thorns in the side at a more abstract intellectual level. Since many defectors were well-educated and intellectual, these matters of ideology were not to be discounted. They include a concern for the welfare of their nation and the quality of government.

21. There was sometimes a point of special conflict between the defector and local or national Communist party leadership. These conflicts were expressed both at personal and ideological levels and, given the subordinate position of the defector, placed him in unpleasant as well as unsafe circumstances.

Defection Circumstances

22. The decision to defect was not impulsive or erratic. It was long thought out and, like events leading to it, cumulative rather than precipitous.

23. The precipitating conditions were usually a job situation getting worse, a political-social crisis placing the defector in an unfavorable position or a developing threat to the potential defector's personal freedom or safety. Often there was an immediately prior blow-up with the supervisor or other boss, e.g. reprimand, refused request, unpleasant exchange, etc. Growing disgust with colleagues, including anger and a sense of impotence (we infer) to prevent or punish some particular bad behavior of colleagues, occurred. Also, changes in work or work assignment viewed as destructive to careers, ideals, plans, safety, etc., may have occurred. Sometimes these were outcomes of more general changes in the organization.

24. Visible changes prior to decision to defect or after it, and prior to physical defection, included mood changes and especially nervousness, depression and irritability. For

the most part, behavior did not call attention to the individuals and was controlled and mature. Unlike the first
study, we have no evidence (or data) on changes in social
habits, being away from home, etc.

25. Prior to defection by a Chinese person, emotional changes
    are least evident, work dissatisfaction is least often ad-
    mitted and observable life changes and new or erratic
    conduct occur least often. On the other hand, work
    satisfactions are most lacking among the Chinese, and
    their situational dissatisfactions are the greatest. It is
    among them that the most elaborate escape procedures
    appear—ones relying heavily on disguise, indirection and
    dissimulation. Prior to defection, changes in perspective
    and changes in behavior occur most often among eastern
    European personnel, as contrasted with Chinese or Soviet
    ones.

26. Prior to defection, defectors pass through an emotional
    crisis in which shifts in political perspective, reappraisals
    of work and career, new views of one's country in relation
    to the regime and to opposition nations emerge. Relations
    with friends and colleagues also appear to undergo a felt
    change, although it is not always noticeable. This crisis
    is best considered a crystallization and confirmation of a
    long-considered solution to the accumulative grievances,
    fears and disgust. The greatest number of shifts appear
    among eastern European defectors.

27. There is occasional evidence for "anniversary" or "holiday"
    syndromes influencing choice of date of defection for some
    persons. This is of clinical significance and suggests the
    symbolic importance of their act to defectors.

28. In deciding to defect, we infer the need to provide
    justification—rationalizations in terms of ideology and, in
    particular, service to the homeland and sometimes even
    to the Party. Justifications stressing the danger to the
    enduring values of country and folk arising from the
    present regime were stressed, so that the act of defec-
    tion could be interpreted by the defector as acceptable if
    not even patriotic or noble.

29. The stated intention in defection was most often either to relieve conscience, that is, to find a style of life more compatible with ideals than working for Communist government apparatus, or to escape from painful, despicable or dangerous job situations.

30. It is the rare case among our sample for the Communist to West defector to be recruited by Western personnel. The defection decision was arrived at independent of these but once made, required the assistance of Westerners, if only at reception points.

31. Knowing a Western language, especially English, was an important precondition. Those not familiar with a language took steps to learn it.

32. Knowing Westerners was an important precondition. Those not knowing Westerners sought information about embassies, tried to meet Westerners, etc.

33. A very considerable facilitation of defection occurred if the immediate family was in the West or could be brought there, or if relations with immediate family were strained or unimportant. There is a hint that defectors not securing escape for those families were not as close to them as would be expected in their culture.

34. In planning, defection misinformation could block or delay escape. Fear of negative reception was also a block, as was concern that local (fellow countrymen) personnel working for Western embassies were Communist agents who might effectively block escape, even if access to an embassy or other outpost had been achieved.

35. In planning defection, confidence in their knowledge of practical matters was essential. Skills in finding and using permits, papers, plans and physical facilities were essential, as was knowledge of escape routes as such crises during escape were common and were related to the mechanics of escape and making contact.

The consistency between round-one data and the partial cross-validation (and expanded) round-two inquiry is evident. On only two counts, the evidence for poor relations with work colleagues and evidence of prodromal changes in social habits prior to defection, is there disagreement.

Westerners to the Iron Curtain

In the preliminary study, the following characteristics or careers of West to Iron Curtain defectors, N=24, were tentatively identified:

1. In the United States, defectors tended to be children of minority, lower class and/or immigrant parents.
2. They had a poor psychological relationship to their fathers.
3. They were maladjusted as teenagers.
4. They showed sexual deviance or inadequacy as adults.
5. As adults, they were intelligent, hard-working and ambitious but also insecure, foolish, greedy, inadequate and "loners."
6. They were sensitive to low status on the job, displeased with career progress and having poor relations with co-workers and especially supervisors.
7. They were recruited by Communist agents or case officers and they defect in place.
8. Prior to defection, they showed increased drinking and spending, and changes in social behavior.
9. During predefection period, they were developing close ties with Communist officers or agents influential in their defection.
10. They were acquainted with other defectors prior to their own defection.
11. They have language skills in Russian, Spanish and/or Chinese.
12. Anniversary or holiday syndromes occur; that is, defection takes place on dates of personal symbolic importance.
13. Motives offered include Communist ideology, response to blackmail, desires for excitement, prestige and money offered by USSR.

Data from the second round of study, N=39, allow the following statements:

As Children

1. Fifty percent of the cases on which data is available

describe the defector's father as abnormal, alcoholic or sociopathic.*

2. Half of the fathers of male defectors on whom there was data were described as socially maladjusted.

3. Most fathers of defectors were lower class; most fathers and mothers were immigrants.**

4. Only one-quarter of the defectors were said to have poor relations with their parents, yet one-third of the families were rated as not normally close and two-fifths of the families were described as unstable. Furthermore, 60 percent of the defectors on whom there is data lost one parent before the age of 16.

5. Forty percent of the families about whom there is data were rated as not giving good care to the individual when he was a child.

6. Half of the families had immediate relatives with records of sociopathy, drug abuse or other visible social maladjustment.

7. Some of the defectors, as children, had visible social handicaps such as being minority-group members, Negro, poor immigrants, etc.

8. As children, to age 12, none of the defectors were themselves described by biographers as maladjusted or anti-social.†

9. One third of the defectors were described as having problems in social adjustment as teenagers.††

10. One-fourth showed drastic ideological shifts as teenagers.

---

* As Robins' 1966 study suggests, such fathers are very likely to produce sociopaths as offspring.

** The risk of delinquency for second-generation lower-class offspring is greater than for the normal population, as the Wickersham report showed (1931).

† Given the high risk of maladjustment for children from families having characteristics as described above, two hypotheses are tenable. One is that their's was a late-blooming delinquency, e.g. the trust violation a prodromal act, or that biographical data was inadequate for the childhood period. An intriguing possibility arises out of the first, since the common criminological pattern is for very early signs of maladjusted behavior. (See the work of the Gluecks, 1950, which is of a special syndrome of masked delinquency.)

†† Depending on the rating used, this would not be higher than normal populations.

As Adults

11. Several homosexuals occur in the sample; in addition, several more defectors were without ordinary heterosexual relations. Only one had his closest personal relationship to his wife, even though most were married. Among western European (as opposed to American) defectors, the closest relations were most often to lovers (female or male). The inference is that the defector sample contains more than an expected number with unusual sexual relationships and roles and a striking lack of close marital relationship .

12. Nearly half of those about whom there is data had no constructive leisure-time activities; the inference is of a frequent defector lack of satisfying normal interests in hobbies, sports and the like.

13. A few defectors were described as having major ideological differences with their parents. This is an unusual pattern and implies not only poor family relations but instability in ideological commitments.

14. One or more of the defectors had been a member of far-out sect, fad or "craze" groups, another sign usually associated with instability.

15. Half experienced profound religious or political conversions as adults.

16. Some had a history of ambivalent relations with police or military organizations, as inferred from joining-quitting-joining-quitting career patterns.

17. The majority about whom there is data were poor credit risks during the period prior to defection.

18.. The majority about whom there is data gambled more than casually.

19. Almost all about whom there was data (8 of 9) were excessive drinkers prior to defection. The alcohol-problem variable is one of the single predicators of trust violation.

20. The majority about whom there is data were described as possessing the following personality traits: weak (character), excitement-seeking, practical, "unrealistic," having poor judgment, easily influenced by others. Many were

flamboyant in conduct. Money was very important to them, although they spent rather than accumulated it.

21. Among most western European and some American defectors there was a history of unreliability in work and social obligations prior to defection.

Delinquent and Criminal Conduct

22. There is little indication of detected criminality prior to defection. Some did have court appearances.

Careers

23. Defectors with low salaries were uniformly dissatisfied with their pay, and many with high salaries were also dissatisfied with pay. Salary dissatisfaction, as such, is more pervasive among defectors than job status dissatisfaction.

24. When supervisors had been critical of their work, defectors were uniformly angry at the supervisors, and in the period prior to defection, none showed a constructive response to adverse work evaluations.

25. For most American defectors, there were many reported satisfactions in their work; for western European defectors, work was not as satisfying (consistent with generally less adequate working conditions in Europe); nevertheless for both groups work satisfactions outweighed dissatisfactions. In the United States there were almost none dissatisfied with the job itself; in Europe (NATO), there were many more job frustrations and strains.

26. Most defectors were rated as having liked their jobs overall.

27. None of the defectors had rancor toward the organization for which they worked in the sense that their organizations had harmed them, their families or their friends. Most were proud of their organizations and had been on the job a long time. Even so, their conduct indicated ambivalence, with loyalty countered on some occasions with hostility to specific features of the organization.

Defection Circumstances

28. All defectors on whom there is data had been acquainted with someone who had earlier defected.

29. Most were recruited by other agents or by Iron Curtain intelligence officers, and most were given instruction in methods of trust violation.

30. Expressed motives often included a desire for money. Ideological reasons are rare. The influence of a lover (male or female) sometimes played a role, as does revenge, e.g. in response to supervisors. It is equally important to note that case analysis for half of the defectors yields no data on motivations.

31. Marital relations were related to defection, either in the many cases with poor marriages where anger and escape are inferred to have played a role, or in some cases where a marriage partnership also worked as an espionage partnership.

32. Prior to defection, the major personal changes noted were in emotionality. Tension and depression were seen most often; irritability was also noted and, in a few cases, bizarre behavior. Mood changes were most common among western European defectors.

33. In regard to life changes, there were few in marital relations and none visible in political interests of commitments. In the work situation, recent discipline or reprimands had sometimes occurred, as had losses in status or power on the job.

34. Conduct changes that were frequent included an increasing drinking problem, the accumulation of personal debts in the year prior to defection, increased extramarital sexual activity and involvement in these and other events with scandal potentials.

35. Among western European personnel, changes in friendship patterns, especially dropping old friends, and in daily habits occurred, including more frequent absence from home and the taking up with new friends and interests. Among western European defectors intense relations were sometimes visible with new persons who, later, turned out to be recruiting agents, handlers, and the like.

36. The American defectors said little that could specifically be taken as warnings, although a few spoke of being

worried. Among western European defectors it was more common to hear of anger about jobs and the desire for revenge; some gave hints of big changes coming in their lives.

37. After defection had occurred, most apparently were in emotional conflict over their behavior and were experiencing psychological guilt. Many appeared to be depressed when the trust violation was detected.

38. Comparing American versus western European NATO defectors it appears that the latter defectors gave more preliminary signs in conduct and emotion of impending trust violation.

On the basis of the foregoing descriptions, it appears that Communist political trust violators differ consistently from Western ones. The former are more often mature men who decide on their own to defect for reasons that at least Western contrast, constitute a group of often sociopathic or psychologically observers would consider realistic. The Western defectors, in unstable individuals who are generally influenced to violate trust, that is recruited during periods of stress associated with their chronic personal maladjustment. Within the larger groups, East-to-West and West-to-East, there are a variety of discernible subgroups, the easiest classification of which is by region of origin and defection. East European, Red Chinese and USSR defectors appear to differ from one another as groups and in ways that are compatible with their cultures and their political situations. Western European, NATO and American defectors also differ. It is of interest that there seems to be some correspondence between trust violation careers, particularly work situations and conduct prior to defection, among NATO and Iron Curtain defectors who are neighbors and, in the case of Germans, fellow countrymen. There are, of course, many individual variations within the groups, but our emphasis here has been on similarities. What is striking is the similarity by culture and region of the defectors. We hesitate to condense the earlier statements into too succinct form, but we stress that American and western European defectors are primarily men from sociopathic family backgrounds whose defection circumstances and personal conduct appear to resemble other forms of trust violation in their culture. Communist defectors, on the other hand, are primarily higher-status personnel caught in exceptionally stressful work situations who, not insulated by ordinarily expected close ties to colleagues and, in some cases, family, defect only after an accumulation of incidents and considerable deliberation.

Attention to differences should not overlook certain similarities among those political trust violators as a whole. There seems to be common ambition, middle- or upper-status positions, work situation ambivalence or dissatisfaction, poor relations with superiors and, to a lesser extent, with co-workers. Lack of close ties to women and to their families are usually observed. The act of defection itself requires opportunities and skills; for example, contact with opposition recruiters or guides, and is helped by a knowledge of language and terrain. In almost all cases, one finds that defectors had personally known another defector, which suggests the importance of pathfinders, learning or response to an example set by others. Escape from problems or dangers is an often-noted ascribed motive and so are gains of safety or wealth; ideological considerations are secondary. One infers a period of intense strain prior to defection, although *visible* evidence of strain occurs most among Europeans and Americans, less among USSR and rarely among the few Chinese in the sample. It is not surprising that after defection full happiness is not always found; some defectors are unhappy in their new homes as well.

Chapter VII

INDUSTRIAL SPIES

INTRODUCTION

INDUSTRIAL ESPIONAGE aims to procure proprietary knowledge or products by methods which are in violation of contractual obligations and/or criminal laws. Although no doubt historically practiced whenever one unscrupulous man had wished to possess for himself the knowledge, processes or products belonging to another, it has only been in recent years that industrial espionage has become a matter of public attention.* One may attribute this in part to the rapid development of scientific technology in which private knowledge and secret processes may play a large role in advancing one business competitor against another.

The range of activities which are included in the ill-defined field of industrial espionage are many, ranging from cases in which an employee applies knowledge associated with earlier employment to some new position, to clear-cut theft of blueprints or the electronic surveillance of conference rooms for the purpose of gaining knowledge of plans, ideas and so forth. Some industrial espionage is difficult to distinguish from conventional political-military espionage, for when industrial plans, procedures or products are sought by foreign nations who have been denied access to them, the techniques employed are part of a more general intelligence operation. The definition of the act probably rests on the application of what is stolen, whether it applies commercially or militarily. Some industrial espionage is difficult to distinguish from ordinary theft, for when an employee steals a new product, his action is considered espionage if he sells it to

---

* In 550 A.D., the Emperor Justinian managed a coup in industrial espionage by engaging monks to smuggle silkworms out of China when the Chinese were trying to protect their monopoly (although India, Persia and Japan early learned sericulture from the Chinese). Justinian's success led to a Byzantine silk industry.

145

another firm or sets up his own plant for manufacturing. If, on the other hand, the new product, for example advanced radio, is used for his own pleasure or sold to someone else for use only as opposed to copying, the act would be larceny only. Popularly defined as industrial espionage are efforts by salesmen to obtain and offer information about competitors to potential buyers; "market research" endeavors which seek to establish the plans and products of competitive industries, which information is then offered for sale; the efforts of industry to hire (pirate) knowledgeable employees from competing companies with the intention of learning about that company's proprietary procedures; the efforts of government-contract officers working on assignment in corporations, who resign their commissions and threaten to go to work for competitors unless hired by the company to which they are assigned; the "moonlighting" application of knowledge from one job to knowledge required for a second job held at the same time or this same application in sequence as an employee quits one job and offers himself to a second employer with his knowledge "in tow"; and the use of a company position as a "cover" for work or sales for oneself or a second company—as for example, when a salesman for X Corporation uses his sales position clandestinely to promote the product of Y Corporation, which may also be paying him or of which he may be an owner. Also included are more direct, crass efforts to bribe or blackmail employees who act as "resources in place" to hand over information or products, the entry into companies by "plants" who gain employment or pretend to do business there with the intention of stealing, the use of call girls or other service personnel to extract information from knowledgeable persons and the employment of electronic or photographic equipment for surveillance, copying and so forth.

To date, no study has been done of any aspect of industrial espionage. One interesting account of methods is to be found in an interview with a professional industrial spy (Anonymous, 1965) who describes his equipment, his methods for spotting informants and the nature and cost of his services. It is of general interest to note that this "spy" first seeks informants among service personnel such as janitors who have access to secret materials but who have no reasons for loyalty and are badly paid. He also secures "in-place" agents by checking employee credit ratings and approaching those who are much in debt. He employs call girls to obtain information (and as a means for later blackmail of the entrapped client), he impersonates service personnel in order to gain access to a plant, and in very important cases where the assistance of an executive is required, he will seek to become part of the man's social group or will become friendly with the man's friends in an attempt to learn of his interests, weaknesses and the like. Technical writers are another group who have access to information but are badly paid, dissatisfied with their work (he says most have literary aspirations) and presumably are not part of a cohesive work group where loyalty might be developed. He is attentive to minority group members in the expectation that they have been discriminated against in the company—or feel they have been—and so may be susceptible to being paid for revenge. He seeks out newly fired employees on the assumption that they will be seeking vengeance. He may also seek the company of key secretaries, not trying to bribe them or solicit information directly but to establish relationships (or to hire others to do so) in which information is conveyed without the secretary being aware of its significance. He also seeks out ambitious men within the company who feel their advancement is slow and who are envious of the positions of others; gamblers are another group of interest to him, as are men so eager to get a better job that they will offer information to the new employer who baits them with offers. His methods are a catalogue of the determinants of trust violation.

Some of the activity which is part of industrial espionage is either unethical or perhaps just in poor taste, as opposed to hard-and-fast violations of contract or law. Furthermore, it must be assumed that much successful theft occurs without being recognized. Finally, it has only been in the last several years that prosecutions have been conducted in which industrial espionage as a charge has been made to stick. As a consequence, there are but few cases of industrial espionage identified as such and fewer cases of persons so identified. Sometimes litigation over patent infringements or contracts have concealed the activities; frequently companies are reluctant to press suits or complaints because evidence is too hard to gather; a company which is sure that it has been victimized may be reluctant to make an allegation for fear of countersuits for slander or restraint of trade. Nor can one assume that the company which alleges an act of industrial espionage is itself without fault. All of these factors contribute to the difficulty of pinpointing industrial spies.

Nevertheless, a study of industrial spies ought to throw further light on persons and settings involved in violations of trust. Therefore we set out to gather a sample of proven or alleged industrial spies, to interview them and their controls and to test our expectation that there would be differences among the two groups in the direction of greater personal maladjustment in the case of the trust violators.

METHOD OF STUDY

We were at the time (and still are) interested in the selection of competent executives for police services. As part of that interest, we had begun a study of outstanding managers of small and middle-size companies (matching the size of most police departments) with particular focus on competent, fast-rising, self-made men rather than those who stumbled upward via the usual tedious bureaucratic shuffling and reward for nay-saying and do-nothingness (the latter being our impression of much large organizational promotion). It was our hope that there were characteristic life history patterns which could be translated into recommendations for police management selection, either at the time of rookie recruitment or in selecting junior executives via lateral transfer (not only from other departments but from industry itself where such transfers have yet to become the practice). We had an idea that competent managers, aside from training, experience and aptitude, would have had notable character-building experiences in childhood and adolescence. We defined such experiences as a combination of early parental support and experience with trauma and adversity which had been overcome. We wondered if the history of the presence of and reactions to early adversity and crisis might not be a better predictor of later competence than the absence of adversity, as for example among protected and advantaged children, assuming equivalent parental affection, discipline and support. We also expected that histories of law-breaking, illness and inadequate relations with others would be symptomatic of poor responses to adversity and would not be found among independent (as opposed to bureaucratically molded and psychologically shapeless) executives. We anticipated that independent executives would report serious difficulties and mastery of them.

Since we were already in the field with that inquiry (one which we regret we were never able to complete), it was an opportunity to interview executives who had allegedly engaged in industrial spying. We therefore included our checklist in a subsample of interviews with those alleged to be spies and with two small matched control groups.

We identified (from newspaper accounts, court cases, etc.) six men whose employers had sued them for acts of industrial espionage (as earlier defined). Three of these had been tried and judgments handed down against the suit defendants. (Four cases had not had a decision rendered.) Controls were sought by matching the alleged spies with persons remaining in the suit-filing company who had equivalent positions and opportunities for trust violation but who had not, as far as was known, violated trust. We could find only 5 such persons. Another group of controls was therefore selected, upon recommendation, from executives in the same type and size of company as the alleged industrial spies (who were all managerial) worked for after they left the suing company. There were 5 of these as well. We grant the original sample to be tiny and the controls to be mixed. We were not in a position to improve upon them.

Only 9 of the 16 sought (6 alleged spies, 10 controls) were interviewed. Three were trust violators, 4 were controls. Two of the alleged spies had disappeared without leaving any forwarding addresses; a third one was elusive, staying at airport hotels and not maintaining any local addresses and was not available for interview. Among controls, there was one who had left without a forwarding address, 2 could not be reached by telephone (we could not get through to them, they would not call back), and the fourth could not see us until a date far in the future. One has the impression that the lost spies were more than footloose and were actually covering their trail. We are at a loss as to why one control (who had left his position which had been the selection criterion) acted in the same way (although there was hearsay that he too had violated company trust). The remaining lost controls were busy and uncooperative but not elusive. If we stand on elusiveness as a discriminator, one finds three of six trust violators lost to the sample for that reason and only one of the 10 controls.

Interviews were arranged with the remaining 9. The interviewer, a layman, was not told which person was an alleged spy and which was a control, nor were any questions asked in the interview about litigation, industrial espionage or the like. The interviewer did know that some among these 9 were alleged trust violators. Aside from completion of the check sheet based on personal history, the interviewer rated subjects as also required by the check sheet. No reliability test was conducted. All but one of the respondents were cooperative; one was curt and evasive. He proved to be one of the alleged industrial spies. In these interviews, as with the ones in the initial personnel endeavor, emphasis was not on check sheet items but on the handling of adversity during the person's career.

ESTIMATING TRUST VIOLATION FROM INTERVIEW CONTENT

Upon completion of all interviews, the interviewer was asked to rank everyone seen in terms of an estimate of who had and who had not engaged in industrial espionage. Those rankings compared to the actual identification are as follows.

Interviewer Ranking Most Likely		*Fact*
Rank 1	Subject AV	Yes, trust violator
2	Subject BV	Yes, trust violator
3	Subject EN	No, not a violator
4	Subject CV	Yes, trust violator
5	Subject GN	No, not a violator
6	Subject FN	No, not a violator
7	Subject DN	No, not a violator
8	Subject HN	No, not a violator
9	Subject IN	No, not a violator

It would appear to be an impressive success for the interviewer were it not for the fact that subjects AV (V for violator) and BV spontaneously brought up during the interview their involvement in litigation with prior employers. The interviewer wisely assumed the litigation reflected charges of industrial espionage. Subject EN (nonviolator) was misguessed because of his strain, defensiveness and suspiciousness. Subject CV was also suspicious and defensive; had he said more or had more attention been paid to his slip of the tongue about stealing from a former employer, the interviewer says he would have ranked in the first three. We must conclude that our experience in post-interview identification has failed, not because of incorrect identifications but because the correct identifications were contaminated by interview content which made it too easy. We had sought identification based on associated personal history and behavior data; we had not sought revelations, for if one were interested in predicting trust violation propensities prior to its occurrence, one would have only personal history and behavior data on hand.

PERSONAL DESCRIPTIONS OF NONVIOLATORS AND VIOLATORS

The interviewer rated each subject on twenty-five items constituting the "personal description" check sheet. Each item could be checked to indicate the absence or the presence of a trait; twenty-two of these implied personal adjustment and maturity. An adverse rating on an item indicates that in the interviewer's eyes, the respondent behaved during the interview or described himself as characteristically acting in a fashion indicating some undesirable trait or personal problem, e.g., vain, foolish dogmatic, insecure and so forth.

Adding together all the adverse ratings for each respondent, we find only five adverse ratings for all 3 alleged trust violators combined, an average of 1.6 each. All violators had at least one adverse rating. For the 6 nonviolators, a total of four adverse ratings were entered, an average of 0.7 each. Four nonviolators had no adverse ratings. The absence of adverse ratings suggests that the interviewer viewed all the sample members as well-adjusted men who did not show extreme behavior on any of the traits on the checklist.

REPORT OF TROUBLE: VIOLATORS COMPARED WITH NONVIOLATORS

Two parts of the checklist required information about the subject's personal background and present habits. Completion of the checklist depended on the respondent's willingness to reply and the accuracy of his perceptions, memory and statements. Content of these items ranged from the stability of job history through delinquency, illness, alcohol use, leisure-time activity, parental conflict, child-parent relations, love relations, economic reliability, religious and political interests and the like. On several items, interviewer interpretation of remarks occurs so that a possible bias component enters. A total of seventy-one items were completed, each one of which might be indicative of a difficult experience or of "troubled" conduct. For example, the early death of a parent would be a painful experience, whereas a history of excessive drinking would be troubled conduct. The two kinds of items are combined in a "trouble" count.

The subjects were all given a "trouble" score consisting of all reported difficulties and conduct problems entered on the checklist. Below are presented the trouble scores for all respondents:

Violator Group		Nonviolator Group	
Subject	Score	Control	Score
A	9	D	5
B	20	E	4
C	5	F	2
Average: 11 per person		G	5
		H	0
		I	1
		Average: 3 per person	

The violators do have higher trouble scores than nonviolators. Had "C" been less guarded, his score might well have been higher. These differences, which are based on self-descriptions rather than trait ratings, are for the most part more objective and less contaminated measures than the interviewer ratings. These differences in life trouble counts do suggest that the trust violators differ from nonviolators; persons alleged to have engaged in industrial espionage report more life difficulties and maladapted conduct than controls.

There is a further possibly interesting feature. All three trust violators were the youngest children; none were only children. The difference in birth order is, of course, only suggestive; were a later study to confirm it, it would be in keeping with Schacter's (1962) theory that sibling position (ordinal position) does affect social behavior. For example, Schacter found that affiliative behavior does differ in association with birth order and specifically that the youngest born will be least likely, under conditions of strain or anxiety, to affiliate, to seek "togetherness." Independence is his preferred course. One can see how that independence might reflect itself, under conditions of career dissatisfaction and frustrated ambition as an employee, in an action which is "disloyal" to the employer and the work group, one which the employer defines as "theft" or "espionage." The subject is himself likely to define that same act as justifiable and even if selfserving, appropriate in a competitive world. In this regard, it is to be noted that each of the alleged trust violators who discussed his litigation involving a past employer did justify his actions, denied wrongdoing and in several cases had countersued the company. Final court action was still pending, but initial court decisions lent support to the alleged trust violator's claim that the company view of proprietary rights represented an improper infringement, being in the restraint of trade. Thus the independent action which had violated trust and which the courts agreed was at least a contract violation might well be partly justified by external legal as well as private standards. This fact calls attention to the need to examine executive trust violations within the framework of executive-employer interaction under the assumption that both parties contribute to the final outcome. Such an approach makes sense if one assumes that what people do is a consequence not only of their personality predilections but of the situation in which they find themselves.

COMMENT ON THE SAMPLE

All members of our sample were corporation executives and all had done well for themselves whether or not they were involved in litigation over the misuse of proprietary information. They were all unusual people because of their success. Compared with the normal population, they all appear remarkably free from instability or disabling psychopathology. Results of the interviews reveal the following: *none* (a) had ever been arrested or convicted (excluding minor traffic violations), (b) had ever had problems arising from alcohol use, (c) had ever had problems arising from other drug abuse, (d) had more than two different jobs in the last five years, (e) had ever spent any time confined in an institution (prison, orphanage, chronic-disease hospital, and so forth), (f) had any serious behavior problems, past or present, (g) had ever been involved in extreme political or social groups (cults, fads, and so forth), (h) had been accident or illness prone, (i) had ever had psychiatric care, (j) had ever been a credit risk, (k) had been gamblers, (l) had ever had major business or investment losses, (m) had ever had serious marital discord and none had divorced, (n) had ever had major shifts in career lines, (o) had ever had frequent job changes, (p) had ever used aliases, changed names or otherwise altered their identity.

Furthermore, *all* (a) were married and able to enter into a continuing love relationship, (b) had children and appeared competent as parents, (c) had constructive ways of using their leisure time, (d) were business successes in spite of the fact that *none* came from wealthy backgrounds. That means that (e) all had risen up an economic ladder, rather than being born to high status.

It can hardly be denied that all of the sample, violators and nonviolators, are quite remarkable for their freedom from signs of social and personal disorder. They have done very well indeed by any social or psychiatric measure—and that in spite of some very serious background difficulties. We have not, in this sample, pursued our general notion that it is not the absence of childhood difficulty but rather the response to it which may be a predictor of executive capabiilty. We think, on the basis of the case histories, that the notion yet deserves that exploration which we were, for other reasons, unable to complete.

The personal excellence of these men make it clear how the

interviewer came to see them as so free of adverse traits in his ratings. It also makes it clear that they are a highly preselected group, among whom it would be impossible for high frequencies of adverse ratings or reported conduct disorders to exist. We have not only been looking for a needle in the haystack in trying to find executives who committed acts of industrial espionage, but once they are found, we see it is unrealistic to expect them to show the same order of maladjustment that one finds so often among offenders as compared to normal populations. The problem we have had in our comparisons is much like that of the university teacher with a class composed of Phi Beta Kappa students. For the teacher to grade on the curve is to force the assumption of a normal distribution on a group which contains only the top one-tenth of one percent of the normal population.

Yet in seeking signs of conduct disorder, some have been found, and that is surprising. Certainly a future study of executive career variations should expect the remarkable preselection of executives and would seek to discriminate those engaging in industrial espionage from others not doing so by applying refined instruments, and on the basis of an analysis not open to us in this study, of situational as well as life history characteristics.

SUMMARY AND CONCLUSIONS

We sought to identify executives who had engaged in industrial espionage to compare them with men in comparable positions who had not done so. A total of 6 alleged trust violators and 10 controls constituted the sample we sought to interview; of these, we were able to see 3 trust violators and 6 controls.

The interview was made part of our larger interest in executive selection for police management. It focused on background experiences and present interests; it made no inquiries about violations of trust as such. Upon completing all interviews, the interviewer, who did not know which sample member was a control and which a subject, ranked all respondents in terms of the likelihood of their having committted industrial espionage. He made only one error—his fourth-ranked man was a violator and should have ranked third. These successes were due to

unexpected contamination; the two first-ranked men spontaneously mentioned litigation with past employers and the interviewer inferred their nature. Each man was also rated on a
personal-description check list. Very few adverse ratings, ones
indicative of personal maladjustment or extreme behavior, were
made for any respondent.

When check sheet "trouble" counts were made, a summary
for each man of potentially troubling early experiences (death
of parent, poor home conditions and so forth) and of troubled
behavior (learning difficulty, excitability and so forth), it was
found that the 3 violators averaged a score of eleven, the 6
nonviolators a score of three; most troubles centered about
childhood experiences. The 2 communicative violators as opposed to the guarded and suspicious chap who had been mis-
ranked averaged a trouble score of fifteen. We suspect, but
have no evidence, that the third guarded violator might have
had a higher trouble count had he talked more freely. All scores
are based on self-descriptions of past experiences.

When the characteristics of the sample as a whole are reviewed, it is found that all of the men were remarkable for their
freedom from disordered behavior, for their ability to maintain
good interpersonal relations and for their capacity for achievement. Obviously, these executives, each in a small company,
were preselected; the presumption being that particular psychological competence is required for the positions they hold. Such
homogeneity of ability, mental health and law-abiding conduct
makes it difficult to discriminate violators from nonviolators in
terms of any gross personal maladjustment or history of socially
inept behavior. Those who discussed the events which led to
their being accused of industrial espionage justified their actions
and countersued the accusing companies. The success of their
counterclaims in court supports the contention that the situation
in which violations occur must be studied along with the life
histories of individuals in order to arrive at an understanding of
events. Violation of trust in this sample has not been criminal
behavior, and no signs of criminality as such are in evidence
among any sample members. In consequence, our exploratory
study of industrial espionage cases is better considered outside

the framework of criminology but within the framework of professional ethics, of disloyalty to group codes, of differing ideas about what constitutes contractual and professional obligations or of outcomes to organization conflicts centering about the highly competent people. Given "deviancy" so considered, there is support for our expectation that persons identified as trust violators will differ in their personal history and life styles from comparable persons not identified as violators. The methodological weaknesses of our study—unavoidable and pervasive—are such as to caution against generalizations from these findings.

Chapter VIII

POLICE INFORMANTS

INTRODUCTION

IN THIS INQUIRY, we set out to gather information on the background, personal traits and group relationships of persons known to be police informants. We wanted to learn how informants began their relationships with police officers who became their contacts. We were also interested in how officers selected potential informants—if they did so—and how they maintained their relationships so as to assume a continuing flow of information. That information would be, we presumed, in violation of trust, and it was for that reason that informants were of interest to us. They were also of interest to us for practical reasons, for we were interested in the problems and operations of police intelligence as a law enforcement activity.

Skolnick (1966) has described the use of informants by police officers; his informative observations on police vice work are recommended. We have been unable to discover any study of police informants as such, and consequently, we had no store of earlier findings upon which to draw.* During the course of some studies on the use of the polygraph in law enforcement (Blum and Osterloh, 1968), we were developing some experience with informants and the officers handling them, and this provided us with further opportunities for work. As a first step toward field studies, we conducted interviews with police administrators who were in charge of operations in which informants were employed; each of these administrators had himself had experience in handling informants and was experienced in supervising men using

---

* Harari and McDavid (1969) have done a study of tattling among children and find that children tattle on low-status peers more readily than high-status ones. They also find a reluctance to tattle if they are being observed by peers.

them. Although these law enforcement administrators expressed considerable interest in the problem posed by the study, they were not able to present any systematic set of facts or theories accounting for informant behavior nor describing police behavior in managing informants. The administrators were unaware of any similarities which either underlie officer approaches to potential informants or which characterize informants themselves.

Our next step was to review selected literature in small-group research, psychology and criminology bearing on personal characteristics and dynamic group forces associated with unstable relationships to family and work groups and to violations of trust. There is little scientific literature bearing directly on betrayals of trust or on the maintenance of "secret" roles, phenomena which we presumed would be present in at least some of the informants' behavior. Nevertheless, there is a large body of scientific literature bearing on unstable primary-group relations and on delinquency-criminality as such.

The major premise upon which we proceeded was that being an informant was important behavior in the life of the person. Our premise was that it would not be accidental activity. If not accidental, it would then be associated with other features of a person's life and (a) would be determined by social and psychological forces and (b) would occur in association with other social and psychological events. These are the premises which accompany almost any study of human conduct which uses methods of the behavioral sciences.

In addition to our premises, we had general expectations about the significance of being an informant as a way of behaving with a group and as a way of expressing personality. We considered being an informant as an unintegrated conflict-ridden adjustment to a group and expected that people with such ways of relating to a group would show past troubles in their relationships to the other important groups in their lives. The best place to look for signs is in situations that count the most, such as family, school, work groups, etc. We also suspected that at least some informants would have special personality problems linked to the peculiar business of being an informant, a business we viewed as playing a "secret" role. We suspected the presence of "identity" problems, an identity problem being one where the person does not feel confident about who he is, and what he wants to be or how he can integrate conflicting impulses and ideas. Identity problems are not easily discerned in the kind of study we were doing, but we considered that as a start, at least one could inquire about shifts in occupations, use of aliases, shifts in ideology and the like. Troubles in past primary-group adjustments and in developing a mature and integrated personality are linked to early problems in individual development, be these defined in genetic, psychological or sociological terms. Nevertheless, it is evident that current events shape action, and so one must expect that the act of being an informant depends upon immediate circumstances as well as historical ones. To be an informant is to act clandestinely in such a way that the people by whom one is accepted are hurt. To be an informant is to do things that run contrary to the interests of at least one group of one's associates. On the other hand, being an informant is in the interests of the law enforcement personnel with whom the informant works and is helpful to these authorities and consonant with the anti-crime values of the larger society. Nevertheless, many informants are themselves criminals. Being an informant implies a response to a complex and contradictory set of determinants. One might guess that there are push-pull forces affecting the informant both in his contact with his criminal associates, in his relationship to the police officer and in acceptance of social morality. This paradigm is, of course, simplified and applicable only to informants who are themselves criminal. We did not assume that all informants would be the same; we did expect some to share common characteristics.

For the purposes of our study, we used these general expectations as guides in choosing particular items about which descriptive data on the informants was to be sought. These items were incorporated as statements and questions on a check sheet which was distributed to law enforcement officers using and interviewing informants. Some of the items required only a "yes," "no" or "don't know" answer; others were open-ended. Most items sought personal information about the informant's history, which required asking him about himself. Some of the items were inquiries about the criminal associates of the subject and his relations to those associates. Some were directed at the origins and nature of the relationship between the officer contact and the subject, and some required that the officer rate the subject as he appeared, in terms of personality traits. There were a total of 164 items on the check sheet. The check sheet, in modified form, was also used in the defector study. Instructions to the officers emphasized that they were not to guess about check sheet items. If they could not complete an item, they were to leave it blank.

Sample selection was indirect; that is, police officers who were not informants themselves were enlisted to cooperate in the study. Approaches were made to three federal, one state, one county and two city law enforcement agencies. Some agencies felt they did not have the kind of informant populations which were of interest to us; in others we could not enlist cooperation. The study finally focused on informants being used by the police department of a major city. Within that department, personnel, for the most part detectives (inspectors), from three main divisions (intelligence, vice, bureau of inspectors) volunteered to complete check sheets on informants they were using. Some of these informants were the same subjects that were being evaluated as part of our polygraph research. These latter subjects were all interviewed by one officer, a lieutenant in the personnel bureau, and not by the contact officers handling them.

A total of 35 informants were interviewed and described in the first round of work. We do not know what proportion of all informants in the metropolitan area these are nor how their characteristics differ from the unknown total universe of informants. We are unable to state what particular decisions and forces led to the selection of an informant for description by his officer contact any more than we can say how those officers cooperating in the study differed from those not cooperating. We must assume the existence of a sequence of biasing factors which have led to our sample being a special one. It is our guess based upon opinions offered within the police department, that officers who more often used informants were most likely to cooperate in the study and that the checklists were more likely to be completed on informants recently used and better known.

Upon completion of the first round, we remained in doubt about the characteristics of our sample defined in terms of their adequacy as informants. We wondered if they included the best ones; that is, persons most adept at those deceptions and violations of trust which we presumed to underlie their role. For this reason, we set forth upon a small-scale second round which was aimed at briefly describing the characteristics and presumed intentions of a sample of prize informants, ones nominated as being among the most able and reliable in the city. To accomplish this, one of our cooperating inspectors identified his own and other officers' informants who met the criteria of long-term accurate information conveyance. Six persons among those nominated agreed to be interviewed. The checklist was not used; rather, an interview schedule was employed, which probed the circumstances of initiation into the informant role, motives for giving information, how information was obtained by the informant, how he maintained his role without being caught and how the officer managed the relationship.

As a final step, capitalizing on opportunity, we asked a sample of 480 drug peddlars (most not incarcerated) with whom we were working on another study, what they thought accounted for informants' conduct. These dealers are among the most sought-after targets of police work and are an often-informed-against group. As victims or potential victims of trust violation, we believed their views would be of interest.

In an exploratory study of this sort, methodological difficulties abound. In addition to the inestimable sampling bias, there are two other error sources which are little different from other studies. These are requiring that people give information about themselves or that others describe them. We have no guarantees that the information put down on the check sheet by an officer is correct. His subject may have lied to him, or the officer may have misunderstood or otherwise been careless. We attempted to assure care in two ways. One was by stressing it in our instructions and the other was by having inspectors turn their reports over to their bureau captains or depty chiefs, who were cooperating in the study, rather than to the research workers directly. Knowing that their own boss was going to receive and review the report—and pay them for it if it was acceptable—we hoped would work to assure maximum carefulness in check-sheet preparation.

The other error source resides in descriptions the interviewer himself makes of the subject. Ratings or observations of behavior are subject to variability, depending upon who is doing the rating, what behavior the rater sees, what else he knows about the subject, the kind of relationship between the two, etc. Even though ratings of personal traits are subject to unreliability, we have employed them. For the most part, the informants are well-known to the officers, and to the extent that familiarity produces stable ratings (although not necessarily valid ones as measured by some other criterion), the data has that advantage.

In addition to calling attention to sources of inaccuracy and possible sampling bias, it is important to point out the limitations of the approach itself. What we have done is to conduct an exploratory study aimed at getting a first look at informants— what they are like, what their relations with their associates are like, what their relations with their officer contact are like. What we have not done because we were not ready to do it was to employ controls or to seek experimental tests of specific hypotheses. That means we do not have satisfactory answers to questions which ask about the differences between informants and noninformants coming from the same social situation, nor about differences between informants who violate trust in lesser or greater degree. There are implicit comparisons in our present data, ones based on the observations of the officers or based on other research about criminals or the general population. These lead to initial statements which require testing by more rigorous procedures. These are second-step developments, the pursuit of which are warranted by the present findings. In the meantime, we have decided not to imply an order of exactness not present in the data by using statistical tests to ennoble our findings. We have limited ourselves to general statements which themselves may serve as hypotheses in later studies.

GENERAL CHARACTERISTICS OF THE INFORMANTS

Summarizing backgrounds, we find that three-fourths of our initial sample were men, most were between 25 and 45, almost half were not Caucasians, the majority had not completed high school, and nearly all were United States citizens born in this country. A variety of occupations are represented, but there are no professional or high-level managerial people. Prostitutes constitute the largest single group, followed by barbers, barkeeps, painters, laborers and the unemployed persons. In terms of major types of occupation, habitual and professional criminals comprise 20 percent of the sample. About half are skilled or semiskilled persons. Estimating socioeconomic class on the basis of occupation and education, all but one of the sample appear to be lower class, working class, or possible lower-middle class. Surprising by their absence are taxi drivers; this is surprising because some police officials have stated that prostitutes, barkeeps and taxi drivers provide a sufficient group of informants to keep tabs on vice and organized crime within a city.

Turning to the nature of the information given, one finds that informants can give information on a variety of criminal activities, not just one event or "specialty." Crimes against property, especially robbery-burglary-fencing followed by vice offenses (drugs, gambling, prostitution) account for the lion's share of information passed by our initial sample. There are a few cases of information being given on homicide, armed robbery and, in one case, political extremism. It is to be noted that this distribution reflects the sampling among police divisions and inspectors; for example, had more inspectors been sought in the narcotics bureau, information on vice would be shown as having been more often given. In regard to the fact that informants, as observers of the criminal scene, give information repeatedly and about different activities, it is also to be stated that they may give it to several different police agencies. We will later see that officer contacts do not recommend it. We do not know how common this multiple-agency use is as opposed to the solitary management of an informant by one contact. As an illustration, the one informant giving political information had also operated overseas in two Communist areas (as an agent, not as a regular government employee) and may be presumed to have given information to at least one government agency. The merchant seaman in our sample can also be expected to be providing information to a government agency, primarily in smuggling cases, whereas for offenses within the jurisdiction of the city, he will report to the police. It is at this point that from the standpoint of police intelligence, the problems of the utilization of informants is raised, including coordination of information received by several law enforcement agencies.

It is important to know in what relationship the informant stands to the person or persons about whom he gives information. In each case, there must be some contact, some reoccurring situation which enables the informer to observe the activities and/or to hear the reports of those involved in criminal (or as we have noted in one case, extreme political) activities. Multiple opportunities may sometimes arise; that is, an informant may be both a wife and a fellow criminal, or one may be both a work colleague and a fellow addict. We see this double opportunity situation occurring in about one fifth of our subjects. For the most part, an informant, at least those in our sample, stands in a single-role relationship to the informed-upon persons. We say "persons" in the plural, since most of the underworld activities described and associated with habitual or organized crime are interpersonal in nature and involve several persons. For example, several men may plan a burglary, one or two more may help conduct it, a wife may be involved in disposing of the goods, a fence will buy them, a salesman may distribute them, etc. It is much less likely that persons involved in solitary crimes are visible enough to be informed upon.

Among our subjects, opportunities to come to know about offenders and offenses came by virtue of (a) working, living and/or spending leisure time ("hanging out") in the same places (one fourth of the cases), (b) being an addict member of a drug-using group (also one fourth of the cases), (c) being a fellow member of a criminal (or extreme political) group (excluding all vice) (one fifth) and (d) being a prostitute (thereby coming in contact with criminals as customers or associates or hearing about them from other prostitutes or associates; (one sixth of the cases). Less often, one finds the informant snitching on relatives (e.g., a wife "ratting" on her husband) or being a hanger-on or provider of services to the underworld, without himself (or herself) sharing an occupation, living quarters or criminal activity. So it is that people "on the fringe" who have criminals as regular customers in settings where observation, acquaintance and conversation are encouraged can be informants. Providers of illicit services in our sample include prostitutes, drug peddlers and gamblers; noncriminal service occupations becoming informants in our sample are barkeeps, barbers, cooks and restauranteurs, card room operators, theater managers, and domestic servants. Not directly service occupations, but possibly closely allied in a functional sense (in terms of access and contact) may be the entertainers and salesmen, the latter perhaps providing illicit rather than licit services, depending on what he sells.

Finally, contact opportunities arise when the informant shares the same jail cell with the offender (and is sometimes put there for the purpose of getting information) or, having shared a past prison experience, is dispatched as an agent of the police to join a crowd of ex-cons.

HOW THE OFFICER-INFORMANT RELATIONSHIP DEVELOPED

Critical questions for the social scientist interested in trust violation and informant careers as well as for the law enforcement officer interested in identifying potential informants and in anticipating how they must be handled to become productive information sources are these: How did the relationship begin, and how was it nourished? The most frequent contact (57%) was an arrest which put the informant-to-be in such a position that the officer could offer a "deal," that is, as an alternative to prosecution, the offender is invited to give information. In a few cases, informants were recruited by other informants, were witnesses, or approached the officer after being "referred" to him.

Becoming an informant appears to require a personal contact and to take place through known persons or routes. It may occur after arrest or during interrogation; or following an introduction

from a friend, a "recommendation" to an officer from his other
informants or criminal contacts, or a "recommendation" to a
potential snitch from his acquaintances about a particular officer.
In any event, some chain of acquaintance brings officer and snitch
(informant) together, either on a referred or direct-introduction
(including arrest after investigation) basis. It can happen that a
number of people participate in "defining" a man as an informant
or an officer as his "contact." We are aware that "walk-in" self
referrals "off the street" also occur, or a witness can offer himself,
or someone calls the police to report a crime or some suspicious
activity. These modes of contact do not appear in our sample
and we must presume that the continuing informant privy to the
criminal crowd is but rarely self-recruited outside of an acquaintance or recommendation chain.

Most arrested persons are not, of course, offered deals. Presumably, deals occur only when the officer is working on a case
where further information is needed in order to "make" it or
when the officer anticipates a continuing investigation (and/or
future criminality) concerning the offender's associates. We have
no data on the actual background of cases in which officers do
offer deals. In any event, the exploration of whether or not a
particular offender might serve as a suitable informant is not
subject to the police officer's initiative alone; arrested subjects
themselves request that a deal be made (see Skolnick, 1966).

With regard to the immediate factors serving as motives for
snitching, several elements may be present at once. A major
element in the case of the arrested persons was the deal itself—
the desire to avoid punishment. Indeed, the element of fear
extends to persons not arrested; some of the sample were offered
a deal by an officer prior to their being apprehended but after
evidence against them had been gathered. The "deal," of course,
is an aspect of the discretionary handling of cases by investigators.
Even though fear of punishment and the desire to gain immunity
or a lighter sentence is a component for fully half of the sample
in establishing their initial role as informants, it need not be the
only component among the coerced subjects. For some of them,
friendship for the officer and appreciation of his fairness played a
role. Money was also important, as was vengeance in motivating
informants. The fact of the subject's confidence in the officer's

ability to protect him also entered in; when the informant is not sure his officer contact will keep him anonymous and safe, information is less likely to be forthcoming. Some also enter into snitching with an eye on the future, trying to build up a supply of obligations on the officer's part or devices for influencing him so that the snitch, when in need, can expect future police favors. For a few, from the beginning, informing has an appeal based on intrigue. The double role, the secrecy and the danger in the game of spying and the fact that being an "agent" is ego-building when the officer flatters the subject for his work—these are features which attract some subjects.

In summary, officers and/or informants say that the early history of the snitch, the establishment of the initial relationship with the officer, comes about primarily because of the threat posed by the officer and the subject's fear. Trust violation, if there be that, is acceptable for self protection. Important, but less often mentioned and quite possibly simultaneously present, are friendship for the officer, gratitude to him, the desire for money, the desire for revenge on the criminal associates, trust in the officer's ability to assure protection and the enjoyment of intrigue and being a police spy and the accompanying enhancement of self-esteem as the officer offers praise. So it is that both positive and negative forces are at work on subjects to turn them into informants.

One of the most important facts which emerge from the observations of the officers is that the relationship with the informant changes over time. It is, of course, not unusual for human relationships to change, and so it is with snitches that the original motives are altered as time goes on. In the case of our sample, the negative influences are displaced by more positive ones. As we indicated, the most common "hooker" or "angle" was fear of prosecution and imprisonment; and the anxiety about that was allayed by the officer's giving immunity in return for information. Another strong emotion was revenge. Both of these appear to recede as the subject continues to work for the officer. New features emerge or, if present earlier, become more important as anxiety and vengeance become less so. The importance of money grows (informants are paid for each tidbit), and it may well serve a symbolic reward function that is not economic, as does friendship for and trust in the officer. In addition, a number of informants come to enjoy "playing cop," a development which we infer arises in part from a process of identifying with the officer himself. No doubt the immediate excitement of being an agent, whereby the subject sees himself in an admirable and adventurous light, continues to be a factor as well. In any event, by working with the officer, the subject does take on a para-police role and is playing cop. For the informants who stay at it, the activity itself can be satisfying.

Another change over time is that the informant comes to view his associates in a different light. Under the "guidance" of the officer, those who are themselves criminal or who are intimate with criminals emphasize the disadvantages in criminal associations and their own exploitation by others. This puts their associates in the position vis à vis the snitch, of "using" the snitch for their own ends—as perceived by the snitch. That is a "bad" thing to do and justifies the self-protective turncoat acts of the informant in violating trust. The shift in perspective serves to loose the ties with the criminal associates and to bring the subject closer to the officer's view of these associates as "bad" people. Exploitation is not all one-sided; the informant may not only be exploiting his associates by informing on them but also may continue to exploit his relationship to the officer as one for building up "brownie points," an "accounts receivable" for future favors, an insurance policy against later arrest. Not mentioned is any feeling on the part of the informant that the officer is exploiting him. That too must occur; perhaps the officers do not see it or it becomes visible only in informants who quit.

There are only two subjects in the entire sample whose relationship with the officer contact went unchanged over time. For all others, changes are important and the most common ones are positive. The emphasis is on the personal relationship with the officer and on the cop-playing role which is exciting and enhances the informant's self-image. Our data does not allow us to say more about why playing cop is so pleasing. From past research conducted by ourselves and others on police candidates (Blum, 1964), it is known that seeking excitement, having power and carrying a gun, being a respected authority and identifying with a punitive morality can all be motivating factors. That some delinquents want to be cops is common enough; so it is that some of our sample may long have had interests in police work; others may have discovered their compatibility for it only after becoming informants. Certainly for persons with a police record, the only way of becoming involved in police work, as other than "the opposition," is as an informant, since legitimate police employment is no longer open to them. At this point, it is worth speculating that the relationship of criminals and the police can be seen as symbiotic. Some offenders and officers seem to feel they understand one another better than they understand or are understood by persons outside. Insofar as such reciprocity of understanding—or interlocking roles or even of life meanings—occurs, the link between officer and the criminal-as-potential-informant exists prior to any arrest. During the relationship there would be a shift only in sides in the game—the subject would join the team.

We asked officers what the biggest troubles were in handling informants. Finding them and arranging the contacts were most often mentioned in reply. Since the relationship itself must be concealed, communication can only be by "'secure" channels. Since some informants are rolling stones anyway and since the officer cannot simply go about searching for his snitch publicly, one can understand the officer's difficulties. Furthermore there must be ways for passing along information that are not subject to surveillance. Other difficulties reported by the officers included the increasing greed of some snitches as they demand more money, separating fact from fiction in evaluating the information brought in by the snitches, providing for the security of the subject(keeping him safe from detection and violence) and keeping him in shape (not incapacitated from alcohol or drugs). Some officers may also find themselves entangled in the informant's personal troubles, being asked to help him in family affairs, homosexual triangles and the like.

These are all problems directly facing the officer as part of his own dealings with the snitch. The snitch himself has other troubles because of his role, paramount of which is the chance that he will be killed or badly hurt if his criminal associates (a) learn of his informing and (b) find him afterwards. A few face minor troubles such as losing their jobs; some are not in jeopardy. These latter presumably have informed on persons who are not prone to violence or who are in no position to mete it out, or whose roles vis à vis one another do not allow the definition of "betrayed" (as in a witness to a crime).*

Officers were asked what they do to protect their endangered informants. For an unfortunate few (six cases), the officer exposes them, saying, "let him take care of himself." Most are not so casual, and they employ security measures which include the use of misleads and other "red herrings" to cover information sources, avoiding direct contacts or other exposure making the relationship visible, keeping the informant himself under cover and anonymous in reporting, not using him as a witness and working with him to assist him in building cover. It may be that physical security measures—overlooking the fact he carries a weapon—are employed.

We had expected that the informant himself might feel very uncomfortable not just because of the actual danger facing him but because of the deprecatory ring of the words describing him—squealer, rat, fink, snitch, stoolie, traitor and other less printable ones. Most people want to think well of themselves and to strive to present to themselves and others a good front or image, an acceptable "self," in other words, not a betrayer. Many officers denied that the "self-image" was a problem, saying that informants were not bothered. In point of fact, most officers did have techniques for dealing with shame or guilt the snitch might feel. First of all, they used their special relationship to counteract shame by giving praise, by showing appreciation and by building up the fellow's own self-confidence. Secondly, they appealed to his own selfishness and "good sense," pointing out that "you come first." This technique rewards "cleverness," "survival of the fittest" and selfishness as the natural thing to be.

---

* Some narcotics officers claim that among addicts, there is little danger for the snitch, since addicts are described as having relationships so distant, individual compulsions so strong, and opportunistic manipulations so rife that the addict subculture expects and accepts double dealing. There is no violation of trust, since there is no trust. We have not sought to test these police contentions.

A third technique was to encourage the informer to feel that he was not an exception but that "anyone in his shoes" would do the same thing. Among addicts, for example, informing is expected and is called "trade bait." Another method is to justify the act by making the betrayed associates appear deserving of bad treatments—justifying revenge arguing that the associates were in fact "using" the informant and betraying him.* By informing, the tables are quite properly turned. Another device is to encourage the identification with the officer himself, to help the informant "play cop." Toward this end, officers using informants refer to them as "agents" or "operatives," words implying heroism and propriety and police identities. "Never, but never" said one supervisor, "refer to him in his presence as anything but an "agent."

The devices the officer has, utilize not only the relationship but typical methods people employ for avoiding psychic discomfort. Not surprisingly, the informant activates such "defenses" and also apparent growth processes on his own (identification, for example, which is itself a "defense" in the psychoanalytic sense). Officers observed that many informants had already concluded that what they did "was the right thing," that life was a jungle which required self-serving acts or that the gratification from revenge was intense enough to exclude any notions of betrayal. Indeed, for some, being an informant had become a "way of life," so that in spite of its physical and psychological hazards, the subject had worked out a continuing adjustment.

In spite of the problems in management and the dangers to the informant, all of the officers are convinced of their value. The most obvious reason is that the officer has trusted access to the underworld where he receives inside information. He can

---

* Prostitutes, for example, who are also often heroin users are said to hate the pushers (heroin peddlers) because they blame them for their being addicted, are angry because the pushers cheat them by selling diluted heroin, and are not kind in their personal relations. They can also be furious at their pimps because if the girl is not making enough money, the pimp insists they solicit on the streets where they then get caught; consequently, the prostitutes blame the pimps for their being arrested. The officers capitalize on this kind of thinking to encourage revenge on peddlers and pimps.

also provide very rapid information if need be, over impending as well as past events, outstripping the police investigator following routine methods. In the case of vice crimes, the informant can also be a witness to events taking place without complainants and will be, upon occasion, used when there is need to swear out a warrant or to make a case in court.

Officers were asked to set forth the principles which guided informant management. The first principle which emerged was one affirming the need to establish and maintain trust by the officer himself, never making promises that he could not keep and always acting with honesty and fairness. As other research has shown, notably in patient-physician and worker-supervisor relationships, this is good advice. It is also estimable morality. One speculates that fewer informants would enjoy playing cop if the cop who was handling them was himself not an admirable man. One suspects that for some of these people, their officer contact is one of the few reliable men they have known. Given the need most humans have for security, certainty, and in some cases heroes, it is a sign of the officers' sensitivity that they recognize their own conduct vis-à-vis the informant as a critical feature in making the relationship work. Protecting informants is another important feature, one which allows the informant to survive and, in addition, to sense the guardian aura of the officer. To allay anxiety is a prime means of creating trust and dependency. Another factor less often mentioned is the need to keep the relationship private and intense, not to dilute it by sharing the informant with others. One can suggest that behind this doctrine there may be something of the psychoanalytic notion of "transference," setting up a relationship with a person who is neurotic or immature in such a way that he transfers important emotions and attitudes to the authority, thereby creating a more intimate (and also complex) exchange than would otherwise have been. Also implied is the one-sidedness of the affair; the officer must not trust the informant but must himself be trustworthy. A similar rule holds whenever a mature person is to deal with a less mature one, including again psychoanalytic transference procedures. So it is that the officers stress that they must always evaluate what they hear, double-check it, and then still act cautiously. Beyond anticipating deception, the officer must also tread warily so as not to be compromised. The willingness of some informants to exploit or manipulate the officer has been cited; so it is that if they get a "handle" or "hook" on him, the officer can be blackmailed. Not trusting the informant includes acting cautiously and discreetly and not being "sucked in" to tempting offers or unprotected situations. This care is part of the picture of dealing from strength, a point several officers particularly make. Remain firm and "run the show" they say. Do not let the informant maneuver himself into being boss. As an overall task, several officers affirmed the need to appraise carefully the informant, so that one understands his situation, his needs and his probable reactions. As a final task, the job is to build the informant's ego, to give him support and encouragement, to go beyond offering praise and money, but to treat him "like a human being," with dignity and sensitivity. Sometimes support goes further, and officers help a subject get a job and to go straight. Insofar as they do, they may lose him through successful rehabilitation. We had not, at the beginning of this study, considered that possibility but, it is now evident that through the relationship, some informants have come to a new and more honest style of life.

RELATIONSHIP OF THE INFORMER TO THOSE INFORMED UPON

Our assumption was that the informant cannot be understood by himself or simply in relationship to the officer handling him. We expected that the people upon whom he informed and his relationship to them would contribute to the sequence of events leading to giving information to the police, an act in violation of trust on at least some occasions. We therefore asked officers to describe the informant's relation to his associates.

The primary criminal activities or the persons informed upon were, as indicated earlier, in burglary-robbery-fencing and in vice, with a few cases of homicide and armed robbery. By criminal occupation, these people are thieves, robbers, fences, addicts, prostitutes, gamblers and strong-arm types. For the most part, the informants do not describe their associates as being part of real groups but as aggregates—criminals and their cronies coming together in casual association; a "subculture" of the underworld constituting its hangers-on, direct participants, merchants, service people and in more distant ways, its clients. Associations there are loose, transient, and ordinarily do not constitute cohesive groups. Some subjects' associates are an exception and do constitute enduring and close-knit associations.

However casual the criminal groups themselves may be, the relationships of the average informer to at least the types of persons being snitched on has been enduring. More than two thirds had known the "crowd" involved for more than six years; almost one third of the subjects knew their crowd for more than twenty years. Stability within the underworld and *demimonde* as a way of life exists even though individuals come and go. How the informant came to be there in the first place is more than we can say; we can only say something about how he fell into a particular place within the larger lower-class metropolitan criminal crowd. Most frequently, association occurs by virtue of living and hanging out in the same geographical area and in pursuing the same kind of interests and life styles. A few are initiated into their particular crowd in jail; two married into it. Again we must emphasize that these are only routes to particular associates, not to the way of life itself. If one were to draw upon sociological studies, and studies of families as well, one would guess that most of the people in these areas had been born and reared within a similar socio-economic and attitudinal setting. A few perhaps may have fallen from higher stations; for a few others, either their present jobs or crime may represent success or upward mobility from even less-desirable positions held by their parents.

It is of interest to be specific in terms of the actual kinds of people snitched on. Remembering that multiple snitching is the rule—that is, one informant will inform over time on a number of different people—one finds (ranked by prevalence) the following to be likely:

1. Most informed on persons engaged in the same criminal occupation as the snitch.

2. The majority inform on persons of the same race and ethnic group.
3. About half inform on persons of the same sex.
4. About half inform on persons in the same age group.
5. About one third inform on persons who work in the same or nearby places.
6. About one third inform on their clients and customers.
7. Over one third inform on their competitors.
8. Over one-third inform on people living in the same place or area—their neighbors.
9. Some inform on lovers, tricks or spouses (persons they have intercourse with).
10. A few inform on those who share the same legitimate occupation as they do.
11. A few inform on spouses and relatives.
12. A few inform on people who work for them.
13. A few inform on their good friends and close partners.
14. A few inform on their fellow inmates (this number would be larger were one conducting a jail or prison study).

The foregoing is an undoubtedly incomplete catalogue of snitching opportunities. It is dictated by access to knowledge about what someone else is doing that he should not do, which in turn depends on physical and social proximity. Whether the relative infrequency of snitching by relatives reflects loyalty on the part of cousins, husbands and wives or whether it reflects their ignorance of the other's criminality cannot be said. One can guess that the infrequency of legitimate work-association snitching or employer snitching simply reflects lack of access to knowledge of criminality. Whether there are situations where group ties, do in fact, protect against or immunize associates against informing on one another (aside from risk of violence) remains an open question.

Describing the crowd informants run with, officers in general are not inclined to be complimentary. "Crummy" and "sordid" are the kinds of words they use, pointing out that underworld associations mean risks of violence, of both false and legitimate arrests, of addiction and of loneliness. Even with these disadvantages, for most subjects his associations are his way of life, and he seeks no other. To illustrate, one officer said, "He's always in the "in crowd"—fast operators, cab drivers, bartenders, waitresses, musicians, gamblers, prostitutes. The square life is too far behind to go back to and he wouldn't be happy as a square anyway." Another said, "She married this war hero when she was fourteen. She didn't know he was an addict. She started (drugs) at eighteen. She supported them both by hustling and boosting. Later she separated from him but she stayed in the group because by then she was an addict and had to run with the other addicts."

Only two subjects are described as being presently interested in finding a better (noncriminal) life. Three have already found it, having left the worst of the underworld behind.

Officers were asked how the informant differs from those he informs upon, given the fact that most come from the same socioeconomical strata and many are criminals recruited after arrest. The officers replied that the informant acknowledges that crime is wrong and considers himself to be acting in a more proper and moral way by giving information about criminals. About half of the sample of subjects can thus be said to either have developed a set of righteous justifications or maintain some conventional morality which is more law-abiding than that of their associates. Should it be the latter, is this part of the psychological identification with the officer which leads to a new (or reaffirms an old) ideology? On the other hand, not all subjects can by any means be described as pursuing a more righteous course. A few differ from their associates only in that they are brighter and perhaps better able to survive by taking advantage of them through informing and securing protection for themselves thereby. A few are just more greedy, taking money for snitching; for some, the importance of vengeance is the only differentiating factor; and for a few (5 of 35) the officer says they differ in no way from their colleagues.

We asked about specific aspects of the informant's relationship to his associates and were told that (a) most informants do not like anyone in the crowd with whom they associate, (b) most are more interested in themselves than in their associates, (c) most subjects do not like the leaders of the crowd they hang out with, (d) only a few are themselves considered leaders in the crowd; most are equals, and one-third have inferior status, (e) some (one-fourth) are oddballs or simply outsiders and (f) in spite of the foregoing, nearly all the subjects are very conforming in terms of acting like their associates. We consider these to be very important factors; in sum, they imply that the informants tend to be emotionally distant from their associates, resentful of the leadership, self-centered and rarely leaders themselves. To the contrary, some are inferiors and oddballs. Nevertheless, they do not express their feelings or admit to deviation but outwardly conform instead, all of the while concealing their snitching and betrayal as well as their negative feelings about the crowd.

Their associates are not particularly likeable, according to officers. The whole (underworld) crowd tends to be selfish, and its members are hardly considerate of one another. There are exceptions; some of the subjects do run with associates who are good-hearted even if "kinky"; few are conventional citizens. The majority of the subjects are said to be in crowds which remain unorganized in the sense that formal leadership is lacking (even though there can be a hierarchy of status). Sometimes factions and cliques exist, these associated with dissension. Most are losers; rarely do any of them "score" by making a lot of money. For them, crime pays but badly. So it is that no one in the crowd has a lot to offer, whether it be money, success, kindness or personal strength. Even so, for many subjects there are gratifications in being part of the crowd and in having friends, even if they are not good friends. These associations are maintained, even though the underworld crowd acknowledges and suspects one another of betrayal, as is said to be the case with about half of the informants' associates. Indeed, one of the strongest reasons that there is no greater amount of betrayal is that there is, according to the officers, an omnipresent threat of violence should one be caught. Again the picture is painted for the most frequent case; some informers are outside the underworld; others are members of groups that are more cohesive and friendly.

THE SUBJECTS' BACKGROUND

In this section, we shall describe the informant sample in terms of their reported personal and family backgrounds and characteristics.* Since our exploratory study did not attempt a complete life history but focused on items of special interest, these background descriptions are not complete. Each background checklist item, as in other sectors of this inquiry, was essentially a test of an expectation that informants woud be alike in some way symptomatic of developmental problems and interpersonal difficulty. Positive findings for these expectations still require comparison with non-trust-violating controls—if such exist in the underworld—which must be a future study.

Home and Parents

Half of the subjects saw their childhood homes as being poor or desperately poor; half saw them as economically average; one subject said his parents were well-to-do. Childhood economic circumstances were stable; in only one case was there any marked family shift in economic position. Two thirds of the subjects reporting (27 out of 35) described their parents as normal people who were not criminal, addicted, alcoholic or psychologically peculiar. Two thirds also said their parents provided good care and affection, especially the mothers, all of whom (with 19 subjects not described) were said to be loving. Most mothers (17 of 25) were also described as providing adequate supervision. Of the fathers described, two thirds (10 of 15) were said to be adequate disciplinarians (neither too harsh nor too lenient) but more (10 of 19) fathers were said *not* to have liked the subject or to have spent adequate time with him when he was a child. About one fifth (6 of 26) of the same-sex parents (fathers for boys, mothers for girls) were described as themselves socially maladjusted. In one fourth of the cases (8 of 24), the subject was very rebellious toward the same-sex parent. Considering the family as a whole, one fifth report criminality among some other

---

* The officers completing the check sheets are often not able to provide the data sought on subject backgrounds, either because they were reluctant to inquire or the subjects were unwilling to report. So it is that the trends or proportions set forth are limited to those subjects about whom data is available.

immediate family member. Alcoholism or drug addiction are present in nearly one third of the cases in some close family member; almost one fourth have close relatives who are shiftless or no-account, and in two known cases (out of 21 described), other family members are also informants.

The family from which the subject comes is usually (21 of 28) said to have been one where there was a normally close family life. Nevertheless, 40 percent of the subjects reporting (12 of 30) spent some of their childhood in institutions and over 50 percent (18 of 30) lived away from at least one parent, one third of these for more than three years. About one fifth (6 of 26) changed addresses five or more times before the age of seventeen. In two cases, the mother of the subject died or was gone during the first two years of the subject's life, a critical period; and in one third of the cases (11 of 28) one parent died or was removed before the subject turned sixteen. Most of the parents shared beliefs and origins; in only one fifth of the cases (5 of 23) were there serious conflicts between the parents over ideology (we had anticipated more). Four of 19 parents on whom data were available had changed their religion.

Childhood History

We have indicated that despite the reported adequacy of most of the parents and homes, more than half of the subjects spent some of their childhood away from at least one parent and nearly half were in some institution. Considering the likelihood that some of these institutions were penal, one asks about early arrests and convictions. Only five subjects (5 of 35) have never been arrested. One fifth (7 of 33) were arrested before the age of fifteen, and including these, two thirds were first arrested while still adolescents. First convictions occur later than first arrests, first arrests occur later than first apprehensions, and these in turn occur after earlier social troubles (see below). For example, only half of the subjects were convicted before the age of twenty. Seven had never been convicted. Court appearances occur more often than convictions; over one third have appeared between two and ten times, another one third between six and twenty times, and one fifth more than twenty times.

Personal difficulties appear early and in many forms. One fourth (8 of 31) were excessive drinkers before becoming adults. The age of the first "official" trouble with authority (school, police, etc.) for the sample was under age 10 for 10 percent (3 of 30), under age fifteen for 40 percent (a cumulative total including the below-age-ten group), and under age 20 for two-thirds. Seven (7 of 30) were never in trouble. School truancy problems occurred in half of the subjects. As very young children (age 5 or under), 4 of 15 on whom data was available were described as abnormally overactive or excitable, and nearly half (8 of 18) were also described as child behavior problems. One fifth (4 of 25) were late readers. Only a few (2 of 24) were accident- or sickness-prone and fewer (2 of 26) had childhood or adolescent psychiatric care. Although we do not have data on the age of the first use of illicit drugs, we find that half of the sample (16 of 33) do have a history of chronic illicit drug use (aside from alcohol) and possible dependency. Since initial illicit use usually begins in adolescence, we suggest that early illicit drug use is an important characteristic of the sample.

Looking at other aspects of developmental history, we find that about one fifth (7 of 21) suffered embarrassing or crippling physical blemishes or defects during childhood. The majority (25 of 33) dropped out of school rather than completing a diploma or degree. As teenagers, 7 out of 25 showed drastic shifts in their beliefs, interests and ideals. Only one, now a political informant, was involved in extreme politics or social movements as a teenager. One third (9 of 26) were lonely children during adolescence, who had trouble making friends. They were outsiders, not insiders. Presenting a false front or playing a secret role may also have begun early; one third (10 of 27) used false documents during their adolescence to alter their ages or identity.

In an earlier paragraph, we spoke of the fact that some of the sample (one fourth) had shown extremely rebellious behavior toward their parents. We are also told that over one third (11 of 29) got on badly with their parents. In some cases, the subjects have made shifts away from the ideology of their parents; one-fourth (4 of 16) have adopted political preferences

different from parental ones; a few (3 of 27) have been converted
to a new religion.

Adult History

Our check sheet included items to reflect personal or social
instability as adults. In terms of jobs, nearly two thirds (18 of
30) have never held a job for more than two years; of those
employed at all (4 are not and never have been), one third
(7 of 22) have had more than six jobs in the last five years.
More than half (17 of 30) are chronic job-shifters or unemploy-
ables. Residence mobility is considerable; as adults, four fifths
(19 of 25) have had ten or more addresses. One third (10 of
31) have a history of marital discord, although only a few have
married three or more times. Most are said to be able to have
relationships with the opposite sex; a few (4 of 32) are incapable
of love or intimacy in sexual relations. Five are older men who
have never married. Over half (18 of 30) are acutely bad credit
risks; some (7 of 34) are compulsive gamblers; two have
histories of repeated major business losses.

On other details, a few (4 of 33) have a history of institutional escapes, 4 having military service offenses (out of 26
males). Some (5 of 34) have officially changed their names (by
other means than marriage) and 55 percent (19 of 34) have used
aliases, a feature we think related to identity problems, even
though it is common in the underworld. None are cultists or
way-out sect members. Two-thirds (21 of 32) lack constructive
ways of spending their leisure time (no hobbies, sports, social
clubs, reading, etc.). One-third are addicts, and an overlapping
one third abuse alcohol. The majority are ex-convicts.

PERSONALITY TRAITS AND BEHAVIOR

We now turn to the checklist description of the subjects
offered by the officers. In some cases, the descriptions reflect
the estimate of the officer about how the subject's own cronies
view him; sometimes it is the subject's own opinion combined
with the officer's; sometimes it is the officer's rating. We do not
know how much agreement there would be on any one subject

if several people were asked to rate him. We can only hope that the descriptions do represent reasonably accurate portrayals of personal traits and behavior.

What are the traits common to the *majority* of informants in our sample? The majority are described as average or above average in intelligence; much in need of praise, needing to feel important, requiring appreciation; excitement-seeking, cannot stand boredom, perhaps depressed if things are dull.

In contrast to the few traits common to most informants, *some* informants (defined as between 15 percent and 50 percent of the sample) are reasonably well-adjusted normal persons; ordinary people, not unusual; ambitious, striving, pushing to get ahead; intensely loyal to at least one person or group; overly eager to please, cannot say "no"; frightened and insecure; vain, conceited; ambivalent about authority—sometimes respectful, sometimes resentful; unrealistic, perhaps idealistic but with half-baked ideas; foolish, confused, show poor judgment; impulsive, easily lose control; flighty, not persevering; vengeful, hold grudges; unreliable, untrustworthy; slippery, sneaky, crafty; lost souls without direction or meaning in life; born losers, "sad cases"; bums, ne'er do wells, floaters.

Very few informants are described as zealots or fanatics; dogmatic or highly opinionated; angry, bitter or discontented; strong characters, forthright, pillars of strength; righteous, blue-noses, prissy, very moral.

Reviewing these items, one sees that there is little communality among our informant sample in terms of personality, excepting the very important features of intelligence, need for praise and need for excitement. These features are consistent with the informant role. Their intelligence (83 percent are so described) makes them useful to the officer and may be presumed to help the snitch stay alive in his delicate position. The need for excitement, characteristic also of persons diagnosed as psychopathic personalities, may well have played some part in their gravitating to the underworld. Clinical observations suggest that some delinquents act out neurotic conflicts and ward off depression through criminal activities. The police themselves may also be seeking excitement. Living dangerously is something the officer and the informant can have in common and may very well be part of the desire to "play cop" which so many informants are said to have. By being an informant and thereby risking violence, excitement through danger occurs. The need for praise and appreciation is a trait of the informant which provides the officer with leverage. Playing cop is not enough; continuing interpersonal gratifications are also required, and the alert officer provides them by praise. He also offers more, as earlier discussed, in terms of money, alleviating fear, giving protection, being strong and encouraging an intimate, dependent role.

If the foregoing are the common elements, the list of traits checked for some but not other informants is a reminder of the variety of people that exist in our informant population. We have listed these "some are" and "some aren't" items in order of what might be called decreasing normalcy or increasing psychopathology. That ordering implies what earlier descriptive material suggested—that some informants are relatively ordinary folk, whereas others are distinctly maladjusted and a few are out-and-out social catastrophes. Perhaps one of the most interesting features is that most do not fit the stereotype of a "fink," for only one fourth are "slippery" characters standing out as untrustworthy or treacherous. Perhaps a known fink is useless (if still alive), and only the discreet ones are effectively deployable. Perhaps, too, disloyalty, like loyalty, is, as Grodzins (1956) contends, a specific rather than a general matter, one resting on loyalty to whom, what about and at what moment.

What snitches are not is a matter of agreement too and should be added to our descriptions of what they have in common. They are not, at least in our sample, informing because of their feeling of superior morality or their ideological commitments. They are not fanatics and they are not angry men. Perhaps zealots do not exist in the rather casual lower-class underworld from which most but not all of our sample come. It is unlikely that any who were rigid moralists could gain admission to criminal crowds for the purpose of informing. A certain flexibility seems required. It is likely that there are many angry and frustrated men in that underworld, but they do not appear among our informants.

Perhaps chronic anger is one emotion which disqualifies a subject from being an effective participant-observer; or perhaps it makes it impossible for an officer to maintain the kind of relationship with him, one of intimate dependency, which the officers here employ. One final thing the informants are not—in spite of a few being ordinary folk without remarkable quirks or social foibles (those being the noncriminal subjects in our group who have access by virtue of physical or social proximity to criminals), they are not (with one exception) strong or healthy people in a psychological sense.

Chapter IX

OUTSTANDING INFORMANTS

U PON COMPLETION OF the first round as reported in Chapter VIII we sought to interview a sample of informants known for their capabilities in that role. One of our police colleagues identified six as among the prize informants within a large metropolitan region. He interviewed them, using a prepared schedule as a guide.

Among the informants is Joyce, an ex-prostitute known to her police contact for ten years. She spends her time with the racket people, entertains a lot and is part of conversations in which offenses are discussed (including those of her husband who is involved in racketeering). She has a long record of petty offenses, is a heavy drinker and has abused other drugs as well. Her current criminality is restricted to boosting (shoplifting); her information is best on robbery and burglary.

Louie is unemployed, a chronic psychiatric patient, who lives in a neighborhood where many offenders reside, rooms with homosexuals and is considered unreliable in many ways. He spends his time walking about and visiting, knows most of the denizens and is very helpful in reporting where persons wanted by the police may be found. He is also well informed on boosting and narcotics.

Robert, a confidence man out of Chicago, is noted for his intelligence and success in crime. A professional criminal "from the old school," his interest is in avoiding big time (long sentences), for which reason he maintains cordial relations with the police and will, on big cases only and with considerable discretion, cop out (inform).

Clyde is a Negro petty thief and con man who hangs around the neighborhoods where professional offenders live. He is a member of the casual groups of thieves, mostly shoplifters and auto thieves. He has a record of many arrests but enjoys his "influence" with the police.

Ed is a cook whose hot dog stand is in a criminal area. He works the midnight to eight A.M. shift when the "night people" congregate. His restaurant is the scene of many illicit deals and transactions. He has a record of offenses, is a pederast and is reliable on burglaries and narcotics and other offenses as well.

186

Larry is a Negro con man, fence and jack of many (criminal) trades. His primary associates are burglars and bookies, but he is well-acquainted with habitual and professional offenders. He informs on a variety of crimes and is particularly useful in identifying suspects not well known to the police.

Rather than presenting information case by case on these people's initiation to, motivation for, and maintenance in, the informant role, we shall summarize that data. In every case, the informant role developed out of routine police contacts. Three were "turned out" as informants because of their apprehension for an offense—caught "dirty," they wanted to get off the hook. One of them was surprised at being given a break by the officer without there being any elbow twisting to produce information; his response to that kindness was a favor in reply, for he offered information which he possessed. In three cases, acquaintance developed during routine investigation in which those in the underworld group were contacted. One informant responded to a request for help by the police because, he said, he realized the officer needed help and approved of what he was doing. "I'm not a fingerman but I'll help the badge, he can't do it alone," said one. Another knew the person who was wanted and disapproving of the wanted man on moral grounds, aided the police. "He was a bad stud so I burned him."

As the relationship with the officer developed, other influences appear. Several developed friendly feelings for an officer and, within the limits of basic distrust probably characterizing these early stages, enjoyed giving a favor (snitching) in return not only for approval but for the feeling one had "juice," i.e. influence over the police. The intention of creating an obligation in the officer exists, one which can be exploited by the informant in return for a favor when he needs it—generally when next apprehended for an offense. In these provisional friendships and imposed shared obligations, however casual, there is a continuing exchange of banter, advice, warning and as a favor, information. This gift-giving (the officer in turn may lend money, buy the informant coffee or begin to pay for snitching) is one way of saying that the relationship will continue and that both parties recognize its value. One informant, the psychiatric patient, particularly enjoyed his "special agent" status which developed, a status recognized by his contact who always swore him in as an agent prior to taking information. Others came to discriminate more finely about what crimes and criminals they would and would not snitch on; in this way, they shared a partial morality with the officer and could justify being snitches because the crimes or people were bad. Acting in this fashion, they, like other citizens, were the moral constituents being served by the police.

One informant spoke of the importance of maintaining ties to his experienced contact, "to get protection from the older cops who keep young heat from busting you." This fellow was defending against social change by using his contact to intercede and to control the young officer newly assigned to the informant's criminal specialty or working area. In addition to the expectation of the favor of no arrest, by way of having taken on the role of the snitch, there was developed a method specific to meeting the arrest danger; that is, the informant can prepare himself with a bank of information, so that if arrested, he can immediately draw on his account. "Then the beef is cooled and I'm off the hook." The officer can do the same, leaning on a reluctant snitch if an important case is involved. Pervasive among men of the world is the understanding of the *quid pro quo*. Snitches can count on more than immunity (within certain limits, for there is a balance of payments, and certain hot or heinous offenses could not be overlooked for any information, although a lesser charge could be bought by turning evidence on another fellow offender), and on more than status, the righteousness of stamping out wrongful crime or bad studs, a continuing friendship or money. They can count on a two-way flow of information; that is, using the officer as a snitch. This is ordinarily limited (although in corrupt departments the reversal may be complete) to information about the informant's own suspect or wanted status, the status of his friends (do you suspect X?) or even if there are new developments in crime and criminal opportunities in the city. Information about the informant's own suspect status not only allows him to estimate whether or not he was hot but to learn if he could relax because someone else had been charged with an offense the informant had, in fact, committed. In any event, the two-way flow of information is not to be overlooked, for therein lies a set of complementary roles in which both parties parlay the snitch role in pursuit of greater gain. That trust is violated on either side seems of little consequence as long as the self-preservation of the offender or the apprehension of large game on the part of the officer is accomplished thereby. On the other hand, the two-way street demonstrates that in police informant use, as in classical espionage, the double-agent role is one that is easy for both criminals and police to move to.

The intention of both parties does not suffice to maintain the relationship; their conduct must make it possible. Officers stress the need to spend a lot of time with their prize informants, to avoid pressure, to be courteous and affable and under no circumstances to express disapproval of the informant himself. It is further necessary for the officer to protect the informant's safety by security measures such as not seeing him openly, using telephone contact whenever possible, and if necessary, making a public display of rousting him, so that the informant's associates continue to believe that he, like them, is an object of police suspicion and harrassment. There is also an agreement, among some, for officer and snitch not to bug one another's work. "You have to play the game" said an officer; "when the police have the hook the other way, they don't hang around where I work to heat me" said his informant. What that means is that the officer accepts the criminality of the informant and does not, under ordinary circumstances, capitalize on that knowledge to interfere with his crime career. It also means that the informant will not plague the officer with calls or requests for help or money, and will not compromise the officer. There are also explicit stipulations about not lying, on either part. The officer should deny the informant's status as a hot suspect for an offense if that is the case, unless the officer is willing to ruin future relationships for the sake of a large immediate gain. The informant, in return for police kindness, precautions and protection, does not lay on a story. "Mr. I. gives me only sound information." The stability of this trust varies with personality and situational need; the agreement, like all contracts, is constantly being renegotiated.

Each Mr. I. discussed how he received his information; that is, how he managed to observe or betray others. Simply hanging around—staying in the presence of offenders by being part of their social and work life—loomed largest. The fence, for example, constantly bought and sold stolen goods and could identify daily dozens of offenders. The snitching wife encouraged her husband to have his friends to the house to drink and gamble so that she could join in—and remember—their conversations. (Note that the contact officer protected the husband as well as the wife.) Several spoke of the importance of flattering their associates, clients, customers or acquaintances; "go along with the notion they have that they're real cool," "let him think he's a big man, let him talk about himself." One mentioned the value of dispensing alcohol generously for such conversations so that the other would speak more freely. For conversational openers, one informant said he has a line, "I tell them what my beefs have been, then they tell me about their action, the scores they've made." Another, specializing in thieves, shows interest as a customer for stolen goods. One speaks of the importance of buying the suspect a drink or dinner, relaxing him, giving him something, to open up friendly discourse. Another's line is to put himself in the suspect role, "say you have a tail on you and they cop out on themselves" or "tell stories and they tell them back." The most active informer says "try to move next to the big guys and you hear the heavy stuff." One remarks, "knock someone you know the suspect hates, then he'll like you and talk." Another says he involves himself in petty crimes with them to establish his trustworthy role. One speaks of the importance of becoming well known so that people get used to seeing one, "say hello to a lot of (kinky) people so they know you're in the right crowd." Another adds, "When you're with a suspect, manage to have one of his friends there with you so that he talks easier." One, quieter, says his modus operandi is to avoid conversation but to observe carefully what (goods) the other has, who he is with and how much money he's spending.

One cautions, "you have to tell a story (to prove your criminality), but just listen and don't let them believe you're too smart."

Informants were asked how they avoided being detected as, over the years, they continued to snitch, leading to the arrest of others. "Listen and don't talk" said most of them. "Don't ask for specifics" or "Don't go too strong and don't go too often." Never, said most, never ever work with officers who cannot be trusted. "Work only with one cop, don't change" or "Avoid exposure to heat you can't trust." Among specific defensive ploys, we have already noted the mock rousting by the contact officer; another recommends that whenever the suspect is busted (arrested) that he be visited, sympathized with and then lent money. "A suspect would never figure you'd loan him money and burn him." Another proposed that after the suspect's arrest or return from jail "you beef at him like hell," telling him that he was stupid and careless in getting busted. One informant, a transvestite, does not identify himself (herself?) and seeks information only when in drag, this is, partially disguised. Aside from being a precaution, it elicits information for "when you're in drag, people talk to you."

SUMMARY AND CONCLUSIONS

In review, one sees that the opportunity to snitch depends upon access to a social role where confidential information is ordinarily imparted. Thus over time, one proves that one is a criminal and in the same jeopardy as the victim (suspect), so that a defensive cohesiveness may characterize the association, along with the assumption of shared values. It is also seen that the prize informants become customers, homosexual lovers, in-drag transvestites, fellow drug users and, in one case, prostitute-turned-wife. Each of these roles allows shared confidences and gives access to groups whose criminality is of interest to the police. It is also clear that ordinarily one moves into the role slowly, gives various proofs of confidences and as it develops, seeks to maximize opportunity. That is done by creating settings where observations and the flow of confidences are enhanced, such as having dinner and drinking together, working in crime together, being a link in a business chain (fencing), taking drugs together and so forth. Precautions are taken so as not to reveal suspicious interests and so as not to allow counterobservations of the informant's connection to the police. There are a number of devices employed to increase familiarity and confidence once access and opportunity have been developed. We have noted parties, sex, liquor, drugs and law breaking as disinhibitors, but so too is flattery, being sure not to threaten (i.e., playing stupid) and being both a good listener and good, quiet watcher. Confidence follows acceptance by the social group or establishment of intimate personal relations. Betrayal follows easily after that as the interests of the snitch dictate. Discovery does not follow betrayal in this prize sample, for these informants have all been at work for years and have yet to be burned. It is evident that betrayal is chronic and self-seeking, that it involves planning and device, that it can be justified by righteousness, pride, status, being helpful, etc., or by any number of rationalizations ("a guy's got to protect himself," "anybody in the same boat would do the same," or in the classical delinquent rationalization, "everybody else does it"). It is evident also that betrayal rests on trust, not just the partially misguided trust of victims but the actual trust of the snitch in his officer contact and, conversely, of the officer contact in the snitch. It also rests on manipulation—by the informant of his associates and of the officer, to secure protection; and by the officer, to get material from his informant. Betrayal also seems to be linked with shared duplicity; others in the criminal environment are also deceiving and those who are betrayed by the snitch may likely deceive him. Likewise, the officer snitches, a little or a lot, on the department, and his informant is by no means always true to him. Finally, betrayal is, in the low level and relatively disorganized underworld here observed, a mixed bag of what is morally good and bad. Through treachery, justice is served. For justice, treachery is induced. The criminal invokes his morality and public conscience to aid the officer; the officer acts illicitly to receive that aid. The officer invokes the law to apprehend offenders; doing so, he gives immunity to an offender. That is the way of the world, or at least of the snitching world.

Chapter X

THE INFORMANT'S QUARRY

W E WERE NOT in a position to interview victims fingered by the 41 informants who comprised our two samples. We were in a position to learn from one sample of potential victims what they thought of snitches and how they protected themselves. The quarry were dealers in illicit drugs who were cooperating with us in a study (to be published elsewhere) of dealer careers and of the drug trade. Some were small-time and naive; some were in the million-dollar-a-year bracket. Most were on the streets, and less than half had ever been arrested on any drug charge. All those not in jail (N=402) were, at a time when narcotics traffic was drawing a lot of heat, prime targets for law enforcement and were therefore targets for informants as well.

We asked dealers what type of person becomes a narcotics and dangerous drug informant, compared to those average drug users who do not. In reply, the drug peddlers most often said (one quarter so stating) that the informants were weaker and felt more vulnerable; that is, that they were cowardly, fearful, paranoid or suspicious. A few dealers characterized informants as more conservative or moralistic; a few said they were selfish or hypocritical. One fourth could only say that snitches were just bad people. One sixth of the dealers contended there was no difference between an informant and other drug users.

What are the reasons for informing? Most of the dealers emphasized that it was a self-preserving response made to beat a rap. A few dealers also noted that informing occurred because of lust for money, personal weakness, a desire for revenge or righteous moralism (in that order).

What signs do dealers look for when they first meet someone (or later) so as to identify an informant? Remarkable in the replies is the absence of a stereotype of an informant and, indeed,

193

of any specific danger signals. Dealers spoke generally about "impressions" made or the "attitudes conveyed," but it was our impression that most dealers in our sample had no way—either empirically or magically derived—for evaluating potential finks. Indeed, about ten percent confessed that they made no effort to do so. A few dealers discussed the warning signals raised by a person who was too curious or too friendly or who came on too strong. Incongruity was also noted; for example, someone who did not dress the part of the person he claimed to be would be suspect. Some few did rely on stereotypes, for example, "shifty eyes" or the astrological sign under which another person was born.

How do drug peddlers protect themselves against informants? By "security" precautions, for the most part. Over half of the dealers indicated that they tried to screen their customers, not accepting unknown or unrecommended customers on the grounds that among these latter, more than among friends and acquaintances, informants might be found. The implications here are several. One is that an informant would have difficulty infiltrating a drug-using group successfully enough to be accepted and trusted; the other is the folk conception of obligatory loyalty (see Chapter XII), which holds that a friend will not betray. Obviously drug dealers in our sample felt themselves to be members of a loyal and stable-enough social circle to expect trust from one another.

A second related precaution which is common is the practice of concealment, the dealer keeping his criminality secret within the drug-using community and restricting his sales to a few major clients and wholesalers who are, presumably, carefully selected. Over time, these may come to constitute an organization or syndicate. Infiltration into such a closed system—except perhaps at the lower level of the street customer—is more difficult and reduces the vulnerability of dealers to identification and arrest.

Less often mentioned procedures to prevent victimization by informants include care in the use of phones (wiretaps are assumed), monitoring the whereabouts of known informants and undercover officers and the harassment of finks once identified ("harrassment" is a term which embraces murder). Bribery of police, either to buy them off or to pay for counterintelligence, i.e. to warn of infiltration by other narcotic officers is also practiced, but only by 5 percent of the sample.

These observations by their potential victims conform generally to the picture the informants have themselves given. If the criminal deals only with people he knows, then the informant or undercover agent must hang around long enough to become known. If the victim is cautious, suspicious of strangers, then the informant must move slowly and show himself to be safe. If the criminal is secretive, withholding confidences, then the informant must become valuable by offering services (or money) and show himself trustworthy, thereby winning those confidences which are then to be betrayed.

As for the motives of informants, the potential victims see these—with significant exceptions—much the same way as officers and informants themselves do, although with less sophistication and insight. Self-preservation out of fear when caught "dirty" (being arrested) looms largest in all the accounts. The dealers underestimate, compared to the "experts," the role of vengeance, money and moral fervor.

Victims appear entirely to overlook informant motives based on the informant's dislike of or unhappy or impoverished relations with the criminal group and, conversely, his strong positive relationships with "narcs" (narcotic officers). Perhaps it is not surprising that dealers do not see that betrayal can arise from social distance and dislike of the dealer and his group, for that would require of the criminal himself the entertaining of the unflattering notion that the criminal and his friends are not likeable fellows. Similarly, failure to identify the importance of a strong positive relationship between officer and informant as a factor sustaining snitching can be understood as a blindness to a kind of relationship which the criminal himself does not enjoy and one which he may not be able to conceive. Both of these failures in comprehension are human enough, but for the potential victim of deception and betrayal—criminal or otherwise—blind spots to the actual feelings of another for oneself and for the opposition or enemy can be costly indeed.

We have mentioned that five percent of the sample protect themselves from being informed upon by bribing police officers. This two-way flow of information is not to be overlooked, constituting, as it does, permeability in the security membrane of two groups, criminals and narcotic squads, both of which make some effort to keep the opposition uninformed. Not only do narcotics officers serve then as in-place agents for the more professional drug dealers but dealers may also "turn around" identified finks to work as double agents for and against the officers who are running them. For example, the doubled snitch (i.e. double agent) can provide intelligence as to police plans to protect his dealer friends while not providing that information to other dealers. As a variant, one to be expected in a competitive business, a dealer may use an identified snitch, with or without the snitch knowing it, as a weapon against other dealers, setting a competitor up for an arrest by using the informant as a channel to the police. Another variant, essentially a brand of counterintelligence, is to use a doubled snitch to identify other informants, i.e. penetrations into the drug-dealing organizations, who had not been identified. Yet another variant, one form of harassment, is to set up an informant in a criminal enterprise which is so blatant that the police must arrest or remove the snitch, for not doing so would expose the squad or officer handler to repercussions within his own department. That removal operation of criminal enterprise may be real or a frame. Be it a frame, it takes an ironic twist, for the would-be betrayer is set up on a bum beef by those whom he does not realize are wise to him and, we are told, may complain afterwards of having been "sold down the river," i.e. betrayed. In this instance, deception is mutual and the act of betrayal is simply a matter of who gets to whom first, and that in turn depends upon who has the most competent, or lucky, informers. Our impression is that among professional dealers, as among successful police investigators, the development of an effective intelligence system is part of the business. The manipulation of confidences thus becomes a weapon routinely employed by organized criminals as well as by law enforcement personnel.

Chapter XI

INFORMANTS AND THEIR QUARRY: COMMENT AND SUMMARY

On THE BASIS of the three samples, average and excellent informants plus their quarry, one begins to get a picture of how informants are identified, put to work or maintained over time. It is clear that there is no single occupation, personality syndrome or social situation which is common to all informants. Were our sample larger and had we used officers from other agencies, we would no doubt have found even greater variety in informant characteristics. Nevertheless, there are features which are dominant and conditions which are common ones. In our sample, the informants shared a way of life with the people they informed on. Some were "in the life," some served its members. All had intimate access to criminal groups by virtue of their common socioeconomic characteristics, their social and physical proximity, their identification as accepted (if not always trusted) fixtures on the scene and their personalities which allowed them free and an easy—but not loyal or affectionate—social intercourse.

Most of the informants had themselves been in trouble with the law prior to the arrest, investigation or introduction which put them in contact with the officer who recruited them or whom they recruited. Indeed, the majority showed a history of personality disorder, social distress and later criminality beginning in childhood or adolescence. Their socioeconomic status and general life styles have remained relatively unchanged since childhood; so has their history of personal disorder and criminality. If we are to infer any change in their life course from the data, it would be on the basis of their own descriptions of their families as stable and close and their parents as neither criminal nor disordered. Some homes and parents were troubled; but these were equal to the number of disordered offspring who comprised our sample. Two questions arise. First, are their descriptions of their parents and home accurate or do they harken back to some "golden age" that never was? Second, if they are correct and their parents were more stable and law-abiding, do the informants differ in that regard from the larger underworld community from which the informants are drawn? That is, is it a special feature of informants that they, more than their criminal associates, have come from more law-abiding origins? Certainly their early histories of disturbance and trouble are not unlike those found for many habitual criminals and underworld types; the critical issue is if for informants these represent shifts from parental behavior. The data tell us little about how such shifts, if they are shifts, occurred. The only clues are in the incidence of rebellion against parents, in the descriptions of fathers as not loving or attention-giving and in the remarkably high incidence of childhood institutionalization and separation from one or both parents. Even so, we cannot here prove that the informants are different from noninformants. From a theoretical standpoint, it would be gratifying if they were, for one could point to their interest in playing cop, to their evident importance of their relationship to a police officer and their possible identification with him, and to the fact that, according to the officer contacts, the informants differed from their associates in their acknowledging that crime was wrong and that by being informants they felt they were doing right. All of these features smack of an early indoctrination in law-abiding "ideology," an early (childhood) commitment to lawful authority and socially approved behavior. Perhaps all delinquents are so educated or at least all of the associates of these informants. Perhaps not. It is certainly worth investigating further. In the interim, we shall assume that one feature in the informant, especially the outstanding ones, is the presence of a moral code not altogether different from the police, one which reflects conventional morality in rearing, suffering perhaps a fall from grace, and the yet viable urge for conventional approval and status.

Our data provide no tests of our questions about identity

problems. Certainly conflicts with fathers for male children, years away from home in institutions, the shifts away from parental political or religious identification, the presence of other informants in the family circle, the early use of false documents and the considerable employment of aliases are consistent with such problems. It is a big jump from something consonant to something proven. We would have to know these informants better and would have to compare them to their peers. In the meantime, we offer the provisional statement that these people are insecure about themselves and their role in life.

As they present themselves, the informants fall into at least three descriptive categories—reasonably ordinary well-adjusted folk who observe but do not participate in the criminal scene; moderately troubled people with personality problems, histories of social troubles, and present criminal propensities; and way-out lost souls with severe personal and social disorders. Besides their access to the underworld by virtue of the people they live with, or where they live, take leisure or work, the three groups seem to share, as we have seen, intelligence, the need for excitement, the susceptibility to praise and the absence of strong character, dogmatism, prudishness and visible anger or bitterness. If their victims' views are correct, some at least are also insecure and fearful. They also share the fact that they are involved in a usually intense and dependent relationship with a police officer from whom they receive various narcissistic "supplies." Furthermore, they have in common the obvious feature that their loyalty to criminal associates is, to say the least, not overriding.

The underworld in which the criminal informants live and which is the only way of life they know does not ordinarily provide a set of warm, accepting or otherwise deeply gratifying personal experiences. It is portrayed as a casual world, close to pain and violence, never near to success, filled with troubled souls acting out their difficulties in various self-defeating ways. Lest that sound too much like a ministerial lament, it must be presumed that satisfactions exist; presumably in being with people much like oneself, in the excitement of disorder and in finding a life style which seems to fit one's capacities. In that society, the informants are not high on the totem pole and are

likely to be hostile to those who are, they are egocentric rather
than sociocentric in terms of whom they value first, and they are
quite likely to be outsiders striving hard, without success, to
look like insiders. As losers socially and personally, they suffer,
and like many in pain, they blame someone else for what they
suffer. If any of this be so, then the group they need is also
the group they hate. It would be no wonder that they respond
to the offer of a strong outsider giving praise, money, righteousness and ego support and are willing for their own sake and his
to turn on those who have disappointed them anyway. This is
especially so when they avoid prison in the bargain and get some
protection for their criminal careers. This is, of course, not the
picture for the better-adjusted subjects. If it is the picture for
the more troubled folk, it is compatible with our early expectation
that the people on whom one informs are a group which is both
attractive and repelling. Speculatively, one proposes that it will
be a group which the informant is not strong enough to leave,
that may very well still offer pleasures; yet others in the group
control these pleasures and possibly have deprived the subject
of access to them. Being an informant, then, would not ordinarily
be a way out of the underworld (except insofar as it led to being
carried out in a box) or of its fringes. It is a way to stay in it
but at the same time to feel superior, to add to one's income
and psychic stores and to become effective by aligning oneself
with power which can strike back; and to do so in the same weak,
sloppy, rebellious or pseudoconforming way one has acted before.
All this is speculation, but it fits the data for many of the
inadequate-appearing subjects.

Neither the subject's personality nor his push-pull social situation are sufficient to account for being an informant. The essential
circumstances are the presence of the police, the fact that crime
investigation uses informants and the opportunity for the subject
to take on the secret role. The opportunity may seek him out, as
after an arrest, during an investigation or while in jail, or the
subject may seek it out once he sizes up the possibilities. For
many, the opportunity, itself a push-pull (approach-avoidance)
situation, becomes an optimal option only when danger and the
accompanying anxiety are manipulated by a clever officer.

Reviewing the material and interpreting it in terms of other clinical theory, one cannot overemphasize the importance of the officer who first creates fear and then offers himself as a means of alleviating it. It is a time-honored means for creating dependency. The officer uses anxiety to initiate the relationship, he uses it to create gratitude, he acts upon it so that the gates are opened up to fulfill other needs. Listen to one officer handler who said, "There are many types of informants and they snitch for different reasons. You must control the informant, and to do that takes time, money, ability and being in the position to offer favors. You find the real reason the person is informing and you cater to it."

One suspects that anxiety never passes, even though it is displaced by the positive gains to the subject. That the officer is "jealous" and wants to manage his subject without others interfering is only to intensify the relationship, to emphasize the intimacy and to keep the one officer in the manipulative position to "control" and to "cater." (Although one-man control also has security advantages which are not to be overlooked.) As the relationship develops, it is likely that different needs or interests are gratified simultaneously (money, excitement, dependency, vengeance, power, self-esteem, warmth, a model with whom to identify, favors to exploit, etc.). Such multiple functions are much superior to relationships through which only one end is gained; the very complexity and many-leveled satisfactions—and fears—operating should serve to intensify and maintain the officer-informant bond. Perhaps not the least of the bond is the ability to explore a new "identity" expressed as two selves at once; the criminal and the secret-policeman self, having cake and eating it too, although not successful at either. The moral-conventional ideolgy which surrounds the police officer is part of the alter ego, one partially incorporated but held at bay as well. Insofar as conventional morality does harken back to the childhood values as well as the powerful contemporary values of the larger society, the act of playing cop is a positive sign in terms of the subject's own renunciation of the underworld. More often, though, it is a symptom of his ambivalence. In spite of the fact that ideological explanations for actions are notoriously untrustworthy as "real" reasons for behavior, we would suggest that when an ideology is part of a personal solution or reflects a preferred social adjustment, then ideology—including morality—does play a strong part in shaping behavior outcomes. Studies of police officers (Blum, 1964) suggest that their morality does play a part in their choice of careers. Officer observations to the effect that informants are pleased to be "doing what is right" do describe moral responses. Perhaps there is also some of the "telling him what he wants to hear" function there.

There are several additional matters. One has to do with the limited occupational and socioeconomic position of our sample. Had our police investigators been interested in economically "higher" forms of crime, nationally organized crime for example, the informants quite likely would be from higher strata. Considering the importance of "service" occupations in snitching, one would expect lawyers, physicians, accountants and the like to be represented. The field of inquiry shapes the choice of informants; limitations of investigatory technique or imagination would account for informants shaping the field of inquiry. The latter is sometimes the case.

A second point is that the officer, as well as the informant, is playing outside the rules. To recruit and use an informant is distasteful; the officer and the informant may share a common moral burden and perhaps a common defense. Furthermore, the rules of law and the stated policies of most police departments (albeit for public consumption) do not allow any officer the discretionary option of not arresting a known felony offender nor of not turning over the evidence to the district attorney. Working in collusion with the district attorney to withhold evidence or prosecution is also outside the ideal standard for administering justice. Nevertheless, to "give up the apple to get the orchard" requires that investigators violate the law. This is not to say they act without the approval of their superiors, the district attorney and the community. Yet the fact that the officer does offer favors means that he is engaged in a delicate if not an improper relationship. That makes him vulnerable to some exploitation by the subject and may further cement the relationship. It also affirms the shared technique of deception and the complementary snitching by both parties that is particularly relevant among the best informants and the contact officers.

A third point has to do with the "one-man informant" practice. By talking to only one investigator, the officer becomes the only channel for the subject's information. If information comes that bears on crimes beyond the officer's range of interest, one would hope that he would pass it along to the division or agency involved. Implied here is interinvestigator, interbureau, and interagency liaison in the management of police intelligence. It is our impression that such intelligence coordination can be sadly lacking. It has also come to our attention that when an informant himself seeks to snitch to several different officers or agencies he may seek to pit one against the other. Again the need for liaison is clear.

A fourth point arises primarily from the interviews with the prize informants. These have been snitches for years and have developed a number of skills which enable them to join groups, become familiar; set up opportunities for observation, overhearing and questioning; and learn methods of elicitation. They become artful flatterers, good listeners, generous hosts, pleasant bed companions and acceptable company for drug taking. They have also developed method of self-protection which rest on realistic assessments of what could give them away to their victims. Their precautions range from disguise through discretion and security measures that would probably make espionage types admire them. These measures are certainly necessary if they are to continue developing and violating confidence; as some of their potential victims have implied, a burned informant can be made to be a very unhappy man.

The presence of an informant system means that a number of consequences occur. One is the inevitable two-way flow of information. The informant uses his officer as a snitch, the victim uses another informer to snitch on an assigned informer, and as this happens, double agents are created. Counterintelligence systems are generated by the underworld, by informants themselves and even by the police. It means that informal rules for the game are adopted, rules well outside stated public policy.

Working within the former, the police allow or protect certain kinds of crime in return for preventing or punishing other kinds, offenders shift their operations to include intelligence gathering as part of the cost of business and potential victims undertake security measures and adopt their intelligence system to prevent penetration or observation. All this is done with the knowledge by the participants of how it works and to some extent who is working it. All of it is functional in the sense that it helps those involved carry on their work. Indeed, for many, it is indispensable to their criminal careers. Betrayal is also functional at an interpersonal level, for if any of our speculations are correct, it is a weapon used by members of groups to alter unfavorable balances of power or sentiment, to remake themselves in the eyes of others by being special agents and part-time righteous folk, or even by using informing as a way of having a decent relationship with an admired male figure who for some is a model guiding them to a measure of honest conventionality. Betrayal is also functional at an intrapsychic level; it is a weapon for the weak, a way of blending incompatible ideologies and selfish interests, an exercise in secret power and a way of experiencing excitement and importance. So regarded, the violation of trust is a repetitive device used by individuals and groups as a business and political method, as a situational opportunity, as an interpersonal lever; and for individuals as both a psychological defense and source of gratification. The latter psychological functions equate it with a neurotic defense, although, since it is acted out on so many levels, it is both more and less than that.

A PSYCHODYNAMIC NOTION

In Chapter X, it was suggested that the criminal who is the quarry of the informant may be blind to the nature of his relationship to the snitch. The potential victim may not fathom that he and his associates may in fact be disliked by the informer, who is pretending friendship and who conforms to the group's style. The quarry also may not conceive of the likelihood that one of his "friends" (the snitch) has a close and positive relationship with the enemy, that is, a detective.

From a clinical theoretical standpoint, these possible blind spots are of considerable interest. For one thing, they would help account for the reactions of shock, hurt and rage which occur in response to the victim's learning that he has been sold out. That reaction is not just to the violation of a culturally learned expectation that friends do not betray one another or to the discovery of harm to oneself (e.g. one has been identified and arrested as a drug peddler), but in addition, the reaction is an emotional shock attendant upon the destruction of one's own illusions. Stated in a more psychoanalytic vein, the reaction, the complaint of betrayal, is charged with the same energy that had been used to maintain the illusion; that is, the defense against knowing what was really happening. The implication is that poor judgment in not identifying one's enemy as such can be purposeful, for it allows the victim to bask in the fantasy that he is loved and his enemies hated. The truth that is denied and defended against is that he is not (universally) loved and his enemies are not (universally) hated. It is an infantile view of the world, and given the likelihood for immaturity and irrationality among large numbers of delinquents, it is not unlikely that such infantile perspectives are to be found among our drug-peddling subjects.

If a person deludes himself by believing that another person likes or loves him and/or ignores simultaneously the possibility that the same individual has a strong positive relationship to one's own enemies, it is the case that the person has put himself in the awkward position of expecting loyalty, of trusting while at the same time creating optimal conditions for being deceived. If a man fails to sense that not he himself but his enemy has the positive relationship to his presumed friend or follower, what signs can he be expected to judge correctly as that "friend" undertakes intentional deception? One asks to what extent people who are deceived ignore the signals (assuming there are such) given by their deceiver that affairs do not stand as one had hoped? We suspect that wishful thinking and unrealistic appraisals of human relations do play a strong role not only in setting the stage for deception and betrayal (deception the process, betrayal the denouement), but in eliciting the often-violent response which attends their discovery. In earlier chapters, we offered evidence both for ignorance and the irrational among confidence victims, but the speculation which arise from discussions with drug dealers suggest a more pervasive relationship between false pictures of one's relation to others and eventual betrayal by those others.

A further proposition is that deception and betrayal are not only significant events between two people which take place the more easily when the victim deludes himself about himself and his relationships but that the deceiver is himself no tower of rationality or psychological strength. We suggest that the deceiver has at least two components, the first a general psychological maladjustment (character insufficiency, sociopathy, etc.) and the second a specific irrational component which is part of his relationship to his victim.

The evidence for the first, the general maladjustment, is strong. Recall the remarkably high levels of psychopathology among the confidence men given the MMPI. Consider the lack of psychological strength and health inferred from descriptions of police informants by the officers who knew them. Consider the evidence that Western defectors to the Iron Curtain are usually maladjusted individuals with histories of disordered behavior. And consider the clinical observation that even among highly successful executives, those who allegedly are industrial spies show a history of maladjustment greater than a control sample. Consider too, as will be seen in Chapter XII, that in a normal population, deception is relatively rare, especially that deception which culminates in betrayal; that is, having a personally harmful, relationship-ruining nature. Indeed, the only evidence against the first proposition is found in descriptions of the personalities of Communist defectors coming West. In any event, we take the evidence to be, in bulk, strong enough to support the proposition that among many trust violators, there will be a character insufficiency which is often associated with their engaging in a culturally disapproved and interpersonally destructive form of deception, namely the betrayal of confidences leading to self-gain for the betrayer and harm to his confidant.

The second psychological component proposed for the betrayer posits a special relationship with the victim. The essence is that the need for guile, that is, an indirect form of influencing the behavior or fate of another, signifies the relative weakness of the trust violator as he perceives his relationship with his victim. It is no news that the weak resort to guile, whereas the strong use force; what is added here is the unconscious corollary that the meaning of betrayal in a personal relationship is not simply to achieve a selfish end. Rather, it functions to *instruct* the victim in the real nature of the relationship which the victim has deluded hmself about and which the betrayer is too weak to announce directly and, further, may not announce until he has secured a strong asset to replace the victim whom he is about to betray. We understand the shock of the victim, then, when he finally gets the message from his weaker half (associate, wife, friend, etc.). Having fought off the same message before, now the revelation that is the betrayal puts it in terms that cannot be missed. The raw hostility of it comes across; the mark is beaten at the killing ground, the espionage agent bashed into recruitment, the snitch burns the dealer, the industrial spy crushes his competitor. The betrayer is now the strong one and the victim is made weak.

The process of deception and the act of betrayal constitute a way of reordering relationships which offers dominance of the victim through the use of outside assets by the deceiver. Just as small nations ally with great powers, so the weaker half uses the power of the person or institution who receives his information to instruct his victim and to rearrange power. But there is more to it than that, so our proposition states. The betrayer not only uses the power of another, but he relates to his new ally in the same way as to his victim, in a weak or dependent fashion. And ordinarily, he waits until he has secured that new home before pulling the plug on his victim.

Alternatively, the betrayer uses the act of betrayal as a vehicle for precipitating a crisis, out of which he hopes for some magical, possibly universally destructive, solution. The Armageddon complex is an example of the latter, saying as it does, "Let us bring disaster to us all, then the strong shall despair

as now do I and all of us shall die." Minor Armageddons are to
be seen daily, for example when an unfaithful wife allows, indeed
insists, that her "indiscretions" be discovered, thereby bringing
a tumultuous and mutually painful end to a marriage she did
not intend to endure. Quite possibly, that wife had acted out
her fantasies of a richer and grander relationship with her lovers,
yet without finding it with them either. One wonders if that wife
did not harbor the secret (unconscious) hope that the crisis she
has manufactured will not itself, like the cry of a hurt child,
invoke a genie, some protector who will respond to her plight
and come forth to be the father-lover, perfect and strong, for
whom she has, again unconsciously, longed. Indeed, if she is
middle class, her crisis may well lead her into psychotherapy
where the therapist not infrequently finds himself cast in just
such a fantasied role. One suspects that these all-destroying
revelations, those betrayals where all parties suffer, are not
uncommon among the angry weak who, it is here proposed,
constitute an uncommonly large part of the trust-violating population. Prosaic Armageddons, suicidal as they often are, are
compatible with the diagnosis of anger turned toward the self
as well as outward toward the other.

One finds that destructive revelation—betrayal—can be mixed
with the more practical effort to build a new tie before destroying
old ones. The GRU officer seeks to secure his escape route West
and builds his relationship with a strong Westerner (cf. Penkovskiy) before passing state secrets, but at the same time, the
death-defying risk is there which eventually proves death and
not the man to be the winner. Can it be that the adventure
of betrayal, when played for stakes when escape is not in fact
certain, conceals a self-destructive wish? Is it not a bit like
compulsive gambling which has destruction built into that
response to life crisis? The police informant who remains in
place may have the promise of reward or protection, but as
the case of Black Panther Alex Rackley suggests, the rewards
may have to be in heaven and not on earth. One suspects that
the deceiver, *qua* martyr, knows this too. It is as martyr that
informant and idealist become one. And it is the martyr-informer
whom we suspect Communist defectors more often to be. Were

that so, it would square the discrepancy between them and the other trust violators observed and it would accomodate them all within the framework of the proposition. By way of note, the hero martyr is a familiar Russian theme and allows us still to view the Communist defector as a hearty idealist.

It is the confidence man who becomes the exception to the proposition, for his talent is in avoiding Armageddons—cooling the mark to do so and using his shade tree. Nor does he use trust violation to reorder his relationship with his victims, for the mark is already dominated and beaten as soon as he enters the game. Consequently, we must repair the proposition and exclude the reordering of the relationship between con man and a particular victim as a feature of confidence deceptions. The repair is made by suggesting that the confidence man views himself as weak, vis-à-vis everyone, and that his beating one mark is but one battle in a war he can never win. Viewed in this way, the confidence game is a struggle for restitution, just as some schizophrenic behavior is (and keep in mind that some of our confidence men were compensated schizophrenics). The restitution sought is not in the judicial sense of funds repaid but psychologically an attempt to replace missing components of personality, in this case the sense of esteem, of interpersonal worth and capability. The message of the game is the same, to instruct the victim that he has been beaten, but the wishful message for the con man is, unconsciously, that if he can beat one man he can beat them all. The con man cannot do this, of course, and daily sees it so; that is why he has the compulsion to continue the battle.

SUMMARY

Thirty-five police informants used by officers in a major city were described in terms of their background, their traits, their relationship to those they informed on, their recruitment into their "snitching" role and their relationship with the officer using them. Special interviews were conducted with six of the best informants in the city. In addition, 480 potential victims, all drug dealers, were interviewed.

Most of the informants gave information about burglary and

robbery or vice activities. They had access to information because they were socially and physically close to criminals, living, working or spending their leisure time with them. Many were themselves criminals; some were ordinary citizens who provided services to the loose-knit underworld society.

Initial police contact with informants most often occurs during crime investigation. When arrest is near or has occurred, either the officer or the snitch-to-be proposes a deal whereby prosecution is dropped if information is given. Some informants are not threatened with prosecution but are brought in or come forward themselves after having been referred. Either direct acquaintance or "recommendations" bring most informants and officers together, so that a personal acquaintance or referral from an acquaintance is the common route to recruitment.

The potential snitch himself, the officer and quite possibly others as well may all participate in the genesis of a snitch. The role cannot be confirmed until both officer and subject agree. The most common initial tool employed by the officer to persuade is that of club-and-candy—the threat of prosecution and the promise of its being dropped if information is given. The officer creates anxiety and then offers a means to alleviate it. This is the beginning, for continuing informants, of an intimate relationship in which the subject is dependent and in which the officer offers a variety of rewards including money, praise, justifications, excitement and friendship. Practically speaking, a good informant secures police protection so that he may continue his criminal career. Some informants enjoy "playing cop" because it is exciting, because it enhances their self-esteem to be an "agent" on the side of law and order, because it may be part of a psychological identification with the strong officer himself and because by informing on their associates, the subjects gain power over them or revenge upon them. He also expresses his own split morality to the effect that crime is wrong—although others rather than himself become the object of punishment.

Not all informants are criminals recruited during investigation or arrest. Those not in danger of prosecution do not need to save themselves from penalties, but they may still seek the approval of the officer, the excitement of playing cop, the self-esteem of being on the side of the right (and the might!), and the monetary rewards for information, and they do enjoy the friendship and fairness of the officer. Some may also exploit him for future favors. Most informant-officer relationships are complex, with several kinds of interests, rewards, motives and fears simultaneously operating. Over time, relationships, at least in our sample, became more positive, with threat and anxiety receding and friendship and playing cop growing in importance. As a critical qualifying feature, for the relationship to be established and to continue usually requires that the subject be confident that the officer can and will protect him from the potential violence of those informed upon. A few officers abandon their subjects to harm. In the rare case, during a good relationship between the officer and the criminal informant, the subject may become "rehabilitated" and no longer criminal.

Generally informants are associated with the underworld because it is their way of life. Their association—in this sample a loosely knit subsociety—provide both pleasures and pains, but generally the quality of personal relations within the underworld is not kindly, stable or deeply gratifying. The associates are, like the informants themselves, mostly troubled people with long histories of personality distress and social maladjustment. The criminal informant fits in but usually not as a respected person who gets a lot out of his way of life. The noncriminal informants are on the fringes and while psychologically normal, are not strong characters or very moral folk. The best informants are expert at insinuating themselves into confidence and in avoiding discovery.

One cannot be sure if the informant sample is any different from those they inform upon. In some groups, slum addicts for example, informing is an accepted practice. For most, self-interest rather than loyalty to others comes first. Certainly the loose-knit underworld composed in large part of maladjusted and unsuccessful people can hardly command much loyalty except through threats of rejection and violence. Nevertheless, it may be that informants as a class are different from their associates; the implication drawn from their descriptions is that they are brighter, more in need of excitement, more in need of praise, more readily identified with lawful authority, and less pleased with how their own associates treat them; yet they are lacking in enough psychic strength or social prestige to handle their associates directly or to escape from them completely. It can also be, although our present data bears but little on it, that the informant sample does suffer more personality problems of an "identity" sort as reflected in their gravitating to double and secret roles, their use of aliases, their simultaneous criminality and playing-cop activities, etc. It is also possible that informant backgrounds differ from those of their associates; one finds a frequent history of childhood maladjustment, separation from parents, and institutionalization, more than expected in terms of the relative goodness and stability of the homes as described. Conflict with the father may play an important role in their delinquent development.

Examination of the process of deception and the (culminating) act of betrayal suggest them to be functional at several levels—economic, political, interpersonal and intrapsychic. Considerable complexity in the circumstances and motivation for trust violation is proposed. With regard to the manipulation of confidences within the narrow framework of police operations, it is apparent that organized criminals as well as police agencies develop defensive and offensive intelligence capabilities which are necessary for their effective work. Violations of trust which occur as part of intentional police investigations pose a moral dilemma, since the problem of bad means and good ends arises. A second look indicates that the means (deception) may not be as bad, i.e. unilaterally destructive, as the first glance may suggest, and as a corollary, the ends, the ultimate outcome, may not be as good, i.e. beneficial for individuals and society, as the moral snitch might hope. Violation of trust as an element in police-underworld relationships is probably an expanding phenomenon, given the combat-and-accommodation structure of that relationship in modern society.

Chapter XII

THE CITIZEN AND TRUST VIOLATION

W E THOUGHT IT well to hear from citizens what their views were of betrayal and related phenomena. We wished to find out what citizens had experienced as victims and perpetrators of trust violation. With limited funds, we set out to learn what we could by interviewing a sample of citizens in one small industrial town. The town was chosen because its police department was interested in fraud and how programs of crime prevention might be designed.

A carefully selected group of police department personnel conducted interviews in mufti. Citizens were assured that information was confidential and that under no circumstances would it lead to reporting of any interview-revealed citizen misconduct. The sampling device was an area design using randomly selected blocks. Interviewers selected every Nth house on pre-selected walking routes. Male interviewers interviewed any adult male, female interviewers any adult female in the dwellings selected. Call-backs were made to dwellings where no one had been at home.

We could only afford to interview a sample of 100. The sample which was gathered was composed, for the most part, of married persons of whom the average had a high school diploma and whose family income fell in the 5,000 to 10,000 dollar range. It was an all-white sample which emerged, predominantly Catholic. The most frequent occupation for women was housewife, whereas the men were, for the most part, skilled workers or white collar employees. The small sample means that our data provide rough, not exact, estimates of the city population's experience or beliefs.*

_____

* The probable error of estimate for the total city population as inferred from the sample data would range maximally ± 13 percent for dichotomous data of the sort where 50 percent of the respondents said yes and 50 percent said no. The probable error will be less for more nearly unanimous replies.

EXPERIENCE AS A CRIME VICTIM

We began with some general questions, from which we learned that 67 percent of the citizens had, at one time or another in their lives, been victims of crime. The offenses most often mentioned were auto thefts (including strippings, clouts), burglaries, other robbery and theft, and vandalism. Ten percent of the men and women said they had been defrauded through swindling, bunco and the like, 9 percent had been defrauded through forgery, bad checks, etc., for a total of 16 percent (three people suffered both varieties of fraud) who said they had been defrauded in their lifetimes. This is a population rato of 160 per 1000. Crimes against person were rarely reported; one man and one woman (2% of our sample) reported assault, rape, etc. One woman said she had been kidnapped.

We may examine our victimization rates in the perspective of information gathered from the much larger scale surveys done as part of the work of the President's Commission on Law Enforcement and the Administration of Justice. Biderman, Johnson, McIntyre and Weir (1967) found among Washington, D. C., citizens that lifetime reporting was not accurate, for people remembered recent crimes but not ones long past. They also concluded that there was underreporting of recent crimes. If we accept these findings as applicable, we can estimate that our sample was also recalling recent crimes and was underreporting lifetime crime. Our lifetime fraud rate (experiencing 16%) is considerably higher than the one year experience found in Washington, D. C., where only 1 percent reported having been defrauded (con games, bad checks, consumer fraud, embezzlement, etc.) within the twelve months prior to interview. The National Opinion Research Corporation (NORC) (Ennis, 1967) undertook a national survey of criminal victimization which returned incidence rates of fraud of 2.5 per 1,000 during a twelve-month period and for consumer fraud as a separate category, 1.2 per 1,000. The NORC survey also identified regional rates, and for western suburban metropolitan areas, which characterizes our survey city, found a rate of 4.2 per 1,000 for fraud and 1.3 per 1,000 for consumer fraud. These twelve-month incidence rates do not approximate our prevalence rate of 160 per 1,000. The easiest explanation is that our sample did recall crimes, so that their lifetime prevalence experience would naturally exceed a recent twelve-month incidence report. It is also possible that our sample had suffered more defrauding—note that the NORC sample shows a higher rate for western suburbs than for the nation as a whole—or that our interview methods and personnel elicited more fraud reporting. With regard to crime experience as such, the Biderman *et al.* study showed that 60 percent of the citizens reported any lifetime experience with crime. This is reasonably close to our 67 percent figure.

When one contrasts the actual experience of these citizens with their estimates of the kinds of crime which constitute a serious menace to their community, one finds a remarkable shift. The menacing crimes, defined in terms of frequency of mention, were narcotics (and dangerous drugs) offenses and murder and sex offenses such as child molesting and rape. These are not the crimes of which our citizens had been victims. Comparable data comes from the Biderman *et al.* study which showed considerable citizen concern about crime, yet also showed that anxiety was unrelated to personal experience as a victim. These investigators concluded, ". . . most people are basing their estimates on the gravity of the crime problem and its dangers to themselves primarily on factors other than their own circumstances and experiences" (Biderman *et al.*, 1967, p. 122). We would add that the concern of our citizens is expressed in terms of awareness of crimes that challenge the moral code, that is, vice and violence.* Fraud, not mentioned once in the spontaneous listing of menacing crimes, is clearly not of major concern to our citizens in spite of its prevalence among them.

Experience with Sales Misrepresentation and Consumer Fraud

Inquiry was made as to citizen experience with "borderline" areas in which acts which were unethical or immoral occurred as part of selling and buying but where the establishment of a criminal act was unclear. The majority of citizens, 44 percent

---

* Comfort (1950), citing Reiwald, contends that emotionally charged crimes are satisfying to citizens because they represent repressed desires. Fraud is unsatisfying as an object of public concern because it is not laden with guilt and is thus more acceptable and less interesting.

of the women and 62 percent of the men, said they had been the victims of being misled, lied to and the like as purchasers of goods or services. About one-fourth of the men as opposed to only 6 percent of the women said they had been victimized through misrepresentation during the preceding year. Of those recently victimized, their bad experiences were more often on a multiple rather than a single occasion. When asked to estimate the chances that in the future they would be victimized by dishonest sales schemes, the majority, 62 percent of the women and 74 percent of the men, were confident they would not be victimized in the future. Twelve percent of the women and 6 percent of the men indicated they thought it very likely they would be future victims of consumer frauds.

Two initial surmises can be made at this point, both of which will be worthy of further exploration. One is that a large number of cases of consumer victimization occur which citizens do not think of as criminal, and secondly, that although more prone to such victimization, men are less likely than women to recognize their vulnerability. We see that although more men report being deceived as purchasers, many of these same men do not see themselves as being at risk of being deceived again. Women, although expressing a sense of greater vulnerability, do in fact report fewer cases of exploitation. Alternative explanations of the same data would be (assuming the reliability of the difference between men and women) that women are more reluctant to report having been cheated as purchasers, or that men, once recognizing that they have been cheated, do learn from experience, so that their confidence as to the future is justified.

Respondents were asked about their particular activities which might have exposed them to consumer frauds which are prevalent in California. They were asked if they had ever purchased real estate without seeing it, had purchased from door-to-door salesmen such items as magazines, baby photographs, toys, etc.; had purchased aluminum siding, roof oil or furnace cleaning home services from salesmen calling to offer these, had paid for mail order schooling or had bought unseen items in response to a telephone pitch. Thirty percent of the sample said they had been cheated by swindlers engaged in these particular sales activities. Most of the women victims had fallen to door-to-door pitchmen;

the men had their bad experiences spread out among more of the swindles. Another item asked about experiences with used car sales deception. Here, in a familiar American lament, 38 percent of the men (and 16 percent of the women) reported having been cheated by auto salesmen.

Experience as a Confidence Game or Vice Victim

We asked respondents if they had ever been approached by others whom they took to be, either before or afterwards, confidence men, flim-flam men, bunco artists and the like. One third of the men and 6 per cent of the women said they had been approached. We directed specific inquiries to activities which often attract confidence men (see Appendix A), asking about their being offered or buying goods known to be stolen (hot), contributing to (unknown) charities, going to fortune tellers, frequenting bars, attending race tracks, speculating on the stock market, gambling with cards, dice, etc., playing carnival games where rigging was possible and, for men, visiting prostitutes. The most frequent exposures reported were for carnival games (the majority of respondents), gambling (two thirds of the men, one sixth of the women), frequenting bars (one third of the men, one sixth of the women) and betting at the races (one third of the men, 6 percent of the women). Only women (8%) visited gypsy fortune-tellers, only men (one fourth of them) had been offered stolen merchandise; of those offered it, about half had bought hot goods. Being cheated (or being aware of being cheated and being willing to report it) occurred with the greatest prevalence, in relationship to exposure—that is engaging in activities which we assumed on a priori grounds to attract confidence men—in connection with carnivals, where half of the total sample believed the games had been rigged; in connection with visits to prostitutes, where half of those admitting such visits reported being conned (or strong armed) without getting what they paid for; and with gambling, where 10 percent of the gambling men and one sixth (1 of 7) of the gambling women said they had been cheated. (In addition, 12% of the men frequenting bars reported gambling losses to strangers in bars.) The only other fraud reported was in connection with charitable giving, where 4 percent of the women and 6 percent of the men said they had given to phony charities.

From these reports, one sees, consistent with earlier data, that the men have a greater exposure to confidence game risk (assuming the accuracy of our *a priori* assumption) and men report greater victimization. If we discount the importance of carnivals where most visitors seem to treat the rigged games as part of the play, for when asked why they partook most implied it was fun in any event, the important risk exposures are, for the men in this sample, visits to prostitutes and gambling. For women, the important exposures are in gambling and (though low-ranked) in charitable giving.

EXPECTATIONS OF OTHERS

We asked respondents if they accepted cheating and deception as part of life, expecting others to act in these ways as part of the normal course of things. Men more than women responded affirmatively, although only a minority were pessimists in expecting most other people to try to lie, cheat or deceive them. The majority of both sexes said they expected a few or some people to do so, 8 percent of the women and 2 percent of the men expected none to do so; 12 percent of the men and none of the women expected most people to try to lie, cheat or deceive them.

As the other side of the coin, we remarked that confidence men often describe people as greedy, wanting something-for-nothing, an attitude which the con men state makes people easy to cheat. We asked respondents if they agreed that most people were greedy and half-crooked or not. Again sex differences emerge; the majority of the women in the sample denied that most people were that way, although one third were critical of others' motives. Among men, on the other hand, the majority agreed that most people were greedy and half-crooked; one third denied it. In a later inquiry, after we had enjoyed considerable discussion with respondents, they were again asked their views of their fellow man, this time in terms of the facts of life about how people really treat each other. Abstracting replies, one finds 42 percent of the men and 28 percent of the women emphasizing the generally unpleasant quality of human conduct with only a few, 14 percent of the men and 8 percent of the women, being optimistic. The remainder took a middle ground, emphasizing human indifference rather than beastliness, or noting that some people were good and some were bad. The women appeared less ready to generalize and were less often pessimistic or misanthropic. We surmise that these replies reflect a more optimistic view of the world among women in the sample, an appreciation among most men of the selfishness and greed of others, and a general awareness among both men and women that some human predators are on the loose; but for the majority of the sample there was no sense of universal danger.

In a series of specific questions, we asked about how common it was for people in particular situations to cheat or deceive. First we asked those who held jobs what the people at their place of work would do, how common was it for employees to cheat, steal from or deceive their boss. The great majority (two-thirds of the men and women) said it was rare. It is well to remark that here, given a concrete case, respondents described others as much more honest than in the previous question, which tapped views of abstract, unknown others.

We then asked about the employers rather than employees, inquiring as to whether the respondent had in his own experience seen the bosses act unethically or dishonestly, as in violating labor laws, administrative codes, tax laws and the like. The majority reported no personal experience with bosses who cheat, although one fourth of men and women said they had observed such goings on, the most often cited being nonpayment for overtime, although some others were much more serious matters. Here we note, as with the preceding question, that in the concrete instance there is less attribution of dishonesty to others, and as in the previous item, sex differences among respondents disappear when faced with real experiences as opposed to the general view. Note, too, that in this item, although almost all respondents were workers rather than bosses, there is no greater attribution of dishonesty to bosses than to fellow employees. One concludes that there is no general distrust of an employer class. Another business item inquired as to whether the respondent had personal knowledge of a business violating local, state and federal regulatory laws, as labeling and product control, safety, waste disposal, air pollution and the like. Only five percent of the total sample reported such knowledge, as for example charging an unrequired tax on services.

The next item addressed itself to customer behavior, asking if respondents had, in their own experience, seen customers steal from, cheat, or deceive stores or businesses. In response, the majority of men (three fifths) and two fifths of the women did report observed customer dishonesty. Asked what dishonesty, shoplifting was most often cited.

Another item reversed the focus on regulatory control and asked about the regulators. It inquired about government officials, such as tax men or local, state or federal administrative officials, being dishonest, as for example in taking bribes, receiving special interests or the like. Only three percent of our sample had personal knowledge of corruption by government regulatory personnel. The next item asked about police dishonesty, inquiring if the respondent had firsthand experience of a cop in a crooked dealing. Only five percent of the respondents claimed such knowledge; an example was an officer taking money on a regular basis in return for ignoring parking violations. Citizens were next asked if they had ever offered a bribe to an officer. All denied it, although at this point the reader must remember that respondents were aware that the interviewers, in mufti, were themselves officers or police department employees.

A final item concerning official corruption addressed itself to the conduct of elected and appointed officials, such as councilmen, mayors and senators. The inquiry did not specify personal knowledge or experience but rather an opinion as to the extent of corruption, the word itself not being defined. About two fifths of the respondents, a few more men than women, believed corruption among politicians was common; more thought it occurred uncommonly; only one-sixth of the sample thought it rare. We would point out that with this item, as with the earlier estimate of widespread human greed and crookedness, there is a considerable increase in the proportion of respondents taking a dim view of the honesty of others whom they do not know. In contrast, in all the specific inquiries except that of customer behavior, personal experience in observing dishonesty in others was limited. However, the majority of respondents had been cheated as consumers, which may be one source of their attribution of dishonesty to others.

POPULAR DEFINITIONS OF TRUST VIOLATIONS

We assumed that individuals would differ in their definitions of what constituted the actions encompassed under our general term of trust violation. We therefore asked them to define corruption, swindling and betrayal. There was a wide variety of definitions of corruption, the most common central element in these denoting a public officer illegally taking money for his private gain in return for exercising some administrative act favoring the bribe-giver. Corruption was also defined as tax evasion, seeking office with the intent of private gain, any business dishonesty, a failure to deliver on promises, any concealed *quid pro quo* activity, mud slinging, nepotism, the violation of confidence, misappropriation of public funds, any concealed action by governmental officials, theft, the exploitation of knowledge gained as an official to benefit private persons or groups, or simply the failure of an elected official to act in the public interest.

In defining swindling, the emphasis in definition was taking advantage of another (that presumably implying special roles of access and trust which enabled advantage to be taken), cheating, misrepresentation or other devious means employed to gain money or property, a failure to deliver promised goods or services, or theft. The elements of intent to deceive, of manipulation through lies and stories and of exploitation of relationships pervade these popular definitions of swindling.

In defining betrayal, the emphasis is on the violation of expectations among persons who are close to one another or who have assumed special obligations of protection or trust in such a way that a person is harmed by the one who holds special knowledge or power. Judas and Benedict Arnold were given as illustrations; the most often cited general case was that of the squealer, mentioned by two fifths of the men and one sixth of the women. Most definitions contained a much stronger component of emotion and outraged morals than did those pertaining to swindling or corruption, for betrayal was defined so as to imply the concealed exploitation of(preexisting) interpersonal ties, as among families, work groups or those in religious or patriotic communities. Thus the betrayal was not only personally harmful but(disruptive) of institutional ties (in the sociological sense) and destructive to assumptions about interpersonal bonds. "Disloyal," "unfaithful," "dishonorable," "a moral issue," ("violating confidence,") "being false," were phrases employed. "It goes against the friendship bonds," "cheating within the family," "you let a person down," are other ways it was put.

Experience with Violations of Trust

Lying

Having established what individuals had in mind as they defined what we assert are correlates of trust violation, namely corruption, swindling and betrayal, we set out to learn more about violations of trust as they occurred in daily life, in contrast to the unusual extreme case of a criminal trust violation. We began with an inquiry about lying. We asked citizens what lies people ordinarily told in a variety of ordinary interpersonal situations. Table III summarizes the lies which respondents most often described as occurring in each relationship. It also shows the percent of respondents mentioning each category of lies, the percent denying lying in each setting (which includes the "don't know" answers which we treated as an absence of knowledge of lying) and the percent of respondents admitting that they themselves told such lies in each relationship specified.

The data in Table III show that lying varies considerably in terms of intent, awareness, admission and sex, depending upon the interpersonal situation involved. That is not a surprising finding. Awareness of lying for all respondents is greatest in the work situation. Awareness and admissions are two different matters, for where women describe on-the-job lying as much

TABLE III

A POPULAR CATALOGUE OF LIES BY KIND OF RELATIONSHIP

Relationship / Content of Lie	Percent Specifying By Sex, Each Category		Percent Mentioning No Lies or Insisting No Lies Occur		Percent Admitting To Similar Lies	
	Men	Women	Men	Women	Men	Women
Worker to boss						
Offering reasons for being late or absent (claiming sickness, etc.)	90%	92%	4%	2%	60%	22%
Claiming more hours worked than actually worked or more work done	14%	0				
Concealing disqualifying information at employment	6%	6%				
Concealing or denying thefts of money or supplies	4%	2%				
Neighbor to neighbor						
Exaggeration of personal earnings or worth (including value of possessions)	42%	40%	46%	42%	18%	14%
Exaggeration, falsification of personal status (other than financial), such as job level or skill, civic importance, importance of acquaintances	14%	4%				
Flattering or otherwise protecting/enhancing esteem of the other	0	6%				
Between casual acquaintances						
Exaggeration of earnings, worth, value of possessions	32%	40%	28%	28%	16%	16%
Exaggeration, falsification of personal status, such as background, travels, skills, importance, etc.	32%	18%				
Between good friends						
Exaggeration of financial worth, value of possessions, etc.	20%	6%	64%	80%	16%	16%

TABLE III (Continued)
A POPULAR CATALOGUE OF LIES BY KIND OF RELATIONSHIP

Relationship	Content of Lie	Percent Specifying By Sex, Each Category		Percent Mentioning No Lies or Insisting No Lies Occur		Percent Admitting To Similar Lies	
Teenagers to parents	Enhancing/protecting esteem of other	Men	0				
		Women	14%				
	Exaggerating, falsifying personal importance, prowess, skill, etc.	Men	14%				
		Women	0	Men	18%	Men	46%
				Women	16%	Women	70%
	Concealing disapproved general activities	Men	66%				
		Women	50%				
	Concealing or denying disapproved friends or dates	Men	18%				
		Women	16%				
	Concealing disapproved school activities or non-achievements	Men	14%				
		Women	16%				
	Concealing disapproved smoking, drinking	Men	16%				
		Women	4%				
Young children to parents	Denying (minor) responsibility, passing blame	Men	12%				
		Women	18%	Men	28%	Men	56%
	Concealing school activities, failures	Men	8%	Women	26%	Women	58%
		Women	8%				
Parents to children	Claims as to parental good behavior as children	Men	4%				
		Women	16%	Men	42%	Men	40%
	False information about sex including parental behavior	Men	10%	Women	50%	Women	22%
		Women	6%				
	Concealing, distorting parental financial affairs and social activities	Men	6%				
		Women	6%				
	Myths of Santa Claus, Easter bunny, etc.	Men	8%				
		Women	0				

Husbands to wives

	Men	Women
Conceal disapproved activities (unspecified)	42%	46%
Conceal infidelity, disapproved relationships with opposite sex	36%	8%
Conceal income, financial status	8%	6%
Conceal how money actually spent	8%	8%
Conceal drinking	8%	4%
Conceal unhappiness, work problems, other matters that would upset the wife	4%	4%

Men 26%
Women 28%

Men to Women 44% 56%
(depending on interpretation of don't know replies)

Wives to husbands

	Men	Women
Budget handling, prices paid, how money spent	30%	70%
General activities, not specified	12%	10%
Infidelity	20%	2%
Ingestion conduct, such as drinking, eating	2%	4%

Men 52%
Women 14%

Women to Men 56% 62%
(depending on interpretation of don't know replies)

Respondent to police, tax collectors, other governmental authority

	Men	Women
Income and property tax	10%	4%
Denial of traffic, other offenses to police	8%	2%

(Asked not as general inquiry but only in terms of respondent's conduct) as men do, only a minority of women admit to it, whereas the majority of men do so. This may well be a function of the much greater rate of employment among men than women in the sample. In the same way, the somewhat reduced admissions rate of lies in another authority situation—of respondent to policing agency—can be accounted for in terms of reduced exposure (as in tax return preparation), although one wonders if other components are present. That women can admit to lying as much or more than men in other settings is evident in the case of their recalling their lying to parents as teenagers. The setting which leads to the smallest entry in the catalogue of lies, defined first in terms of ability of respondents to cite lies, is that of relationships between close friends. There, too, was the greatest insistence that lying did not occur and a low rate of admissions that one had lied to a close friend. For many respondents, one of the implicit definitions of a close-friend relationship is that of trust, and no lying occurs. Such an expectation accounts for some of the intensity encountered in the earlier discussion of respondent definitions of betrayal in which one component was deception practiced by a friend.

We see that the content and function of lies varies considerably by setting, sex and individual. The defensive lie which protects the tardy or absent employee from presumably justifiable censure or punishment is most common at work. Self-aggrandizing lies to earn money or to get a job also occur in relationship to bosses, although far fewer citizens mention these. In the neighbor-to-neighbor and acquaintance settings the most common lies are status-enhancing ones, especially status defined in terms of financial worth. These citizens observe that keeping up with or getting ahead of the Joneses can be accomplished with lies as well as deeds, although few admit that they themselves do it. A different kind of self-enhancement occurs when parents lie to children about parental performance. One may see that claim, as for example that the parent did *his* homework or came in early from dates, as helping build an ideal model for identification for the child, as reducing argument arising from inconsistencies between what parents did and what they demand or as the construction of a more generalized myth of goodness. Other myth construction for children is apparent in parental lies about sex, Santa Claus, divorce, social activity and the like. Parental self-enhancement as a defense against shame or guilt may also be posited, although we have no psychodynamic data on this. Other defensive lying is seen in deception by children, all of which is self-protection against parental disapproval, or in the sample's recollection of their lies when very young, defense against responsibility as such, some of which may rightly be linked, psychodynamically, to a child's reluctance to develop painful internal standards, i.e. a conscience or superego. Defensive lying also emerges in the marital relationship, where among men there is a heavy emphasis on concealment of infidelity or other disapproved activities (gambling, drinking with the boys, etc.). The thrust of womens lies to their husbands is in the budget department. Women rarely mention the possibility of lying about infidelity either by husbands or wives; men, on the other hand, not only admit it but attribute such lies to women far more often than women conceive of them (or admit conceiving of them). To what extent the inference of defensive lying in the marital relationship must be complemented by the notion of exploitative lying cannot be established. Certainly it is true that lies which allow a spouse to continue in extramarital affairs, thus violating the trust of the spouse in at least some cases (those where affairs are not expected or condoned), is manipulative. Although the gain of the adulterous partner is not through direct exploitation of the spouse, the manipulation has that component. The same may be said of other defensive lying, whether by workers to bosses or by children to parents. One final function in the catalogue of lies remains; it is the protective lie, the lie for the sake of the other, either esteem-enhancing through praise or in protection from trauma or worry. It emerges most frequently in descriptions of lies between good friends and occasionally among neighbors. Women, not men, mention it. Protective lies also occur in marriage but were first mentioned only in connection with men protecting their wives, not wives protecting husbands.

The marital lie was further explored in a subsidiary set of questions. Setting up an inferred function based on the circum-

stances under which spouses said they would lie, it was observed
that among men, the circumstances were most often self-
protection against the anger or reproof of wives. Much less
often the function was protection of the other, the maintenance
of harmony or the protection of the marriage as such. Among
women, the protection of another, husbands particularly, but
sometimes the children, occurred with the same frequency as the
self-protecting lie. These were the primary circumstances which
wives said would move them to falsehood. The results of this
probing show that the spontaneous replies presented in Table III
may be misleading, for probing revealed that wives four times
more often than husbands conceived of conditions which would
require other-protecting lies. Wives and husbands to the same
degree, about one fourth of the sample, recognized circumstances in which they would engage in self-defensive lies.
Women, not men, admitted lying for their children's sake; men
not women, lied for the sake of peace and harmony.

As a surmise, we propose that women do differ from men
in what they lie about, that these differences are partly a function of exposures to work, fiscal responsibility and criminal
opportunity (tax evasion, theft at work), but that they also
reflect different self conceptions and roles within the family. It
appears that women are more often required to protect their
husbands by lying, whereas men, by dint of greater exposure
and implied cultural training and approval are required to protect
themselves from wifely censure. Men are thus more concerned
with lies about their activities, infidelity especially, and project
that concern in the form of a belief that wives, too, are unfaithful
and lie about it. Women are either less preoccupied with the
husband's infidelity (either by dint of confidence or acceptance);
are so discrete and capable in adultery that circumstances implicating them, the wives, as unfaithful never arise, leading to
the need to lie; or possibly are so cautious that in response to
our inquiry, they do not even air the possibility of such lies.
As for the facts of infidelity, which we presume to be the primary
form of betrayal in marriage (incest is another but is not
mentioned by our sample), we have no data on our sample.
Generalizing from the Kinsey findings (1948) which did find

adultery more common among husbands than wives, it would seem that the lies and preoccupations of our sample fairly reflect the probabilities of their conduct. It is, of course, the dilemma of this form of inquiry that our inquiries about lies rest upon the presumption that even liars will tell us the truth. Put more optimistically, any confidence in these results rests upon the assumption that the setting of the interview was a setting which differed enough from settings conducive to lying so that truth-telling occurred. Other work (Hyman, 1954) shows that most Americans tell the facts in response to survey inquiries; whether this holds true for what citizens lie about remains to be established by further research.

Betrayal

Each respondent was asked about his own firsthand knowledge of individuals betraying one another, with the inquiries directed toward several settings where these emotionally charged violations of trust could occur. Keep in mind that the queries were about betrayals, not simply swindling or theft. Table IV presents the replies.

TABLE IV

FIRSTHAND KNOWLEDGE OF BETRAYAL BY RELATIONSHIP AND SEX

Setting		Report Firsthand Knowledge
In a business setting (as between partners, co-workers)	Men	30%
	Women	6%
A child betraying parents	Men	12%
	Women	24%
A parent betraying a child	Men	16%
	Women	22%
A wife betraying a husband	Men	38%
	Women	38%
A husband betraying a wife	Men	46%
	Women	40%
A friend betraying a friend	Men	26%
	Women	30%
Yourself: Have you ever betrayed anyone?	Men	4%
	Women	8%

One sees from Table IV that firsthand knowledge of betrayal in any relationship is limited to a minority. That is in contrast to lying by others, which was certainly familiar to a majority. The most widely known betrayal occurs in the marital relationship, with husbands having the edge over wives as betrayers by a small margin. Knowledge of betrayal or definitions of acts as betrayal, which is likely to be one component of replies, differs by sex. The men are more aware of it in business dealings; the women are more aware, or think of actions as betrayals, in the parent-child relationship. As far as admissions of guilt—and because betrayal is defined as a moral act with strong feelings involved, we believe that guilt is felt—only a few are willing to say that they have ever betrayed another.

Defenses Against Victimization in Trust Violations

We sought to learn what these citizens did to protect themselves—or what they thought others ought to do to insure protection—against being cheated, deceived or robbed through trust violation. Our first question was directed at those individuals who had been approached by salesmen whose services were those often associated with consumer fraud; that is, aluminum siding, roof oiling, furnace cleaning, mail order schooling, etc. Seventy percent of all respondents said they had been approached by salesmen offering goods and services on our list but had not made any purchase. We asked why they had not done so and they set forth the following principles in reply (which we have summarized and in some cases clarified). Most frequently, the policy was one of (a) not buying items that they could not first inspect, (b) not buying products not previously known to them, (c) never buying from persons not known to them, including any door-to-door salesmen, by mail or telephone pitchmen, (d) rejecting any salesman using high pressure, (e) being familiar with a particular sales offer or service (e.g. baby pictures) as a consumer fraud scheme, (f) delaying purchase until after consultation with an informed other person, (g) assuming that any something-for-nothing offer is a swindle, (h) being aware of the possibility—either from past experience, information or personal insecurity—that they personally could be victimized, which led them to caution in response to any sales pitch, (i) a generalized attitude of distrust or suspicion toward salesmen and (j) lack of interest in the particular product or service offered but not any generalized principles of wariness.

Condensing these principles found helpful by consumers in protecting themselves against being cheated, we find these sensible people recommending (a) a sense of caution and a response of distrust in dealing with strange persons and unknown products and services, (b) the value of prior knowledge of items, services and sales pitches as ones often associated with consumer swindles and (c) awareness of one's own potential vulnerability to deception, an awareness which leads to rejection of sales advances or reliance upon trusted advisors.

A second set of queries sought procedures through which citizens protected themselves from confidence games and bunco as opposed to the more businesslike organized consumer fraud. Those recommended were much the same as the foregoing consumer fraud defenses and included the following: (a) seeking further information about any approach from knowledgeable persons or agencies, e.g. the police or Better Business Bureau, (b) exercising general caution in purchasing by having knowledge of goods, services and the sales people offering them and not buying without such knowledge, (c) delaying any actions in response to offers to consider risks, including the control of impulses to act quickly based on greed, false hopes for bargains and the like, (d) insulating oneself from risk exposure by general distrust, caution, rejection of strangers, not allowing oneself to be outnumbered by strangers and the like, (e) supporting social-legal policies to develop better laws controlling consumer fraud and to support law enforcement for consumer fraud and confidence games and (f) developing personal qualities which include awareness of vulnerability and unsureness and the ability to be firm, cautious, distrustful, unfriendly and well-informed. What did not receive mention, the more striking since our line of inquiry had stressed exposure, was the importance of avoiding situations which had an inherent risk potential, as in gambling, bar-hopping, prostitute-visiting and the like. We surmise that whatever specific defensive tactics citizens are willing to develop or to propose for others to develop they are unwilling to forego the consistent pleasurable activities, fantasy schemes or compulsive risk-taking which we believe to entail high risk of exposure to interpersonal predators.

In a final inquiry which came at the end of the interview and after considerable discussion of other forms of trust violation (lying, betrayal, informing, etc.) respondents were asked for additional devices by which individual protection might be insured. In addition to the previous emphasis on (a) the danger of strangers bearing opportunities and the need to assess persons before entering into dealings and (b) the importance of keeping informed on current fraud schemes so swindlers could be more readily recognized, the respondents proposed the following as additional procedures: (c) the importance of not divulging personal, precious or otherwise exploitable (threat, theft, blackmail) information to others, especially to others not known and trust-tested over a long time, (d) the need to be self-controlled and realistic, which means not allowing get-rich-quick dreams to guide one's actions nor to let impulses of risk-taking or going along with others override the need for prudence and (e) the importance of keeping funds and private data in secure facilities, as opposed to pockets, bureau drawers, etc.

Two inappropriate sets of principles were also identified. One was a generalized suspicion or distrust of all strangers or, more broadly, of everyone. We assume that orientation to reflect personality dynamics which imply unconscious vulnerability, deficiency and hostility. The second was the recommendation that particular groups of persons be distrusted or kept at arms' length, e.g. politicians, attorneys, newsmen, Negroes, ex-cons, etc. Whether such recommendations reflect irrational generalization from prior bad experience or the operation of prejudicial stereotypes, it may be assumed that they reflect unexamined ideas about other people and styles of living which are at the least restrictive if not destructive. It is important, as we examine these principles which we believe are not appropriate cautions, to see how limits must be set on the cautionary procedures lest defenses inhibit all appropriate intercourse. We suggest that personality problems, whether neurotic or paranoid, or a social atmosphere engendering anxiety and individual feelings of vulnerability and characterizations of a large number of others as dangerous, can lead one to behavior which, even if helpful in protection against trust victimization, would make ordinary living exceedingly unpleasant both for the individual and those around him. It is thus necessary to counsel for balance and perspective in any fraud prevention program, lest it create more problems than it solves.

After discussing with citizens how they protected themselves, or might do so, we asked for their ideas about public policies to assist in preventing and controlling trust violations. They recommended the following: expanded law enforcement, harsher punishment of offenders, careful control of city licensing for businesses and solicitors, care in the issuance of credentials by businesses, an expanded effort to educate citizens to report persons and schemes suspected of trust violation, public-information programs to instill awareness of swindling schemes along with education as to precautionary devices, stringent screening of mass media advertising to disallow misrepresentation, prohibition of access to the mass media for any consumer fraud enterprise, elimination of junk-mail advertising, prohibition of organized telephone solicitation ("boiler rooms"), the development of regulations to control the style as well as the content of all advertising and sales methods and more active government involvement in the evaluation and regulation of products, services and claims offered by business. Missing is any suggestion that perpetrators of fraud can be dissuaded from further illicit endeavors by any means.

It is our impression that these citizen proposals merit consideration. Their possible excellence should remind policy makers of the substantive as well as political value of involving the grass roots in policy development. Whether or not government, including local government, intends to work more effectively, especially in the consumer fraud arena, given the large number of respectable companies engaged in advertising misrepresentation and the subsequent likelihood of massive commercial opposition to such respectable swindling, and given the relative under-emphasis by citizens themselves on the seriousness of fraud as a crime menace, is quite another question.

PROTOTYPES OF CONFIDENCE GAMES

During the course of work with confidence men and their victims, we observed a strongly theatrical quality in what transpired. The con men play roles for which they rehearse and make up, they hire one another to do bit parts, they set up stages for action and, when all is ready, they invite the victim not only to be an audience but to participate as an actor in the star role. The victim, in accepting the invitation, moves from the humdrum into a world of impersonation and fantasied gain. It can be amazing to see how readily ordinary folk enter into these dramas, how easily the theater begins, and how practiced they are in impersonating themselves as they would be if they were what their hearts desired. One must not overlook the fact that the dramas are destructive ones in which at least one person is hurt, yet that action, too, is not foreign but familiar, and both perpetrator and victim may respond to harm with an unexpected fatalism if not grim humor, as though it were a practical joke. In one sense it is just that.

These notions led us to propose that the elements of the confidence game as well as some other forms of trust violation requiring the assumption of false roles, e.g. spying, undercover work, were familiar to most folk. The presumption was that these elements had been learned early in life, formed part of the repertoire of potential interpersonal actions and were a source of some enjoyment. We conceived of childhood experience with "let's pretend," adult experience in posing, impersonating, pretense and putting on, and lifetime experience with practical jokes, ruses and hoaxes as specific prototypes for intimate violations of trust. Given these notions, we set out not only to get rough estimates of prevalence from our respondents but to gain from them insights into why such goings-on might prove useful or pleasant. The inquiries provide no conclusive test of our notion but do provide grist for the mental mills.

No person failed to remember that as a child he had enjoyed the fantasy of "let's pretend." Asked what a child enjoyed therein, the most common speculations were to the effect that it was an opportunity for the imagination to flourish and, by implication, to realize itself (acting out). The goal of this was most often seen as an opportunity to feel older or otherwise more important, glamorous or successful; that is, to achieve through pretending to a role or personality they were not. Some spoke in terms of the child seeking to become like another he admired (identification, imitation) and of the activity itself being exciting or fun. A few spoke of "let's pretend" as a means not simply of being unreal but of avoiding reality or of getting attention or companionship otherwise absent or denied. Our impression was that at least some of our respondents were not talking about children at all, as for example when one said, "Everybody wants to be a winner," or "It's a way to go beyond your means," or "We all want to be heroes." We asked them when they had given up the "let's pretend" games. Women reported doing so at an earlier age than men, most often before age nine, whereas men most often said between age 10 and 15. Ten percent of the men and 6 percent of the women stated they had not yet given up playing "let's pretend" games.

We asked about theater and playacting. About half of the respondents had taken part in school dramatics, the women more often than the men. The women were also more ready to speculate on the pleasures of theater and playacting. Far and away the most common suggestion given—by women almost entirely—was the pleasure of doing something or being something that one could not achieve in real life. Others put the same thought in terms of escape, of feeling important, of a thrill at being someone different. Some also spoke of receiving recognition or admiration from others, of enjoying the limelight, of "showing off" in an exhibitionistic sense. A few spoke of the joys of imagination and fantasy acted out or impersonation as a means of training for a realistic role. Our impression was, as we reviewed what citizens had said, that they had indeed captured the pleasures of "let's pretend," but, further, that many of them were not discussing the psychology of children or themselves as children long ago at all. Rather, with interest and intensity and in the present tense, they were discussing how themselves or others felt as adults.

Moving from the child as play actor to the adult who enjoys

posing, pretending and putting on, we invited respondents to consider why adults would do such things. Again the primary theme was that of achievement through pretense of that which was not available in reality; that is, impressing others, feeling superior, being popular, keeping up with the Joneses and the like. Some emphasized the immediate escape from unpleasant realities, of being unable to face themselves as they were. These themes do not differ from those offered to account for children's theater, except that for children there was acceptance of and preparation for pretending as part of growing up to adult roles, whereas one senses less sympathy, although much insightful understanding, for adult pretense.

The next phase of the discussion focused on the practical joke, the ruse, prank or hoax. Most men and two thirds of the women had acquaintances who had played such tricks on them. For the majority of men, such experiences had occurred within the year, for nearly one third there had been several times recently that they had been the victims of hoaxes perpetrated by friends and acquaintances. With women it was not so. Only 14 percent had ever been a victim of such joking, only two of multiple hoaxing in the past year. Asked about their role as perpetrators rather than victims, half of the men admitted to playing the active hoaxer. Those doing so, for the most part, had done it repeatedly during the past year. Again this was not so with women; only five admitted to being jokers, only two more than once recently.

Our impression from this data is that deception practiced to fool another, an act which seems to draw its humor from an alteration of status so that one man dominates as another man is made the fool, is widespread among men. It may be considered an acceptable form of trust violation, acceptable because it is "done in fun" and presumably not seen as exploitative nor harmful, nor does it create any permanent disruption in relationships.

The understanding of respondents for the functions and gains from posing and pretense are a good source of insights, some into others and some into their own temptations and devices, as exemplified by those who admitted they were still engaged in "let's pretend." How their theatrics and deception differ from those of the confidence man or other habitual deceivers one does not know. Certainly the desires which are ascribed to the pretender are common ones—the wish for recognition and importance, the desire for competitive triumph or personal glory, the fun in fantasy and the achievement of escape from dull or painful reality. One assumes that the ordinary man, moved by these same ends, enjoys their satisfaction sufficiently in ordinary relationships so that he does not have to adopt disapproved or unrealistic devices to attain them. The ordinary man, unlike the confidence man, already is able to maintain interpersonal relationships which are satisfying. Having these, he need not create theatrical pseudo-relationships. Also, he would not jeopardize his real relationships by embarking on a course that would imperil them through more tenuous and risky relationships comprised of fantasy, falsehood and exploitation. Recall that the lies of marital partners are defensive and serve to maintain the institution (as well as private pleasures). Whatever the masquerades of the ordinary citizen, we assume they are less flamboyant, less exploitative, less destructive of interpersonal ties and are more limited and controlled than those whose lives constitute masquerades in a large portion of their human relations. We also assume that these normal masquerades are different primarily in degree rather than in kind from those of confidence men, spies and the rest and do provide a source of training and temptation, as well as insight, for the more grandiose deceptions.

Regarding the ruses, practical jokes, hoaxes and the like, the data show these to be widespread among men in our sample. It is proposed that the hoax functions in some of the same ways as pretense and impersonation, for through the practical joke, one man's status vis-à-vis another is changed. One man dominates the other through aggressive deception, distorting what the other believes to be reality. Trust is violated and the trusting one becomes the fool, whereas the joker emerges as superior. As a morality play, it teaches that confidence in others is for fools. Even so, the joker and his hoax are acceptable; the anger and humiliation must be controlled, for it is socially incumbent on all parties to define the events as humor. It can be handled as humor not only because the sudden shift in status or reality conceptions tickles the funny bone (do not ask us why) but because the joker takes on the responsibility not to harm or to exploit and to return things to normal; that is, to correctly inform the victim as to events so that preexisting relationships and conceptions of reality may be reestablished. This correctibility of situations also allows another feature, which is reversibility. The joker of today may be the ruse victim of tomorrow. Another feature of the practical joke is that there is a socially set limit beyond which the joker may not go; if he does, he suffers a risk of a permanent change in his status. There were three men in our sample who were chronic jokers. Each was, we suspect, in danger of becoming known, if not already so stigmatized, as a joker. That label is a counterbalancing device whereby the victims of the chronic hoaxer assert a crueler dominance, for the man labeled a joker becomes the permanent and paramount jester or fool. He merits neither trust nor respect. These balances and constraints are, we believe, features that distinguish the practical joke from betrayals or the confidence game.

THE CHRONIC VICTIM

Another set of inquiries were directed toward the victim, particularly the "mark" as the con men call theirs. First, we asked our citizens if they knew anyone who was repeatedly conned, a born loser to the swindling game. Twenty-four percent of the men and 10 percent of the women responded that they knew such people. We asked these knowledgeable folk what there was about the person which made him fall victim so easily and often. Only three points were made; one was that victims were "always looking for a deal." That implies an unrealistic set of expectations about opportunities; it may also imply an unrealistic sense of cleverness or conceit in the victim himself or a compulsion to gamble, as one victim was so described. The second point was that victims whom they knew were unable to resist the aggressiveness or manipulation of others, either by being submissive and unable to say "no" or by being too trusting and gullible. A third point emphasized the unrealistic orientation of the victim; for example, one was described as a "do-gooder," the implication perhaps being that in the aggressive service of inappropriate beliefs or false ideals the victim ran afoul of people who exploited him. Rather than learning from experience to reassess the world, the victim preferred to keep his unrealistic idealism intact and to accept his subsequent chronic-loser status.

INFORMING AND WORKING UNDERCOVER

When asked to define betrayal, some of our citizens had cited squealing as a case in point. We pursued views of informants further. We first asked if they thought it justifiable for the police to assign officers to undercover work, posing as criminals or victims, to investigate vice and fraud. No respondent found that practice unacceptable. We next asked if the police were justified in using stool pigeons (persons not officers) to get information. Most respondents found the use of stool pigeons justified, although six percent did not. Asked if, were they policemen themselves, they would be willing to accept an undercover assignment requiring disguise and impersonation, as for example to uncover drug peddlers, most said they would, although 14 percent of the men and 6 percent of the women would not. Asked what they would think of a friend doing undercover work on behalf of the police, most said they would approve, although 20 percent of the men would withhold approval subject to learning the circumstances. Women respondents were not as tentative. We conclude from these inquiries about police undercover work that it is in good grace, especially if the officer himself takes an undercover assignment. When a stoolie is used, there is general approval but subject to qualification and perhaps misgiving, especially by men in the sample.

We asked our sample if they would be willing to inform on their own friends or acquaintances whom they knew to be engaging in criminal activities. One fourth of the sample, men and women equally, said they would. Most said it would depend on the severity of the crime and other circumstances. Pursuing the point further and introducing our question with some remarks on the American tradition of not tattling in contrast to the need by authorities for information, we asked what circumstances would dictate that a citizen should not inform about an acquaintance's criminal activity. The responses indicated that most were, in fact, willing to report another. Qualifying conditions mentioned were that the matter must not be minor, that no one's life (including their own) would be jeopardized, and that a relative or close friend must not be involved in the offense. They were then asked, on the other hand, under what circumstances a citizen had the obligation to tell authorities about an acquaintance's criminality. The compelling circumstance was, for nearly all citizens, a serious crime. We derive from these remarks the conclusion that although citizens may exemplify betrayal in terms of informing and further that most speak of betrayal with repugnance, most are also willing to inform, providing it is in the service of law and morality and concerns a serious offense. Only a very few place the principle of not informing ahead of any circumstance which might call for informing. We surmise that informing ceases to be repugnant, indeed ceases to be perceived or defined as betrayal when real events arise which invoke morality, a sense of danger or felt obligations of the citizen to approved authority. What mitigates against informing is when the danger arises from doing so, as when retaliation is chanced, when intimate relationships are involved or when the events are minor and not worth the trouble or disruption of activities and relationships which is likely to follow. When such is not the case, then it may well be that the situation provides not only justification but prevents any question of betrayal arising, for duty, morality and well-being conspire to make informing a desirable rather than an heinous act.

We proceeded from the hypothetical case of knowledge of a friend's criminality to the case of the bystander observing a crime and not calling the police. This inquiry was introduced by a discussion which included remarks made by confidence men who spoke of the ease of their work simply because observers did not warn victims or call police. Asked why bystanders do not offer aid,* almost all respondents ascribed it to a desire to avoid involvement, fear of reprisal, a fear that an innocent bystander might himself be implicated or come to grief, and unwillingness to become involved in reporting, court appearances and the like underlay the noninvolvement theme. A few suggested lack of confidence in the system of criminal justice, that if crimes were reported the courts would let the offenders go; consequently reporting was wasted. A few suggested that humans were indifferent to one another, a few thought people might wish to avoid the stigma of being called a "rat." We surmise that reporting on an observed crime does not, except for a few, touch on the tattling or betrayal motif. The problem of nonreporting is seen primarily as an act with a high risk of negative consequences and a low probability for positive ones. In this instance, unlike the hypothetical case used in querying about informing on criminal acts of an acquaintance, morality and duty do not come into play. They cannot easily do so, since the question called for an explanation of an implicitly disapproved inaction, not an accounting for an approved action. Nevertheless, the replies dictate that attention be paid to factors such as anticipated danger, inconvenience and pointlessness (just as found in the Biderman *et al.* study of actual victim nonreporting) in determining how situations are defined and what subsequent actions are undertaken. Considering that most citizens appear ready to inform under certain circumstances in spite of the possibility that another might view it as betrayal, and considering that others do not inform when it is morally incumbent to do so, it is evident that principles relating to betrayal and informing operate only as partial determinants of conduct. Present pressures and anticipated future outcomes, the emotions, dangers and gains are strong influences. As a perspective, it

---

* These reasons can be compared to those obtained by Biderman *et al.* (1967) who found that not wanting to get involved was paramount. Others said they did not want to take the time, that they had no responsibility to intervene, and that since the damage was done and it could not be undone, reporting served no purpose. Given hypothetical cases, respondents emphasized the belief that the police could accomplish nothing or that the police would not want to be bothered.

requires that one assess circumstance and setting as well as principles and stated intentions when one wishes to understand violations of trust. That same statement may apply to the judgment of what constitutes betrayal as much as to the actions that constitute it.

Another question on the undercover theme asked citizens (after an introductory discussion which mentioned James Bond, called attention to the excitement of hidden identities and secret roles, and noted that the con man himself is a trickster in an undercover role) what might be adventurous about being in disguise and working secretly against others. Replies suggested pleasures in risk-taking and combat, the importance of a secret role if one felt otherwise unimportant and the use of danger to combat boredom. Other provocative proposals were that it provided an opportunity safely to hurt or triumph over others not normally vulnerable, there was pleasure in tempting disaster (counterphobic conduct), it was a self-destructive act, it was an acting out by the child of parental dreams, it was a response to television glamor or it was a means for easily changing identities for people not satisfied with who they really were. The more common interpretations were more prosaic—that it was one way to make big money or that these were assignments that were simply part of a job or an action in the service of law enforcement or patriotism. Our impression in reviewing responses was one of shared excitement; that is, the respondents could appreciate emotionally the James Bond variety of playacting just as they appreciated the "let's pretend" of children or the masquerades of adults. One has the feeling that while it was not for them (our citizens being settled and adjusted folk), they could see how the Bondian style might be for others—and not without a bit of longing—"I'd love it," "I wish I were in the FBI," "Wouldn't that give you a life?"

SOME PREDICTIONS

In our work with confidence men, we were struck with the frequency with which they themselves said they were easy victims of various "scams," that is, con games. Many were avid risk-takers; all got rid of their money nearly as fast as they won it in crime or gambling. In their case, the losers and the winners were one and the same. One is reminded of Herman Melville's (1857, reprinted 1954) description of his confidence man. "He is not wholly at heart a knave, I fancy, among whose dupes is himself. Did you not see our quack friend apply to himself his own quackery? A fanatic quack; essentially a fool, though effectively a knave." Certainly our data show wide differences in experience as victims of trust violation and in their role as perpetrators as well, defined in terms of their admitted lying and betrayal.

We suspected that the "marriage" of fantasy and impulses which we identified in the relationship *between* victims and confidence men, a relationship which can be conceived as psychodynamically symbiotic might be demonstrable *within* individuals. Essentially it would hold that certain people are more at home than others with deception—in giving and receiving lies, in responding to pretense and impersonation and in sharing unrealistic aggrandizing fantasies. If that were the case, victims of trust violation would also be more likely to be perpetrators of trust violation. The same notion might also be phrased in terms of these people sharing a core of unrealistic and reversible self-aggrandizing interpersonal techniques, of their being a bit "kinky," as the professional thieves would say, or of their being more ready actors in the theater of interpersonal exploitation, be that conceived in terms of reversible sado-masochistic roles or of being part of social groups in which deceptive manipulations were part of a way of life. We also wondered if there would be a relationship between experience as a victim and a set of psychological traits and habits which we proposed *ought* to be related to fraud victimization, items we called the "mark" items (recall that a con man calls his victims "marks"). That "ought" was derived from some clinical observations we had made during conversations with other trust violation victims which led us to believe there was a relationship between such things as loneliness, mild depression, mild psychopathy, etc., and exposing oneself to risk situations.* As a corollary, another notion we had was that there should be a relationship between being a victim and being more aware of corruption, as defined by criticism of politicians, the police, etc., as being corrupt. This latter expectation is compatible with the finding of Ennis (1967) which showed that victims of burglary were more worried about the risk of burglary. Our notion does not require that the link be one of simply learning about corruption from experience. Given our more complicated expectation that being a victim and a perpetrator correlates, then the concept of projection becomes one explanatory device—persons who corrupt themselves project it to others. We also posit distrust as a function of low self-esteem (other studies (Wylie, 1961) have established that liking for others is linked to liking for oneself) related, in turn, to unrealistic and deviant conduct in general and interpersonal manipulation in particular.

As a final question of our data, we asked if, as one would expect, those with reported experience as fraud victims were more likely than nonvictims to have reported experience as victims of other crimes. Recall that trust violation victims included all who had suffered cheating even if it had not been defined by them originally as fraud. Since anyone who had been criminally defrauded was automatically defined as a trust violation victim, those whose only crime victimization had been other than fraud were called crime victims (as opposed to trust violation victims) in this analysis.

Our test of each of these expectations was crude. That was the case because we did not generate our notions until we had completed the study of confidence men and their victims and had examined our experiences and data. By then, the citizen survey was well underway. That meant that we did not incor-

---

* "Mark" items were responses to specific inquiries which indicated that the individual was without constructive use of leisure time, often felt lonely, bored, depressed, looked forward to dying, often went out walking, often shopped without intent to buy, often sat in public places, distrusted banks as a place to keep money, had removed deposited funds without disclosing investment intentions to any family member or trusted advisor, often carried more than 100 dollars cash on his person, had few relatives nearby, saw friends rarely, talked readily with strangers and often felt the need for excitement.

porate a preplanned scale which would expertly measure the gradations of experience as a perpetrator of trust violations or would tap the variety of components which might function as anti-mark characteristics. The study as conducted did give a good variety of items measuring experience as a victim of trust violation or characteristics as a mark as hypothesized. Our method was an after-the-fact construction of indices based on item replies. What would improve the strength of these tentative findings would be the development of improved scales and items, as is done in any scale or test construction. What is very much needed is a cross-validation of the findings to see if they work on a new population. We should have done that, but we were out of money. At the time of this writing, we are still out of money so that the needed refinements await new capabilities, ours or someone else's.

Table V below presents correlation coefficients obtained when comparing frequency-of-victim status, measured by compiling affirmative replies to various experiences in having been cheated (gypsies, salesmen, prostitutes, etc.) with the other crude scales. Each of these is also a count of replies to items we classified as measures of being a mark, an anti-mark, aware of corruption or a perpetrator. In ordering the victim status distribution, keep in mind that 80 persons had some victim experience, 10 had been approached but had not been victimized, and 10 had neither been approached nor victimized.

One sees that there is a relationship such that as frequency of being a victim of trust violation increases, so does the likeli-

TABLE V

STATISTICAL FINDINGS ON EXPECTED RELATIONSHIPS*

Trust violation victim frequency and mark frequency	$r = .27$	(P .01)
Victim frequency and corruption awareness	$r = .29$	(P .005)
Victim frequency and perpetrator frequency	$r = .19$	(P .05)
Perpetrator frequency and corruption awareness	$r = .32$	(P .005)
Trust violator victim in association with experience as criminal victim	$X^2 = 2.125$	(P .05) (one-tailed test)

* Our thanks to W. D. Asher, Ph.D., Department of Statistics, Stanford University, for assisting in data analysis.

hood of the presence of those traits, habits and self-descriptions which we predicted were those of the mark. The relationship is not profound but is statistically significant. We see that as victimization increases, so too does awareness of corruption. Being a perpetrator of trust violation is also related to being more aware of corruption. We see that frequency of victimization correlates positively and significantly with frequency of perpetration of trust violation. We also find that trust violation victims more often report criminal victimization by crimes other than trust violation.

We take it that our hypotheses, if we may elevate them to that exalted status, are supported and that we have evidence that being the victim of trust violation, that is, being lied to, cheated or betrayed, is related to certain predictable traits and habits. It is also related to an increased sense of corruption among others, to being victimized in other crimes, and to being a liar, defrauder or betrayer of others. Our evidence is tentative and requires further validation with better measures. An important next step would be to rule out the possibility that people who are willing to report experiences as victims are simply also more willing to report other unhappy events or feelings. Were this latter the basic factor operating, then the apparent correlations would be artifacts.

For the present, we presume that the data set forth here and in combination with the observations in other chapters, present evidence that there is a more-than-chance likelihood that people who are deceived by others are also deceivers of others. Conversely, the betrayer is likely to have been betrayed. What we do not know, but what we would expect to find, is that deceivers of others are more often also self deceivers. We also believe that those who are deceived have traits and engage in conduct which makes it appear that the risks they take which result in their deception are not accidental. Given the links to loneliness, depression and excitement seeking, and the absence and seeking of social contact, one would say that those who are cheated are willing to take risks in order to achieve interpersonal satisfactions which they do not have or in order to combat unpleasant moods through social stimulation and exciting risk-taking. The phenomena of delinquents combatting incipient depression through dangerous actions is clinically known, as is that of the lonely heart seeking romance in desperate ventures. We should not be surprised if these are part of a more general principle which has it that those who need special stimulation, presumably linked to fantasy, the acting out of impulses or the defense against despair, will seek it in more risky and deviant trans- actions, for obviously the offerings of the humdrum world of friends and family are insufficient or absent.

The links between being deceived and being a deceiver, being more willing to attribute corruption to others, and to being more often victimized by thieves (since crimes against property are common and those against person are rare) suggest that the cheated one is more exposed to and involved in the world of quick and easy dollars and pleasures than is his less-deceived and less-deceiving neighbor. Whether people gravitate to such social settings or whether they are produced by them—or both— is immaterial. There are different levels of human intercourse, and one way of defining these levels is in terms of participation in exploitative versus nonexploitative relationships. Those in- volved, like slum dwellers who are more at risk of being robbed and being robbers, or of homicides who are more at risk of assaulting and being assaulted, are likely to be doing and watch- ing lies and betrayals more often than the good citizen who neither gives nor takes of corruption—or at least not so much!

SUMMARY

A random sample of adults in a small California industrial city were interviewed in order to learn about their experience with trust violations and their perspective on it. Although most were concerned about the menace of crime, fraud was not a primary source of concern, even though 16 percent of the sample reported having been victimized through criminal trust violations. The majority further reported having been cheated through consumer fraud. Many had been exposed to confidence and bunco games in risk situations; of these, the greatest rate of loss had occurred through carnival games, gambling and in visiting prostitutes. Men reported greater exposure to, and greater victimization through, such trust violations. Women expressed a greater sense of vulnerability, in spite of a lower prevalence of exploitation.

A review of personal experience in observing cheating showed that few had seen cheating or stealing in work settings or by police or government personnel, but many had observed customer deception in stores. A catalogue of lies observed and admitted by kind of relationship revealed different functions by setting and by sex of the respondent. Awareness and admissions are greatest for employees vis-à-vis the boss. In the marital setting, women more than men reported other-protecting lies. With regard to betrayal, a much more serious matter than lying, observations of what others do far exceed admissions. Most widely known is the betrayal of wives by husbands through adultery. In a review of procedures used to protect against victimization in various forms of trust violation, a number of apparently successful principles were set forth, some of which deserve translation into action programs, as, for example, in consumer fraud and bunco protection. Speculation about possible prototypes of confidence games, impersonation and hoaxes led to inquiries showing these practices to be widespread. The prototypes provide psychological satisfactions similar to ones achieved in con games but are limited by cultural and ego constraints.

An examination of views toward undercover police and informants indicated most citizens were in support of these practices and would themselves be willing to inform, providing the offenses were serious. Deterrents to informing include anticipated trouble and danger. It appears that obligations of civic duty to identify offenders or contrary ones not to betray friends are, as abstractions, less relevant to the understanding of informing and trust violation than are definitions of the situation by the person, which rest at the very least upon kinds of relationships to persons involved, moral seriousness of events and risks of negative or zero responses subsequent to informing, compared to chances for approval or effective action subsequent to informing. As in the review of lies and cheating situations, relationships and needs in relation to values appear to influence not only whether trust violation occurs but whether or not the individual perceives it as such or whether others judge it as such.

Based on expectations arising from interviews with confidence men and victims, as reported in other chapters, a set of predictions were made as to the relationship between being a victim of trust violations and (a) showing traits or habits which are associated with victim predilection, (b) being aware of corruption in others not known to one and (c) being a perpetrator of trust violations. Positive and significant correlations occurred in each case. Corruption awareness was also correlated with perpetrating trust violation; trust violator victim status was associated with experience as a victim in other crimes. These relationships, although not powerful, suggest a matrix of relations among trust violation and personality, consistent styles of interpersonal relations and exposure to criminality as perpetrator, observer and victim.

BIBLIOGRAPHY

Adorno, T. W.; Frenkel-Brunswick, E.; Levinson, D. J., and Sanford, R. N.: *The Authoritarian Personality.* New York, Harper, 1950.

Almond, G.: *The Appeals of Communism.* Princeton, Princeton University Press, 1954.

Anon: Business espionage. *Business Management,* October, 1965, p. 58-66.

Aydelotte, F.: *Elizabethan Rogues and Vagabonds.* New York, Barnes and Noble, 1913.

√Barbash, J. T.: Compensation and the crime of pigeon dropping. *Journal of Clinical Psychology,* 8:92-94, 1952.

Bauer, R.: Some trends in sources of alienation from the Soviet system. *Public Opinion Quarterly, 19*:275-291, 1955.

Bauer, R. A.; Inkeles, A., and Kluckhohn, C.: *How the Soviet System Works.* New York, Vantage Press, 1956.

Biderman, A. D.; Johnson, Louise; McIntyre, Jennie, Weir, Adrianna: *Field Survey I: Report on a Pilot Study in the District of Columbia on Victimization and Attitudes Toward Law Enforcement.* Prepared for the President's Commission on Law Enforcement and the Administration of Justice. Washington, D. C., U. S. Government Printing Office, 1967.

Blum, R. H.: *Police Selection.* Springfield, Ill., Thomas, 1964.

Blum, R. H., *et al.: Drugs II: Society and Drugs.* San Francisco, Jossey-Bass, 1969, Chap. XII.

Blum, R. H., and Osterloh, W. J.: Keeping policemen on the job: some recommendations arising from a study of men and morale. *Police,* May-June, 1966.

Blum, R., and Osterloh, W. J.: The polygraph examination as a means for detecting truth and falsehood in stories presented by police informers. *Journal Criminal Law, Criminology and Police Science,* 59(1):133-137, 1968.

Boveri, Margaret: *Treason in the Twentieth Century.* Trans. by Jonathan Steinberg. New York, Putnam, 1963.

Brannon, W. T.: *Yellow Kid Weil. The Autobiography of America's Master Swindler. Chicago,* Ziff-Davis, 1948.

Bromberg, W.: Liar in delinquency and crime. *Nervous Child, 1*(4):351-357, 1941.

Bromberg, W., and Keiser, S.: Psychology of a swindler. *American Journal of Psychiatry,* 94(2):1441-1458, 1938.

Brothers, Joyce: Assassin's reasons often not political. *North American Newspaper Alliance,* n.d.

Brunswick, R.: The accepted lie. *Psychoanalytic Quarterly,* *12*:458-464, 1943.

Campion, D. with Stearns, M.: *Crooks Are Human Too.* Englewood Cliffs, N. J., Prentice-Hall, 1957.

Carlin, J. E.: *Lawyers' Ethics.* New York, Russell Sage Foundation, 1966.

Comfort, Alex: *Authority and Delinquency in the Modern State.* London, Routledge & Kegan Paul, 1950.

Conner, G. A.: Embezzlement: the crime of honest people. *Credit and Financial Management, 12*:27-28, October, 1961.

Cressey, D. R.: *Other People's Money.* Glencoe, Ill., Free Press, 1953.

Daniels, A. K., and Daniels, R. R.: The social function of the career fool. *Psychiatry,* *27*(3):240-243, 1964.

Debray, R.: *Revolution in the Revolution.* New York, Grove Press, 1967.

Dulles, A.: *The Craft of Intelligence.* New York, New American Library, 1965.

Ennis, P.: *Field Surveys II: Criminal Investigation in the United States: A Report of a National Survey.* Prepared for the President's Commission on Law Enforcement and the Administration of Justice by the National Opinion Research Corporation. Washington, D. C., U. S. Government Printing Office, 1967.

Elkins, H. T.: Study conducted by the Office of the Attorney General of the State of California, 1965. See also testimony in the Superior Court, Los Angeles County, California, State vs. Marketmakers, Inc., #874572. See also Aluminum Siding Fraud Investigators' REPORT.

Erikson, E. H.: *Identity: Youth and Crisis.* New York, Norton, 1968.

Erikson, K. T.: *Wayward Puritans.* New York, John Wiley, 1966.

Franey, P. J.: Testimony before the Grand Jury of Los Angeles County, September 28, 1965.

Fromm, E.: *Escape from Freedom.* New York, Holt, Rinehart & Winston, 1941.

Gentry, C.: *The Vulnerable Americans.* New York, Doubleday, 1966.

Gibney, K.: *The Operators.* New York, Harper and Brothers, 1960.

Giffin, K.: Recent Research on inter-personal trust. Paper presented to the Annual Convention of the Speech Association of America, Los Angeles, December, 1967 (mimeo.).

Giffin, K.: The contribution of studies of source credibility to a theory of interpersonal trust in the communication process. *Psychological Bulletin, 68*(2):104-120, 1967.

Glueck, S., ond Glueck, Eleanor: *Predicting Delinquency and Crime.* Cambridge, Harvard University Press, 1960.

Goffman, E.: On cooling the mark out: some aspects of adaptation to failure. *Psychiatry, 15*:451-463, 1952.

Gottschalk, L. A.: The use of drugs in interrogation. In Biderman, A. D., and

Zimmer, H. (Eds.): *The Manipulation of Human Behavior*. New York, John Wiley, 1961.

Granick, D.: *The Red Executive. A Study of the Organization Man in Russian Industry*. New York, Anchor Books, 1961.

Grodzins, M.: *The Loyal and the Disloyal*. Chicago, University of Chicago Press, 1956.

Harari, H., and McDavid, J. W.: Situation influence on moral justice: a study of 'finking.' *Journal Personality and Social Psychology, 11*(3):240-245, 1969.

Hart, H. L. A.: *Law, Liberty and Morality*. Stanford: Stanford University Press, 1963.

Heiss, J. S.: The dyad views the newcomer: a study of perception. *Human Relations, 16*(3):241-248, 1963.

Hoffeld, D. R.: Effect of incentive upon information use in a choice situation. *Psychology Reports, 13*(2):547-550, 1963.

Hubner, M. J.: *A Study of Over-Extended Families*. Detroit, Merrill-Palmer Institute, 1965.

Hurst, W.: Treason in the United States. II: The Constitution. *Harvard Law Review, 58*:395-444, 1945.

Hurst, W.: Treason in the United States. III: Under the Constitution. *Harvard Law Review, 58*:806-846, 1945.

Hyman, H. H. *et al.*: *Interviewing in Social Research*. Chicago, University of Chicago Press, 1954.

Inkeles, A., and Bauer, R. A.: *The Soviet Citizen. Daily Life in a Totalitarian Society*. Cambridge, Harvard University Press, 1961.

Inkeles, A., and Geiger, K. (Eds.): *Soviet Society: A Book of Readings*. Boston, Houghton Mifflin Company, 1961.

Janney, J. E.: Swindlers. *Psychology Bulletin, 39*:599, 1942.

Jaspan, N. with Black, H.: *The Thief in the White Collar*. Philadelphia, Lippincott, 1960.

Jaszi, O., and Lewis, J. D.: *Against the Tyrant*. Glencoe, Ill., Free Press, 1957.

Jenkens, R. L.: *Breaking Patterns of Defeat: The Effective Readjustment of the Sick Personality*. Philadelphia, Lippincott, 1954.

Jones, P.: The city state in late medieval Italy. *Transactions of the Royal Historical Society, 15*:71-79, 1965.

Karpman, B.: Lying. *Journal Criminal Law, Criminology and Political Science, 40*:135-137, 1949.

Kiesler, C., and Kiesler, Sara: The role of forewarning in persuasive communications. *Journal Abnormal Social Psychology, 68*(5):547-549, 1964.

Kinsey, A. C., *et al.*: *Sexual Behavior in the Human Female*. Philadelphia, Saunders, 1953.

Kinsey, A. C.; Pomeroy, W. B., and Martin, C. E.: *Sexual Behavior in the Human Male*. Philadelphia, Saunders, 1948.

Lane, R., and Sears, D.: *Public Opinion.* New Jersey, Prentice-Hall, 1964.

Lauterpacht, H.: Allegiance, diplomatic protection and criminal jurisdiction over aliens. *Cambridge Law Journal,* 9:330-371, 1947.

Lear, F. S.: Treason in Roman and Germanic Law. In *Collected Papers.* Austin, University of Texas Press, 1965.

Leonhard, W.: *Child of the Revolution.* Trans. by C. M. Woodhouse. Chicago, Henry Regnery, 1958.

Lester, J. T.: Behavioral research during the 1963 Mt. Everest Expedition. *ONR, NR:*171-257, 1964.

MacDonald, J.: *Crime is a Business. Stanford,* Stanford University Press, 1939.

MacLeod, R. B.: The phenomenological approach to social psychology. In Taguiri, R., and Petrullo, L. (Eds.): *Person Perception and Interpersonal Behavior.* Stanford, Stanford University Press, 1958.

MacMullen, R.: *Enemies of the Roman Order. Treason, Unrest and Alienation in the Roman Empire.* Cambridge, Mass., Harvard University Press, 1966.

McCloskey, H.: *Personality and Attitude Correlates of Foreign Policy Orientation.* In *Political Inquiry.* The nature and use of survey research. New York, Macmillan, 1969, pp. 70-125.

Manis, M., and Blake, J. B.: Interpretation of persuasive messages as a function of prior immunization. *Journal Abnormal and Social Psychology,* 66(3):225-230, 1963.

Mannheim, H.: *Comparative Criminology.* Boston, Houghton-Mifflin, 1965.

Markel, N. M.; Meisels, J., and Houck, J. E.: Judging personality from voice quality. *Journal Abnormal Social Psychology,* 69(4):458-462, 1964.

Matza, D.: *Delinquency and Drift.* New York, John Wiley & Sons, 1964.

Maurer, D. W.: *The Big Con: The Story of the Confidence Man and the Confidence Game.* New York, Bobbs-Merrill, 1940.

Maurer, D. W.: *Whiz Mob. A Correlation of the Technical Argot of Pickpockets with Their Behavior Pattern.* New Haven, College and University Press, 1955.

Meehl, P. E.: *Clinical vs. Statistical Prediction.* Minneapolis, University of Minnesota Press, 1954.

Melville, H.: *The Confidence Man.* New York, Hendricks House, 1954.

Merenda, P. F.; Clarke, W. V., and Hall, C. E.: Cross-validity of procedures for selecting life-insurance salesmen. *Journal of Applied Psychology,* 45(6):376-380, 1961.

Merz, F.: Uber die Beurteilung der personlichen Eigenart unserer Mitmenschen" (Judgment of personal characteristics of associates). *Archiv fur Gesamte Psychologie,* 114(2):187-211, 1962.

Milosz, C.: *The Captive Mind.* Trans. by Jane Zielonko. London, Secher & Warburg, 1953.

Mullins, C. J., and Force, R. C.: Rater accuracy as a generalized ability. *Journal Applied Psychology, 46*:191-193, 1962.

Myers, J. H.: Predicting credit risk with a numerical scoring system. *Journal Applied Psychology, 47*:348-352, 1963.

Nepote, J.: Interpol versus the underworld of narcotics. *UNESCO Courier,* May, 1968, pp. 24-29.

Norfleet, J. Frank: *Norfleet: The Amazing Experiences of an Intrepid Rancher with an International Swindling Ring.* Sugar Land, Texas, Imperial Press, 1924.

Packer, H.: *The Limits of the Criminal Sanction.* Stanford, Stanford University Press, 1968.

Penkovskiy, O.: *The Penkovskiy Papers.* Trans. by P. Deriabin. New York, Doubleday, 1965.

Peterson, V. W.: Why honest people steal. Chicago, Crime Commission, 1947.

Podalsky, E.: The swindler: a fascinating sociopath. *Pakistan Medical Journal,* October, 1957, pp. 5-8.

Polsby, N. W.: Toward an explanation of McCarthyism. In Polsby, N.; Dentler, R. A., and Smith, P. A. (Eds.): *Politics and Social Life: An Introduction to Political Behavior.* Boston, Houghton Mifflin, 1963.

Poole, Lynne, and Poole, G.: *The Magnificent Traitor.* New York, Dodd, Mead, 1968.

Pratt, L. A.: *Embezzlement Controls for Business Enterprises.* Baltimore, Fidelity and Deposit Company, 1952.

Quinney, R.: Crime in political perspective. *American Behavioral Scientist,* December, 1964, pp. 19-22.

Reiss, A. J., Jr.: *Field Surveys III: Studies in Crime and Law Enforcement in Major Metropolitan Areas.* Prepared for the President's Commission on Law Enforcement and the Administration of Justice. Washington, D. C., U. S. Government Printing Office, 1967, Vol. I.

Rim, Y.: Machiavellianism and decisions involving risk. *British Journal of Social and Clinical Psychology, 5*(1):30-36, 1966.

Robins, L. N.: *Deviant Children Grown Up.* Baltimore, Williams and Wilkins, 1966.

Roebuck, J. B.: The Negro numbers man as a criminal type: the construction and application of a typology. *Journal of Criminal Law, Criminology and Political Science, 54*:48-60, 1963.

Roebuck, J. B., and Johnson, R.: The 'short con' man. *Crime and Delinquency, 10*:235-248, 1964.

Scarne, J.: *Scarne's Complete Guide to Gambling.* New York, Simon & Schuster, 1961.

Schacter, S.: *The Psychology of Affiliation.* Stanford, Stanford University Press, 1962.

Schisas, P.: *Offenses Against the State in Roman Law.* London, University of London Press, 1926.

Schlesinger, H. J.: Developmental and Regressive Aspects of the Making of Promises. Photocopy of a manuscript, 1969.

Schmideberg, M.: Sincerity. *American Journal of Psychotherapy, 12*:297-299, 1958.

Schur, E. M.: Sociological analysis of confidence swindling. *Journal of Criminal Law, Criminology and Political Science,* September, 1948, pp. 296-304.

Selznick, P.: *The Organizational Weapon. A Study of Bolshevik Strategy.* Glencoe, Ill., Free Press, 1960.

Shaplen, R.: *Kreuger: Genius and Swindler.* New York, Knopf, 1960.

Simmel, G.: *The Sociology of Georg Simmel.* Trans. and edited by K. H. Wolff. New York, Free Press, 1964.

Simon, W. G.: The evolution of treason. *Tulane Law Review, 35*(4):669-704, 1961.

Skolnick, J.: *Justice Without Trial.* New York, Wiley, 1900.

Smith, A.: *The Wealth of Nations.* New York, P. F. Collier, 1909. First published in 1776.

Stricker, L. J.: The true deceiver. *Psychological Bulletin, 68*(1):13-20, 1967.

Strømnes, F. J.: Development and differentiation of acquaintance in engaged and married couples. *Scandinavian Journal of Psychology, 7*(1):34-52, 1966.

Sutherland, E. H.: *White Collar Crime.* New York, Dryden Press, 1949.

Tarsis, V.: *Ward 7.* Translated by Katya Brown. New York, Dutton, 1965.

Ullmann, W.: *The Individual and Society in the Middle Ages.* Baltimore, Johns Hopkins Press, 1966.

Waelder, R.: *Progress and Revolution. A Study of the Issues of Our Age.* New York, International Universities Press, 1967.

Walker, D. F.: *The Modern Smuggler.* London, Secher & Warburg, 1960.

Walster, Elaine, and Walster, B.: The effects of expecting to be liked on choice of associates. *Journal Abnormal Social Psychology, 67*(4):402-404, 1963.

West, Rebecca: *The New Meaning of Treason.* New York, Viking Press, 1964.

Wickersham, G. W.: *Full Text of the Wickersham Commission on Prohibition.* Gerard, Kansas, Haldeman-Julius, 1931.

Wile, I.: Lying as a social phenomenon. *Archives Neurology and Psychiatry, 20*:1283-1311, 1928.

Wile, I.: Lying. *Nervous Child, 2*:293-313, 1942.

Wilensky, H. L.: *Organizational Intelligence.* New York, Basic Books, 1967.

Williams, G.: The correlation of allegiance and protection. *Cambridge Law Journal, 1*:54-76, 1948.

Wise, D., and Ross, T. B.: *The Invisible Government*. New York, Random House, 1964.

Wrightsman, L. S.: Personality and attitudinal correlates of trusting and trustworthy behavior in a two-person game. *Journal Personality and Social Psychology*, 4:328-332, 1966.

Wylie, R.: *The Self Concept*. Lincoln, University of Nebraska Press, 1961.

Zaegel, R. J.: A point rating system for evaluating customers. *The Credit World*, October, 1963, pp. 9-13.

Appendix

CONFIDENCE GAME SCENARIOS
AND ILLUSTRATIONS

Gypsy Bunco

Most of the crime committed by the criminal element of the gypsy society is in the form of a confidence game of some sort and nationally this is known as "gypsy blessing." This starts with the fortune-teller. The fortune-tellers advertise widely in newspapers, by handbills and by word of mouth. They will stop people on the streets or in the stores and ask to tell their fortunes.

The fortune is the forerunner of the "gypsy blessing." It is the gimmick that gets people into the fortune teller's establishment. The gypsy wants someone who has some type of trouble—physical, mental, marital, or it may involve other members of the family. For it is a troubled person on whom the "gypsy blessing" is perpetrated. When the fortune-teller does get a person who is genuinely troubled or worried, then it is time to get started on the gypsy blessing. Through years of training by their parents, the fortune tellers have become practical psychologists, and it is relatively simple for them to discover where the area of trouble or worry may be. The next pitch is to burn candles.

The gypsy fortune-telling establishment is set up with an altar, and no matter what the religious belief of the troubled one is some object from this religion can be found on the altar. The room is usually in semidarkness, and it is simple to substitute a cross for a Buddha or vice versa.

If the victim appears at all susceptible, the gypsy asks for an amount of money to burn candles. They charge for these candles by the pound and are told that these candles are imported

NOTE: The materials in this appendix were prepared by bunco squad officers working in cooperation with the researchers.

from abroad and that the gypsy will say prayers for the person while the candles are burning.

If the victim agrees to the candle burning, then he is asked to bring a certain object and an amount of money with him on his next visit to the fortune-teller. Many of these people (victims) have had a recent death in the family which they have already talked about during the fortune-telling, and the gypsy is very skillful in finding out if there is insurance money or an inheritance as a result of this death. If this is true the victim may be told to bring as much as 500 or 1,000 dollars on his next visit.

Gypsies use two objects in this money scam. A raw egg and a tomato are their favorites. The victim is told to pin the money to his clothing for a certain length of time and at night to put it under his pillow while he sleeps. At the same time they are told not to tell anybody about the money or what they are doing about their bad luck, or the charms will not work.

When the victim next appears at the fortune-teller's, he has his money and the object that the fortune-teller told him to bring—the raw egg. The gypsy takes the egg and the money and lays it on the altar on a handkerchief. She tells the victim that his bad luck is in this evil money and that she will bring out the bad luck and his troubles will be over. The gypsy may pick up the egg and pray over it. While she is doing this, she puts some foreign substance with it—this may be a piece of hamburger, a lock of hair or a small figurine in the form of the devil—and then replaces the egg on the handkerchief and wraps the handkerchief around the egg and the money. The handkerchief is placed on the floor and she asks the victim to step on it. The egg is broken when the victim steps on the handkerchief and when the handkerchief is unfolded, there is the foreign substance mixed with the egg. The gypsy says that this is the evil that has been withdrawn from the victim's body, and she begins to chant a prayer against evil.

The gypsy says that this money brought by the victim is evil money and must be done away with. She may suggest that she will bury it in a cemetery or she may suggest that she give it to her church and this will make it good money again. If it is to be destroyed in front of the victim, play money will have been substituted for the real money.

The victim has been known to go back to the gypsy again and again, and losses up to the sum of 75,000 dollars have been reported.

PIGEON DROP

Victims: Usually middle-aged or elderly women who might have a savings account.

Contact: Made on the street, in a store. Con woman mistakes victim for a friend, to start up a conversation. In a store, she may discuss the merchandise. May ask for directions to a certain place. May ask for help. Sometimes has a sympathy story.

Props: Almost always involves a package or a purse purported to contain valuable papers, currency or bonds which has been found on the street or in the gutter, etc. Con woman #2 is the one who comes up with the found item after con woman #1 has made the contact.

Development: The victim, snagged by con woman #1 is played between #1 and #2 until they have her confidence. Suggest getting advice from someone higher up as to what to do, the value of the package, etc. To share in the proceeds, the victim must put up money to show her good faith.

Preventing a Complaint: The victim, greedy for some "free money," is made to realize that the entire procedure must seem to be off the record, although it has been "blessed" by a higher authority such as a "boss," "big businessman," etc.

Illustrative Cases

Victim: Elderly woman.

Contact: Made at the jewelry counter of an exclusive store. Con woman #1 approached the victim and addressed her as a friend. The victim said she was not her friend but continued talking to her. They moved through the store to another counter and were approached by con woman #2 who said she had found a bag with a lock and key and wanted to share the contents with them.

Development: Victim refused the offer, but said to open the bag and see to whom it belonged. Con woman #2 opened the bag and claimed it contained federal papers. Con woman #1 then picked up the bag from #2 and with the victim and con woman #2, walked outside the store where the contents could be looked at more carefully. It was decided that the contents might be important and the conversation continued among the three and revolved around money investments. Con woman #2 left, saying she was going to talk to her banker about the bag contents. The victim and con woman #1 went to another department store. In this store, a little later, con woman #2 approached them again and reported that her bank would hold the bag and try to find its owner, and that her banker had told her his bank would double the interest on any amount of money. Con woman #1 gave con woman #2 some money to invest. They asked the victim if she had some money to invest and the victim became interested. The three took a taxi to her home where she picked up her bank book and went to her bank. Con woman #1 went with her into the bank to make sure she would withdraw all her money and computed interest which amounted to 3,066.49 dollars. Then they got back in the taxi where con woman #2 was waiting and drove off. While in the cab, victim's money was placed in con woman #1's purse by con woman #1. The cab dropped the two con women and the victim back at the large department store, and con woman #2 left them, saying she had to make a phone call. Con woman #1 went up to the sixth floor of the store with the victim and said she had to make a phone call too, but would be right back. When victim waited for a while and realized what had happened, she became hysterical and the Security Officer of the store was called.

Victim: Elderly woman (71).

Contact: Victim was standing on a street corner when con woman #1 came up to her and called her by a name foreign to her, and when victim stated that was not her name, con woman #1 said she looked enough like her to be her twin sister.

Development: Once the conversation was started, the con woman #1 gained the victim's confidence by telling her that her husband and small child had been killed in an auto accident, and she began crying. The victim tried to calm her down, and just then con woman #2 came up and said she had found 10,000 dollars and would share it with them. But she said they would have to put up money to show good faith. Con woman #1, who earlier had said that she had 7,000 dollars as a result of the auto accident that killed her husband and child, immediately put up what she said was 3,000 dollars and con woman #2 gave her what she said was 6,000 dollars. The victim agreed to put up money but had to go home to get her bank books. Con woman #2 had a car, and the three drove to the victim's home where she picked up her bank books. Then they went to the two banks where she had her accounts and she drew out 2,415 dollars at one bank and 1,600 dollars at the other. Con woman #1 accompanied her into both banks. Back in the car, the victim put all her money in an envelope and gave it to con woman #2. Then they drove to a certain intersection, and the victim was instructed to go to a loan company about three blocks away where her money would be given to her by a loan company officer. She walked to the address and found there was no such address nor any loan company. By the time she walked back to the intersection where she had left the con woman, they were gone.

Victim: Middle-aged woman.

Contact: While walking on the street, the victim was approached by con man who asked her if she knew where the missing bureau was. She asked him what bureau and the con man went on to tell her that he had found some property and produced a white envelope. He said he did not know what was in it.

Development. The con man then opened the envelope and the victim saw a large amount of money in currency and United States Savings Bonds. The con man said he worked at the telephone company on the coin machines and he would have to talk to his boss, but that he did not see why they could not split the money. Then he asked the victim if she had any money and she told him she had a small savings account of 400 dollars. Con man said that if they were going to split the money, she would have to produce a bond of 400 dollars to show that she was interested in the deal. The victim withdrew her 400 dollars from the bank and they went to the telephone building. He told her to wait there while he and his boss counted the money. When he returned he told her there was 25,000 dollars in the envelope and that he would take 400 dollars as part of his cut. She would get her share when she telephoned Mr. White at a certain number. The con man drove off with her 400 dollars, and she went to contact Mr. White and was informed that no such party resided at that address.

Victim: Middle-aged woman (58).

Contact: At the notion counter of a department store. Con woman struck up a conversation about the materials and the prices.

Development: While conversing about the merchandise, con woman #2 approached them with a small brown paper package in her hand and said she had found it in the gutter outside. The package had what appeared as shorthand writing on one side and was ready for mailing. She (con woman #2) said she had taken it to the Post Office, but they had given her the runaround and she did not know what to do with it. She turned the package over and con woman #1 called their attention to a white envelope tucked into a fold of the package. When all three looked inside the envelope, they saw what seemed to be a large amount of currency. Con woman #2 said she was going to take it to her boss who was in the building next door and ask him for his advice and told con woman #1 and the victim to wait for her. Five minutes later she reappeared, and said that her boss had counted the money and there were 12 1,000 dollar bills. He thought it was best for her to split it with the two women she had told about finding it so that they would keep quiet but that they should show good faith by putting up some money to show that they would keep quiet and were responsible people. Con woman #1 said she had 5,500 dollars on her and showed a large bundle of money. Con woman #2 then asked the victim if she had any money in the bank and she replied that she had a little over 3,000 dollars. Con woman #1 gave her money to con woman #2 who said she would go and show it to her boss while the victim and con woman #1 went to the victim's bank to withdraw her money. They were to meet on the mall and when they rendezvoused there with con woman #2, she gave con woman #1's share back to her and then took the victim's money, saying she would show it to her boss. Con woman #2 returned in five minutes and said that her boss had the money and her share of the 12,000 dollars but that he was tied up in a meeting with some men. If she would go to the eighth floor and wait by the elevators, her boss would bring the money out to her. After going to the eighth floor and waiting for twenty minutes, the victim inquired for the "boss" and found there was no such man nor such an office.

CHINESE BUNCO

Tin Sin Kuk

Tin Sin Kuk (Heavenly Swindle), as perpetrated in Hong Kong, is a carefully prepared swindle conducted by a group of professional confidence men. The victims are Canadian, American and Filipino Chinese who return on a visit or retirement with their life savings in their possession. There is reason to suspect that their suitability as victims is made known to the syndicates before their departure for Hong Kong by contacts in overseas Chinese communities.

Victims who have reported their experiences to the police have been so confused and demoralized by the swindlers that their explanations have been clouded by untruths, half truths and exaggeration. For this reason, convictions are nearly impossible.

Tin Sin Kuk is, basically, cheating at gambling, with fan-tan being the most commonly used game, although sometimes a dice game is used. The number of persons comprising a syndicate depends on the intelligence of the victim, the amount of money involved and the length of preparation involved. Sometimes only two or three of the group are actively in the game, but if a full-scale operation is necessary, six people are used, playing the following parts:

1. The "Speaker" or "Introducer," who is the smooth talker who contacts the victim in the course of business, generally

during the time the victim is visiting flats or houses with the intention of investing some of his money in real estate. The Speaker introduces himself as a native of the victim's district, speaking the same dialect and being willing to help the victim meet other friendly businessmen to enable him to purchase real estate on favorable terms.

2. The "Contact Hand" who is eventually responsible for persuading the victim to gamble.
3. The "Old Man," who is the elder statesman of the group and gives the impression of being world-wise and experienced.
4. The "Money Hand," who gives the impression of being extremely rich and also very generous. He operates during the opening stages of the swindle to bolster the confidence of the victim and instill in him trust in people with whom he is dealing.
5. The "Tail," who is introduced to the victim before gambling commences and plays the part of a rich, inexperienced and stupid visitor, in possession of a vast fortune, who has gambling fever and is indifferent to his losses. He is the bait in the trap.
6. The "Assistant," who comes into the picture after the swindle is complete. He acts the part of a "fix man" and "helper" to the victim by offering to negotiate in his behalf for the return of part of his losses and at the same time persuading him it is unwise to report to the police, as the prosecution will be costly.

Development: After the victim has had several meetings with the Introducer, he meets the Contact Hand and eventually learns that the Contact is worried about the actions of an acquaintance of his who is losing vast amounts at gambling and spending more money on women and drink. Would the victim be willing to help them teach this man a lesson by systematically cheating him at gambling? They explain that after they get his money from Tail, they will give him back 50 percent and split the other 50 percent among themselves. This way perhaps the man can be persuaded to reform.

Once the victim has decided to help in the reformation of

Tail, he is introduced to Old Man who teaches him how to cheat at fan-tan in a way that ensures that the banker never loses. Fan-tan is played with counters and revolves around the number 4. The victim is shown how to manipulate one counter so that he always can beat the Tail and win his money. When he has attained enough proficiency, Tail is introduced to the victim and the conversation turns to the subject of gambling. The tail is persuaded to play fan-tan with the victim for small stakes, and at first the victim wins a considerable amount of money.

Tail soon indicates his dissatisfaction with the size of the stakes and begins to talk of amounts running into tens of thousands, refusing to play unless the others can produce a stake which will equal his own. He produces large wads of bills. They decide to meet later and play for larger stakes.

After Tail has left, the remaining members of the group persuade the victim to invest all the money he has available in a common "kitty" into which they place equal or greater amounts with a view to teaching Tail his lesson at the next meeting.

Lucky as he has been at this first game, the victim is easily persuaded to invest his life savings. His money is deposited with the group and they add what appear to be large sums of money. When Tail appears for this session of gambling, the stakes are very high and after a few initial wins, the victim finds that despite his manipulation of the counters, he loses his money and his friends' money too. Tail departs with all the money.

Now the victim is blamed for losing. The others claim he has made mistakes in manipulating the counters and they find counters in his trouser cuffs or on the floor. They allege he has been careless and dropped the counters. The victim, appalled by his losses, really believes that he is to blame. He promises to mortgage his property, to borrow money, to do anything he can to obtain another stake to play once more with Tail and win back the money for himself and his friends. After raising more money and losing it again to the Tail, the victim realizes that he has been the subject of fraud. And at this stage the Assistant appears, who tells the victim he has been cheated but that through his help he may be able to get part of his money back if he agrees not to go to the police. It is arranged that the victim get back 10 percent to 20 percent of his losses, and he is sent to a solicitor's office to pick it up. He is given a predated IOU to take with him, properly signed by the Old Man and payable on the date the victim goes to the solicitor. The solicitor writes a letter to the Old Man demanding payment of the amount due on the IOU, the amount is paid and a receipt given to the victim.

The amount returned to the victim depends on his character and his potential as a source of trouble should he report the incident to the police. The negotiations to recover even 10 percent take a long time, many meetings are held, and other persons introduced who offer to act as go-betweens and who give much advice. The confused victim finally feels he is lucky to have even this pittance and that he has done reasonably well in the whole affair.

Other Forms of Tin Sin Kuk Swindle

Running second to Fan Tan is a dice game using loaded dice influenced by a magnet held under the table, and here the victim is taught to utilize the magnet, enabling particular results to be obtained. Of course when he plays the big game with the Tail, the dice are substituted.

Another form of Tin Sin Kuk involves an invitation to the victim to invest in an illegal operation such as the importation of dangerous drugs which are later reported to have been seized by the government and therefore the investment is lost. In this operation, the victim is made to part with more money by pretending it is to be used as a bribe to insure immunity from arrest for participating in an illegal operation.

Illustrative Case

Victim: Elderly Chinese, furrier, owner of rental property.

Contact: Victim advertised vacancy in paper, two Chinese women phoned and asked about the property, saying they were from Singapore, but they really wanted to buy property. They asked what business the victim was in and when informed that he was a furrier, they wanted to know where the store was located.

Development: The next day, the two women called at his store and looked at some of the furs. They admired the furs and told the victim that they had a friend who wanted to buy some expensive fur coats; he was a wealthy owner of a rice plantation in.........and would the victim be willing to bring several of his best coats to..........to show to him?

The furrier went to the address the next day, taking several fur coats with him and was introduced to the wealthy plantation owner. He said the coats were to be purchased by his rich nephew, who was not there at the moment, and that when the victim showed him the coats, he should charge 10 percent over the actual cost as his commission. He gave a lengthy story about his nephew, how he was throwing his money away on women and gambling, but that he always listened to him. Arrangements were made to meet the nephew the next day, but when the victim arrived the next day the story was that the nephew had lost 10,000 dollars gambling the night before and he had just been to the bank to get money to pay the gambling debt. He showed the victim a large roll of money and put it back in his pocket. Then the con man started talking about teaching his nephew a lesson; that he knew a gambler who would show them how to win his money from him. The con man said he would phone the man, and he did, and in about half an hour, a Chinese appeared on the scene. He showed the victim how to play fan-tan (4 points) and explained how to signal about the number of buttons left so parties could bet on them and stick the nephew.

Con man #1 suggested that the victim bring about 5,000 dollars and between the four of them, the woman, con man #1 and con man #2 (the gambler), and the victim, they would have 20,000 dollars and could beat the nephew out of 50,000 dollars and teach him a lesson.

The victim was told to get the money and return the next night for the game. When he did not return, the con men called him several times, but he told them he did not gamble and did not want to play.

✗ BANK SWINDLE OR TREASURY AGENT BUNCO

This swindle is based on enlisting the aid of "reliable" persons to trap dishonest bank employees. (But of course the one who is really trapped is the "reliable" person.) The *modus operandi* for the bank swindle is thorough and painstaking background work plus a carefully timed and executed plan when working the scam.

There are at least two con men, sometimes three or four involved in this game. The two main con men enter a town separately and check into one of the finer hotels. After renting a car, usually a Cadillac or other impressive-appearing model, they go on a tour of the town looking for either a lower middle-class rental area where they try to find out who owns the buildings or a middle-class residential section where the homes are well-kept. They jot down the addresses of several of these homes and then go to the public library and obtain the names corresponding to the addresses from the city directory. Then a bowling alley, restaurant, bar, etc., with a readily available phone is located, near the area where they will be working. Another method of obtaining names is to go to an outlying bank. the one where presumably these people do their banking, and stand in line at the teller's windows in an attempt to observe account numbers and amounts of deposits and withdrawals. The victims selected are preferably 60- to 80-year-old widows.

Having obtained a list of victims, a handy phone and the bank to be dealt with, the two con men retire to their apartment, and a very important part of the swindle begins. This is telephoning the victim, and usually one of the con men is a specialist at this. Posing as a Federal agent or a bank security officer, the con man telephones the victim, advises her that the bank suspects one of its tellers to be an embezzler and asks her to cooperate in trapping him. If she agrees, she is told to go to the bank, withdraw a specified sum of cash and take it home in an envelope. Adding a touch of realism, the man may caution her to wear gloves. He says they will send a taxi to pick her up and take her home again after the money is withdrawn, or sometimes they use their own car with a man hired from the local underworld as the driver. Arrangements are made to pick up the envelope at her home so that the money can be checked for fingerprints and serial numbers and then returned to her saving account. A different underling is used for this job; sometimes to make the elderly victim feel that he or she is playing "cops and robbers" he will identify himself as being Agent So-and-So or even identify himself by a code number. The phone staked out near the victim's house is the one used for this call, since the con men can ascertain when she comes home from the bank and call as quickly as possible. Many times, the victim is offered a reward for her help and in this case she is told that the amount will be deposited along with her money after it has been checked by the "bank examiner."

The con men have an almost foolproof way of ascertaining if their victims have enough money to really bother about. When the con man who is the telephone specialist calls, identifies himself as being with the Treasury Department, he says that they believe one of the bank tellers is shorting the customers and that the victim's bank balance is several hundred dollars short. The victim is asked to check his bank book and give the amount of balance shown in the book. If the balance is too small to bother with, the con man says the victim is lucky, it is someone else who has been shorted, but if the balance is high, the answer will be that the victim's account is short by a certain amount and then comes the pitch to try and catch the guilty teller. He (the victim) is cautioned to say nothing to anyone in the bank when he draws, say, 2,500 dollars from his account, and he is also asked how he wants his reward check made out. In some cases, this spurious check is given to the victim plus a receipt for the money he has drawn out when the con man goes to the victim's home to pick up the money, check it, and redeposit it. This bank swindle is usually worked on a Friday, since with the banks closed on the weekend, the average victim will not try to contact either the con man or the bank until the following Tuesday. By then the con men are in a different area, working a different bank.

A variation of this swindle has occurred when the victim has a very sizable bank account. On the first run, she is told to go to a certain teller—that he is the one the bank examiners are checking. After she has turned over her money, they call her later in the afternoon and report that the teller checked out all right and ask her to go through the same process the next day with another designated teller. For a third time, they tell her she has done a wonderful job but that the fingerprints were smudged and they will have to repeat it, "you will have to do it again tomorrow."

The success of this swindle is primarily because once the victim is set up, she is never out of surveillance by the con men or their employees. Someone watches her house, one is outside the bank and having observed her in the bank can call off the game if she has talked to the teller by giving a hand signal to the con man in the car who will follow her home. If anyone goes into her home when she comes back from the bank or if anything appeared unusual during the withdrawal of the money, the con men will abandon the attempt.

This swindle did not originate in the United States but in a neighboring country, and most of the money swindled was sent there by Western Union under code names and addresses. However, the cities along the western coast have been systematically worked the last three years; the game has been "taught" to native con men, although they still seem to have one of the foreign cons in each group. Another gang is working on the east coast with as good results for the gang.

Illustrative Case

Victim: Elderly widow.

Contact: By telephone.

Development: The first step was telephone contact by someone saying he was a bank examiner and that he had discovered someone was tampering with her account. He said that they needed her to withdraw money to complete their investigation and that she would receive a 500 dollar reward if she did this. The victim said she would help and called her bank, asking to withdraw 7,800 dollars. Mrs. X gave the wrong account number, although she did have an account at that bank; she asked that the money be delivered to her home. In this instance, the assistant cashier felt that something was wrong and called the Fraud Detail, who sent two men over to Mrs. X's house to check with her. She repeated her story and was convinced that she was about to be victimized, after the game had been explained to her. It was suggested that she go along with the con men, but she said she did not want to because she had a bad heart. While the two men from the Fraud Detail were at the house, the phone rang seven times. Once she was instructed to go to the bank and she said she could not because of her health. The caller called back and said he would send a cab to pick her up. A policewoman was summoned and came and heard some of the phone conversations, and it was arranged for her to pose as Mrs. X. The con man sent a cab and the policewoman went to the bank. The teller to whom she went was aware of the circumstances and gave her a brown envelope containing a one-dollar bill and six bank writing pads. The policewoman picked up the package and came back to the house. She said she thought she was observed in the bank but was not sure. As soon as she was in the house, the phone rang and Mrs. X answered. Yes, she answered, she had the money, it was in a brown envelope and in hundred-dollar bills.

She was told that a man named A.......... would call to get the money and he would be Code 3. In five minutes he arrived and said he was Mr. A. .... The policewoman had put on one of Mrs. X's dresses because she had said she would be wearing a gingham dress, and she ushered Mr. A in. She questioned him as to whether he was the bank examiner and he said yes, he was Code 3. The money, she said, was in the other room and as they walked into the other room and he reached for the brown envelope he was arrested.

The "bank examiner" turned out to be a minor criminal and had been hired for 100 dollars to come to the house of the victim and pick up a package. He was to walk a block to the next corner where he was to give the package to a man in a 1963 Ford. In his pocket was a fake badge which said "Detective," and he said he had been instructed to show it to the victim if she did not want to give him the package.

The other members of the gang were picked up later by police at two separate apartments and in two cars.

However, before being apprehended, the con men had been successful in fleecing many elderly widows of many hundreds of thousands of dollars.

Since the telphone call to the victim in a bank swindle is all important in setting up the game, the following script (found on an arrested con man) is included:

> Hello, Mrs. Jones? Mrs. Jones, this is the bank calling. We're having a little trouble here in the accounts that we are trying to straighten out. Do you have your bank book handy? Would you get it please? I would like the last entry date in your book. The date was? Fine, Mrs. Jones, now what is the last balance in your book? Twenty-two thousand dollars and forty cents? That's fine, Mrs. Jones. Your account is correct. Right, sorry to have troubled you, goodbye.

After this initial contact, the con man phones again and, again according to this script, says, in part:

> Hello, Mrs. Jones, this is the bank calling again. Are you alone? Are you free to talk? My name is Sherlock, ma'am. I am with the security police. There has been quite an amount of pilfering from the accounts that we have been called upon to investigate. . . . This is what we intend to do. We are going to take your card out of the master file and substitute another card. The card that will replace your card in the master file will show a balance of only two thousand two hundred and six dollars and forty cents. Now I want you to go to the bank—I'll send a car for you—and make a withdrawal of four thousand nine hundred and forty dollars. If the particular teller that you go to honors your withdrawal, knowing that the card shows only a balance of two thousand two hundred and six dollars and forty cents, then of course we will know that she is one of the thieves. . . . Now do you have a pair of gloves that you would wear? . . .

The script goes on, spinning a tale of intrigue that often sounds quite believable to elderly people who may lack the mental alertness to deal with clever con men.

MEXICAN CHARITY BUNCO

This bunco is so named because the victim is almost always a person of Mexican or Latin-American descent, and the con men involved are Spanish speaking and of Mexican appearance.

The Mexican charity bunco is usually a leisurely affair; several days may be used meeting in coffeehouses, churches, etc. In fact, the Catholic church in the town or area where the con men are working is often used as a rendezvous. In one case, the con men and the victim spent two hours in the church praying and lighting candles to the success of their undertaking. In fact, several intended victims were left "sitting in the church" when the con men felt something was not going right and called off the game.

Contact with the victim may be made on the street or in a department store, and the conversations are almost always carried on in Spanish. Contact is usually a plea for assistance, and the assistance is associated with death or sympathy—funeral payments, abortions, doctors' bills, go home to see a dying relative, settling estates and buying tombstones, etc. The "honesty and good faith" of the victim is always appealed to.

Small purses are involved in this game—the switch purse is a small purse (small enough to go under a coat or shirt) and is found to be sewed shut and filled with cut-up newspaper.

Illustrative Cases

Victim: Elderly Mexican woman.

Contact: In large department store.

Development: A Mexican woman, speaking excellent Spanish, approached the victim in the store and asked help in looking for Dr. ....; she had just arrived from Mexico and did not know how to go about finding a doctor in a city. On the victim's offer of help, she told her the following story: Years ago, her (the con woman's) father had worked in the city hospital as an orderly and, finding 500 dollars under the mattress of a patient, had stolen it and went to Mexico where he prospered and became a very rich man. After a heart attack, he confessed his theft to his priest who advised him that if he gave a large sum to charity, his sin would be forgiven. So her trip was to find the doctor and give him 8,000 dollars to be given to any reliable charity. The important thing is not necessarily finding the doctor but seeing that the money (she shows a roll of bills) goes to a worthy charity. Just then a Mexican man (con man) came up and asked in Spanish if he could be of help. After hearing the story, he suggested that he and the victim each be given 1,000 dollars for their trouble and they would take the 6,000 dollars left and give it to charity and needy people. The con woman was delighted—now she can go home before her father dies knowing that his wish is taken care of and that his sin will be forgiven. "But how can I trust you?" asked the con woman. The con man said he had cash and showed a roll of bills. The victim said she had money in a savings account and she was persuaded to draw 2,000 dollars from her account and meet the con man and con woman in the coffee shop of the department store in an hour. When she had drawn out her money and returned to the coffee shop, the con man took her money and put it in his wallet with his money, handed it back to the victim to hold and said he had to do a small errand and would be back in a minute. In five minutes, he was back and the victim handed the wallet back to him. Then the con woman asked the victim to buy a small box of Kotex for her, and when she came back she would give them the 8,000 dollars. When the victim returned, both were gone.

Victim: Elderly Mexican woman.

Contact: In front of a bank.

Development: Con man #1, nicely dressed, neat, approached victim, asking for help. Spoke excellent Spanish. Said he had just arrived from Costa Rica, was looking for his runaway sister and would pay 6,000 dollars to find her. When victim suggested contacting several agencies, con man #1 "confessed" that his sister had run away from home because she was pregnant and her father threatened to kill her boy friend. He further "confessed" that she had died after an abortion and what he really wanted was someone to take care of paying the doctor bills, funeral expenses, etc., so he could return home. Anything over, the victim could keep. Just then con man #2, also Mexican, came up and he was told the same story. He was very smpathetic and offered to help out of the kindness of his heart and to prove his goodness, he went in the bank and came out with a roll of money, which he said was 4,000 dollars. Victim went into the bank and withdrew 4,400 dollars. Con man #2 put this money in a white zippered money purse with his own and they returned to con man #1. The money of con man #1 was put in the white purse and con man #1 showed the victim how to conceal the purse under her coat for safety. Then he gave her an identical white purse and the two con men left. The purse was found to be sewed shut and to be filled with newspaper cuttings.

Victim: 86-year old man of Mexican descent.

Contact: Outside store as old man was window shopping.

Development: Con man #1, speaking Spanish, said he was looking for a man with money. He (con man #1) had just come to the United States from San Salvador to purchase a tombstone for the grave of his boss's daughter but he was being pressed to return home and had to find an honest man who would take care of the tombstone placing for him. He showed the victim a roll of bills which he said was 9,000 dollars—this he would give to a dependable person for buying and placing the tombstone and for making a contribution to the Church and for needy people; the rest he could keep for himself. However, he did require that the person produce 3,000 dollars to qualify for the task. Con man #2 approached and talked himself into the game. When the victim advised con man #1 that he could get only 1,500, con man #2 volunteered to put up the rest of the amount. All adjourned to a coffeehouse, where con man #2 produced his 1,500 dollars and urged victim to get his money. He accompanied the victim to his home (for his savings account book) and back downtown to the bank where the victim withdrew 1,500 dollars.

At the second meeting at the coffeehouse, the victim produced his money and it was placed in a small plastic zippered purse by con man #1, along with the rest of the money in his possession. Con man #1 then asked to borrow the victim's watch because he had to take medication at a certain time and did not have his watch with him. Victim volunteered to pay the cafe bill, but was refused by #1 who asked to inspect the victim's half dollar and kept it without the victim's realization.

The three left and walked to the Catholic church two blocks away, where victim was given the zipper purse (switched) to put inside his shirt. He was told to walk in, opposite direction to allay suspicion and con man #2 walked with him a short way and said he would meet him at his house to divide the money; then he followed con man #1. Three blocks further, on his way home, he met a friend and told him of his marvelous luck. They both inspected the purse which was found to be sewn shut and contained cut-up newspaper. Also gone were one watch and fifty cents!

Victim: 68-year-old man of Latin-American descent.

Contact: Business area of the city.

Development: The victim is accosted by a man asking to be referred to a trustworthy bank because he had a lot of money which he feared to lose. Con man #1 displayed a large roll of money, insinuating that it was in excess of five or six thousand dollars. Then he asked the victim if he knew a man named Antonio Saenz, who was reportedly in the real estate business, adding that this money was to be given to him for certain purposes. He indicated that he, himself, was from South America. The victim was unable to tell him of a man by that name and started to walk away, whereupon con man #1 hailed a second stranger and asked him the same questions. The full story was that the money was to be given to Antonio Saenz. Of it, 1,500 dollars was to pay the hospital bill of his recently deceased sister and 1,500 dollars was to be spent for funeral expenses and a monumental stone. An additional 1,500 dollars was to be given to Mr. Saenz for his trouble." Con man #2 suggested that the money be given to the victim, as he appeared to be an honest man and could handle the jobs easily.

The next day (Saturday), the three met and continued the conversation. They decided to talk more about it on Monday and at that time talked once more about the items to be taken care of with this sum of money. On Saturday, it had been decided that con man #2 and the victim would divide the 1,500 dollars originally meant for Mr. Saenz, but now, at this third meeting, con man #1 became concerned about entrusting the money to the victim and requested that the victim prove his solvency by withdrawing any savings he might have in the bank. He was not satisfied at seeing the passbook, he wanted to see the money, and so the victim agreed and withdrew 950 dollars from his bank.

Now the three went to the Catholic church where for two hours they prayed and lit candles, asking God's blessing on their undertaking. On leaving the church, con man #2 developed a toothache and the three went to the nearby hospital to see if he could get relief. The wait in the hospital appeared to be long, and the victim was advised to go home and wait for them. Con man #1, still fearful of losing his money, gave it to the victim to hold until they were through at the hospital. In giving the victim his money, con man #1 reached under the victim's shirt, showing how he should carry the money so as not to lose it. At the same time, he managed to mix his money with the victim's money, placing it all in a handkerchief and then tying a knot in the handkerchief. (Obviously the switch was made at this time.) The victim arrived home, and desiring to see the money, untied the handkerchief and found nothing but a stack of blank checks.

GOLD SWINDLE

The gold swindle con game is based on buying gold ore at below the market price and reselling it at the market price.

Illustrative Case

Victim: Owner of a tourist park.

Contact: Con man stopped at the tourist park which had in conjunction with it a small "museum" where there was a display of western relics, among them a display of gold coins. Conversation was begun over this collection of coins when the con man "tourist" said he knew where some gold could be bought cheaply and then resold at the regular market price.

Development: The victim became interested in this gold deal because he wanted to set up college trust funds for his two children and this sounded like a good way to guarantee them. The con man said he would have to make some phone calls and see if the deal was still offered—if the gold ore was still available at the below market price. After several phone calls and several return visits by the con man to the tourist park, he said he had it arranged and gave the victim his instructions. He was to take his money—his life savings of 30,000 dollars and meet in a certain

town with a young couple who knew the "gold salesman" and
they would take him to the place where the gold ore would be
turned over. According to the con man's instruction, the victim
wrapped his money in neat packages and went to the designated
town where he met the young couple and a man who said he
was a physician and the owner of the gold ore. The four got in
the car of the young couple and drove up into the hills where,
in a deserted area, the "physician" took out a gun, identified
himself as an FBI agent, took the 30,000 dollars and drove off
in the young couple's car. Along with this swindle, the tourist
park owner had paid out 3,000 dollars in fees to the con man
who originally contacted him for "expenses" in working out
the deal.

The young couple had been "hired" for 2,000 dollars to carry
out their part in the swindle—although they swore they didn't
know it was a swindle—and on the loss of their car, they reported
their part and returned their fee.

GOLD MINE SWINDLE

Westerners are particularly apt to go for the gold mine
swindle, for since the days of the Forty-Niners, there have been
tales of lost gold mines. The tale of the Lost Dutchman gold
mine is familiar to many persons. This gold mine swindle
involved the Padre Del Oro mine, a fabulous mine that could
be a bonanza if the money was available to reopen and rework it.

Illustrative Case

Victims: from all walks of life, investing amounts large and
small in the grandiose dream of the Padre del Oro mine.

Contact: The con man presented himself at a Catholic church
several years ago, saying he had just come to the parish and
wanted to be a good parishioner. He offered to make a sub-
stantial contribution to the church. He mentioned the sum of
25,000 dollars which would be available as soon as he completed
the financing for the mine.

Development: One priest was so impressed with the tale of
this mine that he got another priest to go in with him and they

invested 5,000 dollars. Several other church officials, many parishioners, and many others invested. For the money they gave him, the con man gave each one a promissory note and a grant deed on a mining claim. He said that he needed 3,000,000 to begin taking gold out of the mine. He offered to return 10 percent on any investment within thirty, sometimes ninety days. A partial listing of these "loans" came to 316,700 dollars. The number of actual investors in the mine is not known, but action was brought by thirteen, one of whom had gone to the State Division of Corporations. The mine was not even on property owned by the con man and was a worked-out placer mine which no one would bother working.

The con man for this "gold mine swindle" had a "tongue of gold," for he stalled off his victims for four years after they had invested their money before any question as to his honesty was raised.

COIN SMACK AND/OR MOVIE PRODUCER SCAM

Victim: The victim in this type of bunco is approached, for example, at a busy downtown intersection. If the con man is a "specialist," he may pick only victims from say, Australia, usually identified by the typical Aussie dress, with the victim usually carrying a Quantas or BOAC flight bag and sometimes taking pictures of the street scene.

Contact: The con man makes contact with the victim with general conversation and tells the victim he is also Australian, making sure that he is from a different part of Australia than that of the victim. After a brief conversation, the con man asks the victim to have a cup of coffee at the nearest restaurant. The victim is agreeable and they proceed to the restaurant.

Development: During this interval, there is a "Tail" (con man #2) who goes ahead to the restaurant, and when con man #1 and victim arrive at the restaurant they seat themselves at a nearby table. During the conversation in the restaurant, the con man tries to learn whether the victim is on vacation and when he is planning to leave town. (Most of the victims are on a tour of the United States and England and have a planned itinerary, travelling in a group.) Usually included in the itinerary is a short trip to Los Angeles. The con man asks the intended victim, during the conversation in the restaurant, if he is interested in Hollywood and would he like to meet some movie stars and visit one of the studios. If he is interested, he (con man #1) can arrange it, as his son is a movie producer and will be in town the following day and he would be glad to get tickets for him (the victim). At this point, the victim gives the con man his address (hotel and room number), his name and telephone number. Con man #1 tells the victim that he will telephone him the following morning and bring him the tickets.

About ten o'clock the following morning, the con man phones the victim from the lobby of his hotel (usually a major hotel) and asks him to meet him downstairs in the lobby. As soon as the victim arrives, con man #1 tells him that his son will be a little late and they should have a cup of coffee while they are waiting for him. The two leave the hotel, go to a coffee shop, order coffee and begin conversing.

At this point, con man #2 enters the scene and states "he's from Texas and could not help overhearing what they were talking about," and wants to buy them another cup of coffee. He joins the party and the conversation eventually turns to sportsmanship, whereupon con man #2 tells the victim and con man #1 that he had heard that "all Limies and Aussies" are bum sports. Con men #1 and #2 begin flipping coins and #2 loses about 25 dollars. At this point, con man #1 whispers to victim, "Let's show him what good sports we are; you hold "Heads" and I'll hold "Tails" and we'll take his money and give it back to him." During this operation, con man #2 loses about 500 dollars while the victim is holding the money. Angrily, con man #2 gets up from the table and starts to walk away, saying he is going to get the police, because he thinks that if he had won, they would not have paid off.

Con man #1 hurriedly produces a roll of bills, and the victim produces a book of Traveler's Checks. In his Texas drawl, con man #2 says, "Those ain't cash and they aren't good." Con man #1 asks the Texan if he would forget about calling the police if he can prove to him that he can cash the traveller's checks.

The two con men take the victim to the bank and cash the money orders and return to the restaurant. Con man #2 says, "I'll flip you once for five-hundred dollars," and the victim, feeling he cannot lose, flips while con man #1 holds the money for the victim and con man #2. Con man #2 does lose, and he makes a scene and then runs toward the door, saying he is going to get the police. Con man #1 tells the victim, "Let's split company —I'll meet you in the hotel lobby in five minutes." After the victim has waited for an hour in the lobby for con man #1, he calls the police.

Note: On certain smacks, the con man will call the victim at his hotel and tell him that the "Texan" was hit by a car as he ran into the street and that "it looks bad—I don't think he will live." There were many police around asking questions when he (con man) left to make this phone call. This call is made to the victim intending to scare him into not calling the police.

COIN SMACK

Game: The quick buck.

Contact place: Bus stations, amusement parks, bars, airports, train stations.

Victims: Prefer person from out of town or on way out of town; usually young males (students, sailors, soldiers) or older men (of apparent foreign descent). Victims are usually unavailable for later information since they are on the way to or from someplace and are thus reluctant to lodge protests.

Illustrative Cases

Victim: Tourist at Disneyland, Canadian, male.

Contact: While victim was "doing" Disneyland, con man #1 struck up conversation and asked if the victim was interested in the movies. On receiving an affirmative answer, he said that he was a movie producer and if victim would meet him at the ....Hotel he would show him through his studio.

Development: Victim met con man #1 at the hotel and they went, on the suggestion of the con man, to a nearby coffee shop where they ordered coffee and began talking. In a few minutes, they were joined by con man #2 who insinuated himself into the conversation. Con man #1 and #2 began matching coins, using nickels and showing the victim how the game worked. After victim joined in the game, con man #1 kept raising the price of the coin flip, and before he knew it, the victim had lost 600 dollars. He signed over traveller's checks to cover loss.

Victim: Young white college student.

Contact: Outside bus depot.

Development: "Where are you bound for?" On reply of a certain state, the con man said, "That's where I'm going too; how about a cup of coffee while we wait for the bus?" Since the depot restaurant was crowded, the con man #1 suggested that they go to a nearby pancake house—it would be less crowded and they could talk about their trip. On the way, they met con man #2, and con man #1 and con man #2 started matching coins. After many games, con man #1 won 500 dollars from con man #2. Immediately con man #2 started complaining that he had been gypped and did not want to pay up—perhaps he had better get the police. Whereupon con man #1 says, "Tell you what I'll do. If our friend here will let me count the money in his wallet, I'll subtract the amount from what you've lost and pay you the rest. Okay?" Con man #2 calmed down and said he will go along with that and not make any trouble. Victim gave con man #1 his wallet, counted the contents and returned it to the victim. Con man pays con man #2 the difference ($365) and he goes on down the street. Con man #1 goes in the opposite direction and the victim starts back for the bus depot. On the way he checks his wallet and finds that the contents, $135, are gone.

Victim: Young white male (17 years old).

Contact: Inside bus depot.

Development: Con man #1 approached victim and asked where he was going. Victim said he was waiting for a bus to an eastern state, but that it did not leave for a while. "Good," said the con man, "I want to buy a dress for my daughter who is about your age. Come and help me pick it out." On the street, they were approached by con man #2 who sauntered along with them, telling them that he was from Canada and that his sister had died and left him real estate and he had about

1,100 dollars and wanted to know how to spend it. Con man #1 said, "Let's flip coins for it." Victim and con man #1 started matching against #2, and the victim soon lost all his money. Con man #1 said reassuringly, "Never mind, kid, we're partners," and then said to con man #2, "Let's match for 500 dollars." They matched and con man #2 lost and said "How do I know you could pay me if *you* lost?" Con man #1 showed a roll of bills and con man #2 says, "I still think I've been conned; I'm going to call the police." As con man #1 and the victim went down the street, con man #2 followed them, complaining bitterly. Finally con man #1 said to the victim, "We've got to shake this guy. You go back to the station and I'll meet you there and give you your share of the money when I get rid of this guy." Victim complied, and on the way back to the station realized he has lost 54 dollars.

Victim: German male in his middle thirties.

Contact: Outside bus depot, at phone booths.

Development: The victim, speaking broken English, was obviously having trouble in placing a phone call. Con man #1 offered to help, and found out that the victim is newly arrived in the country and trying to phone his new employer, the owner of a bakery. Con man #1 said he would be glad to put the call through for the victim and told him to go sit down on a bench along the outside wall of the depot and he would call him when he gets his party. In a few minutes, he comes out and said he could not get the call through, but that he would try again in a few minutes. While they were sitting on the bench, con man #2 approached, appearing very drunk, and sat down with them. Con man #1 and con man #2 start matching coins. When con man #1 loses his money to con man #2, he asked victim for the loan of his money and victim complied. Con man #1 won all of con man #2's money and con man #2, acting drunkenly, said he has been gypped and he was going to call the police. Con man #1 told victim to go back into the depot, he would get this character calmed down and then come in and give him back the money he had borrowed from him. Victim complies, and of course con man #1 never comes in.

Note: The con man's mention of the police caused victim

to comply readily with their moves. He was not anxious to get involved with the police, coming into a new country and starting on a new job. Speaking broken English, he was also at a disadvantage.

BLOCK HUSTLE

Most con men or bunco men, when they first arrive in town, size up what the action is and use what is called the "short con" for expense money.

The block hustle is sometimes a false jewelry scam. In most major cities, a con man can buy a set of rings for about 2 dollars, and for an additional 50 cents can purchase the box. These rings are tagged with a blue tag, with the price written in white ink. The pitch is that the peddler was employed by a crooked Jew who had beat him out of some money and now he (the peddler) is going to beat him. The con man also infers that the rings are stolen. He will ask the victim (sucker) for any amount he can pay, with the con man making between 10 dollars and 75 dollars for this dodge.

A variation of this is the block hustle of a watch which looks beautiful and is made just for this type of pitch. These watches are known in the trade as "pin levers" and contain no jewels. A good watch hustler can make up to 100 dollars a day.

Other Phony Sales

Perfume Scams: Another variation of the block hustle is the block perfume hustle. This is perfume packaged to look like a well-known brand, such as "Jade East," which is a best seller. The block brand is named "Oriental Jade." All these perfume hustles have a large price tag on the bottom of the bottles, along with a French label. Some hustlers have gone as far as to show a full-page ad of the perfume taken from one of the large magazines. These ads are reproduced by the hustlers to show the merit of the product. Chanel #5 is always used by hustlers, with a perfect reproduction of the bottle and with a very plain white label. At holiday time, this brand is the greatest hustle in the perfume racket, with the hustlers easily making

100 dollars a day. Another block perfume is called "White Christmas," which, of course, the sucker believes to be "Christmas Night."

Barking Dog Scam: Most hustlers fall back on the barking dog toy, which is hustled on the street. The dog jumps and barks so loud you cannot believe it. Do not believe it! The bark is produced by a whistle in the hustler's mouth which cannot be detected by the buyer because the buyer is watching the dog on the sidewalk. The hustler is careful to place a whistle in each box, and if the customer complains, the hustler will refund his money on the spot. Of course the hustler is continually moving and changing locations.

Razor Scam: Along with the above pitches is the electric razor hustle. The razor is packaged in a beautiful case along with a guarantee and a large price tag on the bottom. This little item is made just for this type of hustle and costs the hustler about 3 dollars. He usually gets 20 dollars for these razors. The name of this razor is "Underwood," and of course the customer confuses this name with the regular Remington electric razor.

JAMAICAN SWITCH

The Jamaican switch is so named because the participants sometimes pose as sailors off ships just in from British Guiana or some part of the West Indies. Sometimes the pair of con men will consist of a Negro and a white. This is also true when the participants are women.

Illustrative Case

Victim: Negro male.

Contact: In street, in district frequented by mixed races.

Development: The con man came up to victim as he was leaving his car and showed him a piece of paper with the words "EAGLE ROCK HOTEL, PEERGREEN ST." He asked the victim where it was, and when the victim told him he did not know, the con man, who spoke with a Jamaican-Spanish accent, said he would give him 50 dollars to go to a phone booth and locate this hotel. They walked up the street until they found a phone booth and the victim entered the phone booth, with con man #1 standing in the door. Con man #1 spoke to a man who was passing (con man #2) and asked him if he knew of this hotel. Con man #2 said he had been a cab driver and asked to see the slip of paper and said, after reading the address, that there was no such hotel or address. Then he asked con man #1 how long he was going to be in the city. Con man #1 said he was a seaman on a banana boat docked at the terminal and would be in town for thirty days. Con man #1 then flashed a large roll of bills and asked con man #2 where he could get a girl. Con man #2 said that he should put the money in the bank, that someone would rob him; he even offered to put the money in the bank for him. Con man #1 stated that he would give con man #2 100 dollars if he would get him a redheaded white girl. Then con man #2 asked the victim if he had a car. If he had, he could fix the sailor up in no time. They drove to a certain address and con man #2 went around the corner and came back in ten minutes saying that everything was fixed, that he had located the girl. He told con man #1 to leave his money with the victim so he would not be robbed. Con man #1 said, "How do you know I can trust him?" and that he had a money belt with 4,000 dollars in it and 1,500 dollars in his pocket and that the Captain of his ship had told him that he could not trust "niggers." Con man #2 then said that he would give his money to the victim and con man #1, and they could drive off and return, showing he trusted both of them. On returning, the victim returned the money to con man #2. Then con man #1 stated, "You niggers don't own anything in this country—the white man wouldn't give you anything. If you can show me 2,000 dollars, I'll give you 1,000 dollars." The three go to the victim's home and he shows them his bank book which shows 2,150 dollars. Con man #1 kept saying that that did not mean anything—"You can't withdraw money from the white man's house." The victim kept insisting that he could get the money, and con man #1 said, "Well, if you can get the money and this fellow here can get me the girl, I'll give you the money I promised you." The three go to a bank, and con man #1 stays in the car while con man #2 goes into the bank with the victim, who withdraws 2,000 dollars. Upon returning to the car, victim shows con man #1 the money and he still argues about it, saying that the "white man" had just loaned the money to the victim so he could make 1,000 dollars. Finally, con man #2 convinces con man #1 that the money was really withdrawn, and #1 says, "Okay, let's go and get the girl," and they drive to a certain street corner, park the car, and both con men get out. Con man #2 tells con man #1 to leave his money with the victim and con man #1 says, no, he still does not trust either one of them. Con man #2 asks victim for his money and says he will hold con man #1's money as well. Victim hands over his 2,000 dollars and con man #1 gives his money to con man #2 as well. They tell victim to wait in the car, as they will be right back, and of course they never return.

Reported Abortive Cases

Victim: White middle-aged male.

Contact: On public street, while waiting for a bus. Approached by young Negro male who spoke with a Jamaican accent and struck up conversation with the victim.

Development: Con man asks for street directions, telling the following story. He was a sailor from a banana boat from British Guiana and was on his way to visit his sister in a southern city. He had met a colored streetwalker who solicited him for 20 dollars. He gave her the money plus extra for whiskey and she had told him to go to the Elkhorn Hotel on Peagreen Street. But he did not know where it was; if the victim would help him look up the hotel address in the phone book he would give him 20 dollars. He insisted on walking up a block or two in case he would see the hotel while they were looking for a phone booth. While they were walking up the street, the victim asked a Negro male coming out of a house if he knew where the hotel was. The con man exhibited a large roll of money and both the victim and the colored man told him to put it in a bank. The con man said, "No, banks are only for Jews, they steal from colored people." When the conversation revealed that the victim had less than 100 dollars in the bank, the con man said he didn't trust either of them and hurriedly walked away.

Notes: The victim went back to wait for his bus and reported that he saw the con man walking down the street with a different colored man. Obviously the victim spoiled the game by accosting the man coming out of the house; he was not a con man. Apparently not enough money was involved to be interesting, as the victim had only 100 dollars. There was a racial overtone— "Banks are for Jews, they steal from colored people." Prostitution was involved in con man's story.

Victim: An elderly woman, 81 years old.

Contact: On street, while walking near church.

Development: "I am looking for a nursery school for my three children," said the white con woman." How long have you lived here? Maybe you could help me." During course of conversation said she knew someone who had found 600 dollars. They walked toward victim's home and outside were approached by con woman #2, a Negro. They talked about the money. They were invited into the victim's home and there was more talk about this remarkable find of money. Con woman #2 said she was going to call her boss and if possible she would take 200 dollars and give each of them 200 dollars. The victim suggests they call the police. Con women #1 and #2 left shortly, after cautioning her to keep quiet about the money. Victim reported she saw a large roll of bills in con woman #1's pocketbook.

Notes: This was an approach that would appeal to the elderly grandmotherly type who might have some money in the bank. The con women evaporated at her suggestion of calling the police.

MARKETING OPPORTUNITY SCHEME

The Marketing Opportunity Scheme is based on an endless chain of progression. For a nominal sum, a person can participate in the marketing opportunity and then by bringing in more participators, he is promised that he will profit from their joining, making money for doing nothing more than bringing in five new members. The vision ahead for an original joiner is tremendous, since he believes that he is going to profit from every new member in his "chain" and thus is eager to interest new people in the scheme.

Marketing Opportunity meetings are conducted at various locations by "area coordinators." Let us say that this particular opportunity dealt with the "Hydrolife Whirlpool Bath." At the meeting there would be testimonials given for the efficacy of the product, attestation to its cure-all effectiveness, and signed statements read (from well-known sports figures, etc.) as to its benefits.

There are speakers at these meetings, and each has a certain task to perform. First there is the man who says "there is nothing to buy, nothing to sell" in the marketing program. He introduces a man who paints a glowing picture of the immense amounts to be made by participating in the program—figures running into the thousands of dollars for part-time participation. He explains that all the participant has to do is bring in five members at the next meeting. Each participant in the scheme is required to rent a Hydrolife machine for a monthly payment of 10 dollars as long as he is a member of the marketing program, but the primary inducement is the lure of large profits to be derived from payments of money by later entrants to the program.

The next speaker might be introduced as "Dr. So-and-so" and the audience told that after hearing this distinguished man, they would be anxious to join the marketing program. This speaker tells the audience that he has been a special agent for the "Pan American Sécret Service," that he has worked with crime commissions, that he belongs to many national organizations and that he has investigated this marketing program and checked it out with the Better Business Bureau and all agencies— state and federal—and that "it checked out perfectly."

The persons at the meeting are lulled into a sense of security after hearing this "expert" and are ready for the next step. In the marketing organization, members are known as "distributors" and "supervisors." A distributor must pay a license fee of 298 dollars for a three-year license. For this license fee, the distributor may profit by inviting other persons to attend "opportunity meetings." For each new prospect who becomes a "distributor," the person who had originally invited him to the meeting is entitled to receive a 50 dollar commission from the marketing organization. At the end of the month the original "distributor" is entitled to receive 4 dollars for each direct distributor he brought into the program. And when the direct distributors invite other people to opportunity meetings and these join, then the original distributor is entitled to receive a 2 dollar monthly commission for each as long as he continues to pay his monthly rental payment for the Hydrolife machine.

The next step is the supervisor. If a direct distributor becomes a supervisor—for an additional "release fee" of 2,000 dollars—the original distributor receives a "release commission" of 600 dollars. For each person in the chain of a direct supervisor, the original distributor receives fifty cents per month as long as that person pays his monthly rental fee; for each person in the chain of an indirect supervisor, he receives twenty-five cents per month, etc. As a supervisor, the participant is entitled to a 60 dollar commission for each person he invites to a meeting who becomes a distributor. At the end of the month, he is entitled to 5 dollars for each direct distributor joining the program during that month. This system of "commission" payments extends back along the chain, so that the original "member" can see ahead of him endless payments for bringing in more people.

Fancy brochures, called the "Opportunity Manual," are put out by the marketing opportunity organization stating "your success will be guaranteed," that as a participant you "can grow and build your organization to an astronomical size" and that the plan is designed so "that all may prosper in direct proportion to the energy, interest, time and enthusiasm put into sponsoring new distributors." Included in the brochure are selected testimonials from persons purported to have made vast sums from the marketing opportunity plan and testimonies from people who have used the Hydrolife machine.

The final pitch is that "anyone who gets in here in the next six to eight months will make a fortune." And it is explained that if a distributor wants to leave the program, he can do so, but the organization would keep his 298 dollar license fee and give him title to his Hydrolife machine which would retail between 265 and 298 dollars. This sounds fair enough to the person attending the meeting, and he leaves to recruit members with his head filled with astronomical figures of the money he is going to make just by getting five people to come to the next meeting.

One other important thing takes place at the meeting. At some time during the evening, the speaker calls out several names of distributors and they are asked to come forward and are given checks or cash as their commissions for the month. The amount of the commission is announced by the speaker as being 10,000 dollars or even more. The sucker goes away with dreams of easy money.

The article used in the marketing program is not important as such—it might be in an entirely different field than the "Hydrolife" machine. What is being sold is the opportunity to cash in on getting something for nothing.

Certain rules for recruiting members are made. One person originates the program and enlists five persons. At the beginning of the second week, the newly recruited five begin to recruit five more persons each to join. During the second week, the original recruiter does not recruit again. At the beginning of the third week, the newly recruited 25 begin to recruit five more persons each, and neither the original recruiter nor the first five newly recruited persons recruit again, etc., etc. Before the end of the twelfth week, the total population of the United States would be involved if all went according to plan!

For the persons who devised the "marketing opportunity," the money is, of course, in the license fees paid by the persons who become "distributors" and "supervisors." When an area is milked, they move on to another part of the country, perhaps with an entirely different product.

ART FRAUD

The Art Fraud is a type of long con.

Victims: Persons interested in art—paintings, prints, drawings—usually people with plenty of money but no real knowledge of art; interested in acquiring a collection for prestige value.

Groundwork: The gang moves into an area and rents a store

where its "art works" can be displayed or arranges to have some of its stock displayed in a small art gallery or a store dealing in supplies for artists. Sometimes an ad is run in the local paper, describing the collection and stating that it will be on view at certain hours on certain days. Sometimes the con will advertise an auction sale of paintings, and at this sale will see and locate prospective victims. The auction sale draws in people looking for art at a lower price and people who believe they may pick up something valuable at a "steal."

Contact: Made at auction sales, with people who come to look and hope to buy later; or outright sales at the auctions, galleries, etc.

Development: If a con man does not make a sale outright at the auction, he may strike up acquaintance with the victim and tell him that he has just as valuable and beautiful a painting at home and that he will sell it because he needs money; and if the victim will loan him some money, he will put up the painting as security. Sometimes the victim would buy the painting outright, lend the money or guarantee a note at the bank. When this latter deal is made, the bank is not out the money, but the guarantor. When a victim appears dubious of the authenticity of a painting, forged appraisals are offered, or a spurious appraiser (one of the gang) will be brought in to authenticate the painting. Sometimes the victim will be sent to a small art store to have the painting appraised and authenticated; this will be a store where one of the con men poses as an authority on painting.

Once the victim has the painting, becomes suspicious and goes to an art expert who says the painting is a fraud, the victim may be so embarrassed he may do nothing about it; if he does go back to the auction and complain, he will be given back his money; the gang wants to operate for several weeks in a picked location and can afford to return the victim's money to prevent his going further with his complaint. Since two art auctions brought in 50,000 dollars to one art fraud gang, return of money to one or two disgruntled customers is insignificant.

Behind the art fraud is a picked gang who obtain the paintings, etc. This gang consists of forgers, painters and copyists, as well as some artists, for some of the goods offered are *real*.

LOST AND FOUND

Victim: Any man all dressed up, accompanied by a woman, both of them drinking and in an expensive place, for instance a well-known bar, or perhaps if on the street, where strangers are taking pictures.

Development: Using a "block hustle" ring, the con man drops it in the dark next to someone who is preferably a little bit drunk. When the con man picks it up, he says, "I'll bet that is worth a thousand dollars." Then he goes to the rest room. Con man #2 comes in and starts looking around on the floor for a ring he says he lost a little while ago. (If con man #1 is a Negro, con man #2 should be a white man.) Con man #2 says the ring was worth 1,000 dollars and his wife had bought it for him and she will be sick if he does not find it. After looking futilely for the ring, with the people saying nothing about one being found, the con man leaves. Then con man #1 returns to his seat next to the couple he has selected and who saw him find the ring, and says nothing. In a few minutes, the victim says, "Do you want to sell that ring?" (The con man has figured on this happening; the other would be that the couple would send con man #1 into the rest room to retrieve his ring.) Con man #1 says no, he thinks he will have it appraised. The victim, brave with drinks, offers him 300 dollars. The con man says no, he would have to get at least 400 dollars. If the woman becomes interested in the deal, the con man will try for even more than that.

Once a price has been decided on and the victim says he does not have that much cash on him, the con man hustles the pair out to cab and goes with them to get the money. Then he hands over the ring and leaves.

PADDY HUSTLE, "MISS MURPHY," CARPET GAME

Victims: Men looking for prostitutes.

Contact: Anywhere—on the street, in a bar, hotel, etc.

Development: After the con man has discovered through casual conversation that the victim would be interested in a girl, he praises the girls at his hotel "where he is the manager." He says that the girls are not only good looking and know their jobs but are all health inspected. "It is a top-notch place."

For this particular variation of the paddy hustle, the con man has located a hotel where there is no night clerk on duty. If he is working with a partner, he has him slip behind the desk from a seat in the lobby when he sees the con man approach with the victim, or if he is working alone, he himself goes behind the desk when they go into the hotel. He tells the victim that although this is a first-class place, he would feel better about the deal if the victim would give him all his valuables to keep while he is upstairs. He brings out an envelope for this purpose. He takes out the fee for the girl and then puts the victim's money in the envelope and writes out a receipt for it. Again he stresses the cleanliness of his establishment and says that before the victim can go upstairs he must have a VD inspection. Then he talks about the various girls and tells the victim he can have his choice, but that he recommends one in particular. If the victim says that is the one he wants, he says, "Fine, I'll have her ready for you when you have had your VD examination." Then he directs the victim to go to the first-floor bathroom and says that a nurse will be along in a moment or two to give the VD inspection. The victim willingly goes to the rest room to wait for the nurse, and once he has closed the door, the con man takes off.

Illustrative Example

Victim: Fairly young male, walking alone on the street.

Contact: By Negro male, asking if he would like a girl.

Development: When victim said he might be interested and asked what the set-up was, the con man said it was less than a block away but that he had to be careful who he let go up there. The two walked along the streets and the deal is developed. The victim said he would pay no more than 15 dollars and would want to stay all night. They finally settle for the 15 dollars and the time was to be four hours. While walking down the street, the con man said he could have a Negress, a white girl, a Spanish girl or whatever he wanted. He asked the victim where he worked and when he found that the victim worked for an electronics company, he seemed reassured, saying that he did not want any sailors or soldiers going up there; it was a nice place and he didn't want anyone who would make trouble. Then he asked if the victim had the 15 dollars, and when he was shown the money and the ID card, he was reassured. By now they were near a certain hotel. The con man said "Now, just to be safe, put your money in this envelope—all your money—and when you get in the hotel, walk through to the elevators and when the operator says what floor, you tell him "four" and give him the envelope and he'll take care of it for you, and take out the fifteen dollars and give it back to you when you come down again." The con man produced an envelope and wrote 15 dollars on it and put the money in it. Then he reached under his coat for his pen again and wrote 81 dollars in the other corner. He handed the envelope back to the victim, saying, "Now you're all set." When the victim said, "What do I owe you for your trouble?" the con man said, "Nothing, nothing, I just want to help you." The victim gave him what change he had in his pocket and went into the hotel and, following directions, went to the elevators and found they were self-operated. When the night clerk told him there were no girls at this hotel, the victim left. On the street, he opened his envelope and found it full of newspaper. (The switch had been made when the con man reached under his coat for his pen.)

THE SPANISH PRISONER GAME

The Spanish Prisoner game is an old con game, and in recent years the "Spanish Prisoner" may have become an "American Prisoner," but the game is essentially the same.

Props: First, worthless but impressive negotiable papers worth a large sum of money (purportedly). Earlier this might be a map to buried treasure, family jewels, etc.; second, a purported smuggled letter from a dejected prisoner (usually a Latin-American) and a picture of the prisoner's beautiful daughter.

Contact: The victim is told a touching story of the deprivations the "beautiful daughter" is undergoing in "this villainous country." The "smuggled letter" promises the victim his daughter's hand and a sizeable portion of his estate, the negotiable paper, the treasure map, family jewels or whatever if the victim will send a certain sum of money by the courier (the con man with the letter and the map, paper, etc.) so that his daughter may be rescued. To show the good faith of the "Spanish Prisoner," he will leave the map or negotiable paper, etc., with the victim while the daughter is being rescued and on her arrival from "prison," they will be wed. (The picture of the daughter is always of a ravishing beauty.) Perhaps the daughter is to bring with her the family jewels or further map directions, etc. At any rate, the game is the same; money for bribery must be given to the courier before the daughter and the family treasure can arrive.

Sometimes the Spanish prisoner becomes a wealthy man "who is in jail for income tax evasion." In this case, the victim is drawn by the idea that he had salted away money before he was jailed and part or all of this money would be available to the victim if he helped the prisoner's daughter.

This scam goes back to the days of the Spanish Armada.

DRAGON BLOOD, "VOODOO" OR "HOODOO" SCAM

Victims: Superstitious persons, usually in a poor neighborhood, preferably one of Negro residents, Latin-Americans, Mexicans, etc.

Contact: Con man lets it be known around the neighborhood that he is in the business of protecting people from bad luck. He may go from door to door selling "dragon's blood" to put on the doorsill to keep the enemy out; it will also keep the dead out. With him, he carries his "curry," "querie" or cury bag in which he carries his own lucky pieces—and he lets it be known that he has lucky pieces for sale to others. He goes on the supposition that his victims are superstitious and religious but also believe in black magic.

Development: Once the con man has established that he is a dealer in lucky charms, black magic, etc., the victims come to him. They are usually people in some kind of trouble—with their wives or husbands, with their boyfriends or girlfriends, and the trouble might be over lost love, getting a new love, jealousy, etc.

The answer to any of these problems is to buy from the con man a lucky charm, a lucky potent or preferably a whole bag of lucky charms. The victim is told that for the charm or potent to work, he must bring an article or token of the one the charm is to work on. In the case of a woman, he may ask for a lock of hair, a pair of panties, something very personal. The con man, on the customer's first visit, will rub his forehead with "sweet oil" and pray over him. If the victim goes for this kind of thing, the con man knows he has his victim snagged and can proceed with the whole bag of charms.

When the victim comes back with the token of the person he wishes the charm for (or against), the con man takes the token, puts it in a handkerchief and puts the handkerchief in a glass of water. Then he prays, or may read from the Seventh Book of Moses, or from "Seven Keys to Power." The victim pays for each charm he buys and after repeated visits may invest in the whole cury bag which is to be worn around the neck. He may invest in a lucky potent, too. The whole atmosphere is one of religion, with the con man praying, singing and invoking help for the victim. In this way, the victim, by paying for each charm and by making repeated visits, is bilked of most of his savings. He may be sold candles to burn (as in the Gpysy Blessing scam) and he may be sold incense—"number" incense on which numbers appear as it burns. He may be directed to do certain things on the day that the number appears in the incense. Some of the lucky charms are called "High John the Conqueror," "Low John the Conqueror" (price paid?) the Devil's Shoestring (a root), etc.

SWINDLE AGAINST RELIGIOUS ORDERS

Victims: Members of religious orders—Catholic sisters and Catholic priests who are in teaching orders.

The Con Man: Masquerades as a priest, wears the proper clothes if and when he needs to; has a directory of all Catholic schools and Catholic churches. The con man is familiar with the Catholic faith (may be a washed-out priest).

Contact: Made by telephone, usually to the head of a teaching order. He poses as a priest and says he is "Brother........" and that he is calling from the office of the head of that particular teaching order. He tells the head of the teaching order that one of his teaching brothers (or sisters) is in serious, very serious, trouble and hints that there might be a morals charge involved. Then he tells the priest that a representative of the order will get in touch with him shortly and explain to him how the matter can be worked out.

Development: The con man gambles on the fact that Catholic priests are afraid of things like moral charges, and so within an hour, he calls the priest and identifies himself as "Brother ...." and that he is calling for Father.......... from the head of the teaching order in a far-off state. The Father has delegated him to take care of this serious matter and he has worked out a plan so that the church will be able to settle the matter quietly and without any publicity. When the details are all arranged, he will call the priest back, and in the meantime he should get 2,500 dollars in cash and be ready to follow through on the plan to save the errant brother. In a few hours, the con man calls back and says that he has made the arrangements; some of the money is to be used to take the errant brother back to the headquarters of the teaching order and the rest is to be used to "take care of the charge" against the brother. He is to go to a certain phone booth in the lobby of a hotel in a nearby city and at a certain time will be given instructions over the phone. According to schedule, the phone rings in the designated booth and the Father answers and is given his instructions. He is to put the envelope of money behind the seat in the phone booth and return to his school; in a few hours the Brother who is arranging the matter will stop by the school to pick up the Brother, who is to be returned to the headquarters of the order.

Although reluctant to follow such an order, yet afraid of publicity deleterious to the Church, the priest leaves the money and goes back to his school to await the visitor who will come to take the erring Brother back to headquarters of the order.

FURNACE FRAUD

Typical Structure: The furnace fraud has a very small office, usually one room with one phone and a clerk, in a large metropolitan area. This organization employs few people and does not use the boiler room method of operation. The fraudulent furnace operation is usually done by door to door solicitations by a salesman who is selling a cleaning contract for the furnace at $29.50. However, he is actually planning to sell the victim a new furnace. The home owner is told that because the furnace company is in the area cleaning furnaces, he, the salesman, can give the home owner a very good deal on cleaning.

The salesman is particular in selecting homes five years old or older. Thus he convinces the victim that the furnace needs cleaning and then cons him into believing the furnace is dangerous due to its age.

Typical Victim: The furnace-cleaning case requires the victim to be a home owner who lives in the low-class to middle-class area. He prefers the middle-class area because they have enough equity in their homes to purchase a new furnace. The reason they are interested in the middle-class community is because this subject can usually raise 700 to 900 dollars for a new furnace, thus eliminating the writing of the deed of trust or having to finance it through a finance company.

Initial Contact of Swindler with Victim. The salesman goes to the door of the victim's home selling a cleaning contract for the furnace. The salesman usually contacts housewives in mid-morning while their husbands are at work. When the victim agrees to have the furnace cleaned for the low price of $29.50, the salesman asks the victim for the use of the victim's phone so that he can call his office collect to see when the cleaning crew can come. After the call has been completed, the salesman usually tells the victim that the truck will be there in about two hours. The salesman then leaves the home after having secured a contract for the furnace cleaning.

Approximately two hours after the initial contact, a truck from the furnace company rolls up to the front of the house and a man advises the victim that he is there to clean the furnace. The victim shows the cleaning man where the furnace is and he proceeds to work on the furnace for a period of 30 to 45 minutes. The serviceman calls the victim to show her that the furnace is extremely unsafe by showing her some trumped-up problems. With the use of a small mirror he not only shows the victim but also convinces the victim that there is a crack in the furnace wall.

In other cases, a small smoke candle, approximately one and one-half inches high and approximately one-half inch in circumference, is placed in the bottom of the furnace and lit by the serviceman. The serviceman calls the victim and shows her how the furnace smokes, telling her the fumes could be fatal to the family.

In another case, the serviceman disconnected the furnace, carried it out to the back yard and called the lady out. She witnessed him fill the furnace chamber with water and saw that the water was leaking out of the furnace. The serviceman explained to her that this was how poisonous gases were escaping from the furnace.

He tells the victim at this point that the furnace is old, and for her own safety and that of her family, she should purchase a new one. He then asks the victim if he could use the telephone to call his boss collect. He calls his boss and advises him that this furnace is extremely hazardous and he should come out and talk to the victim. The telephone call is usually to a phone booth or a coffee shop where the salesman is waiting for the call.

Establishing Victim's Interest and Willingness to Buy. The original salesman returns to the home, where he is met by the serviceman. In the presence of the woman the serviceman explains how hazardous the furnace is to the salesman. The salesman thanks the serviceman for being so efficient and the serviceman excuses himself.

The salesman then fast-talks the woman into contacting her husband and tells him about the problem. The salesman also tells the victim that if they decide to purchase the furnace from his company, he will add the $29.50 towards the purchase of a new, nationally known brand furnace. He also tells them that because they are working in the area, he is able to give them a discount on a new furnace. In most cases, the woman asks the salesman to return when the husband is at home and she will discuss this with him.

The salesman then comes back that evening to strike when the iron is hot, now that the victims are psychologically primed to the fact that their lives are in jeopardy. In most cases, they agree to purchase the furnace from the company. The price of the furnace is anywheres from 700 to 900 dollars depending upon the type of blower they select and the input of BTU's.

Paying for the Furnace: As soon as the victim agrees to purchase a new furnace, the contract is signed and an appointment is made for the next day to install the furnace. The victim is told that if he can get the cash without a long-term contract, they will deduct an extra 50 dollars from the price of the furnace If he does not have the cash, they slip a deed of trust in on the victim. The furnace is then installed on a C.O.D. basis. The person does not usually realize that he has been victimized until somewhere along the line he reads the price of a new furnace. He then becomes inquisitive and checks, to find out that the furnace he has purchased costs approximately 145 dollars. He then realizes that he has been swindled.

Preventing Complaints: Actually, there are no steps taken in this particular type of fraud case to reduce the likelihood of the victim's complaining because if the furnace is installed and does work properly, there is no reason for complaint. However, if the furnace does not work properly, the serviceman is sent back to correct the malfunction. If it is a disagreement over the price of the furnace, the victim never gets to speak to the salesman himself.

Prosecution is almost never carried out in these cases due to the fact that they are unable to identify the salesman in most of these cases. Not only that but the victim is very reluctant to broadcast his stupidity of being taken by a fast-talking salesman. Therefore, he very seldom complains.

Illustrative Example

The victim was contacted by a representative of a furnace-cleaning company and was advised that the company had a truck in the area and was offering a special price of $29.50 for cleaning the furnace. This cleaning job included cleaning all pipes and cold-air return, cleaning and decarboning burners and pilot lights, cleaning combustion chamber and flues, and checking all valves and thermostats. The victim agreed to have the furnace cleaned at the above-mentioned price.

Approximately three days later, a red maintenance truck

with a blower attached arrived at the victim's residence and a man identified himself to the victim as the serviceman there to clean the furnace. Upon completion of cleaning the furnace, the serviceman called the victim and advised him that he was going to call the company's furnace technician and have him inspect the furnace to see if it was operating properly.

That afternoon, a man arrived and identified himself as the technician from the furnace company and stated that he would like to examine the furnace to see if it was operating properly. The technician made an examination of the furnace and advised the victim that the furnace was warped and the seams of the firebox were separating. He further stated that the victim should purchase a new furnace.

That evening, the technician came back to the victim's home and in the presence of both the husband and wife, told them that their furnace was faulty due to a warped and split heat exchanger which could be fatal to their family.

During the course of this conversation, the victim and the technician entered into a written contract whereby the victim agreed to purchase a new furnace described as a 90M BTU gravity-flow furnace for a total price of 640 dollars, which included installation. Since the victim was unable to pay cash, he was given a time contract for a period of 36 months, which brought the total price of the furnace, including installation and finance charges, to a total of $805.68.

Note: Prior to the installation of the new heater, a representative from a local natural-gas company was contacted and he examined the same heater. He found the heater to be up to standard and in no way faulty.

As a result of the legitimate inspection from a reputable business company and the swift intervention by local police authorities, a case involving fraud was brought against the individuals involved.

CARPET FRAUD

Typical Structure: In most cases, there is no business front in carpeting cases and no personnel offices whatever. They have a group of independent contacting salesmen that are given contact cards out of the boiler room telephone operations where evening appointments are made for the salesman to show the carpeting to both the husband and wife.

Typical Victims: In carpet fraud cases, the victims are the lower-middle-class and middle-class people that would be interested in having wall-to-wall carpeting in the relatively modest home.

Initial Contact of Swindler with Victim. The salesman goes to the homes and tells the people what a lovely house they have, how nice they are, gets on a first-name basis and gets very chummy. He tells them just how beautiful they are going to make their home by installing the lovely carpeting he is showing throughout their entire house.

The salesman brings samples of the carpeting with him. The carpeting, in all instances, has been found to be continuous-filament nylon-tufted carpet. They use a burlap-type base and just poke continuous-filament nylon yarn through the weave of the carpeting and then past on to the back of that a second piece of burlap or material with some rubber-type glue. Some of the types of rugs are chenille with the loops cut on the top; others are the Wilcon type with the loops uncut. They are all in the stark colors—solid green, solid red, with very rich hues and tones. They immediately look very opulent in a typical rug sample of 2 feet by 18 inches. They bring in a big, thick pile of these things and plop them out on the floor.

Establishing Victim's Interest and Willingness to Buy: In each instance, the salesman tells the people that this is a brand-new introductory offer of special nylon carpeting put out by this firm and that this type of rug has been sold strictly on a commercial level and how strong it has to be to be used on floors of big theaters and other public gathering houses. They lead the people to believe that this carpeting is something special from their warehouses and factories. The fact is that they have no warehouses or factories.

The carpeting can be bought from any carpeting company who makes known carpeting in the United States at roughly 3 dollars per yard at dealer price. The mark-up on this carpeting is fantastic, and this price does not include the padding they use. They do not use the foam-rubber padding because they cannot get it as cheap as they can Ozite or Coco pad, but they tell the people that they have a 64-ounce pad specially made. They show them a sample of this with a kind of nonslip gummy substance on one side. The edges are all bound up, so it looks like it will never fray.

The salesman tells the people that they can let them have this rug at a very low price to introduce this commercial-grade carpet to the consuming public. They get them interested, make a quick measure of the room, and draw a fast diagram of the rooms involved.

They tell the people that their commercial carpeting is cut in vast lots at the factory so they sell it in factory units. In some cases they tell the people that they can let them have it for 10 dollars a factory unit and work their way down to 5 dollars a factory unit for the rug, pad and wall-to-wall installation. The only gimmick is that a factory unit is two square feet not one square yard, so if you figure two square feet goes into nine four and one-half times at the price of 10 dollars a yard or 10 dollars a factory unit, they are quoting a price of 45 dollars a square yard with pad and installation. When breaking their price all the way down to 5 dollars or even 4 dollars a factory unit, they still end up with approximately 17 dollars per square yard, which is a very stiff price for a rug that you could buy in a consuming market on sale at around 6 or 7 dollars a square yard installed.

Paying for the Carpet: No money changes hands. The victims sign a contract that very night.

In the carpeting deal, if the price is under 200 dollars, they would not have a deed of trust signed. It is only if the deal goes up over 500 dollars that they would slip a deed of trust in on the victim.

When they get a contract signed, they go out and sell the contract to some local carpeting installer. He goes to the home and measures it accurately, gets the right color, type and the model of the carpeting and then buys the carpeting from a local carpet dealer. He then goes and lays the carpet and gives the so-called carpet company the bills.

The carpet company, in the meantime, has sold the deal to a paper-buying mortgage company who sends out a payment book to the victim. This is generally when the victim first becomes aware that they have been defrauded—when they receive their payment book and notification.

The carpet company ends up with its virtually 100 percent profit on the deal and having done nothing at all.

Preventing Complaints: To reduce the likelihood of a complaint by the victim, if there are any squawks, the swindler comes out and is very liberal in making adjustments. They can stand to be on the profit they are making. If the victim gets really nasty and claims fraud on the part of the salesman, the outfit advises the victim that the salesman does not work for them anymore. They tell the victim that he was an independent contractor and they do not have any responsibility for him.

Usual Outcome of Cases Where Complaints Are Filed? There have never been any prosecutions in this area.

Illustrative Example

The victim in this carpet fraud case was contacted by a representative from the carpet company and asked if a salesman could come to the residence and show their carpeting to both the wife and husband some evening. The victim agreed, and an appointment was made for a salesman to visit the victim's residence and show rug samples to them.

The victim reported that when the salesman arrived, he was exceptionally friendly and immediately got on a first-name basis. He displayed his rug samples and proceeded to tell the victims that the carpeting he was showing was an excellent carpet and that he could sell it at a very low introductory price because they were introducing this commercial-grade carpet to the public.

The victim agreed to purchase the carpeting, and the salesman took measurements of the room and told the victims how much they would need. The total price of the carpeting, which included installation, was $824.95. A contract was signed that very night.

The carpeting was laid and the victims were very satisfied until they received a payment book and notification from the mortgage company. At this time, the victims called the local authorities and reported a possible fraud. Investigation of this revealed that a fraud had been committed and prosecution for fraud was obtained. However, the home owner was referred to civil authorities to seek advice as to what action could be taken to settle the matter of his property.

ALUMINUM SIDING

Typical Structure: The aluminum siding fraud has a typically small business store front, in a first-floor business area somewhere in a metropolitan area. Personnel offices are virtually none. Few people are employed. A girl is out front with a desk and telephone, sometimes a counter. There is a back room where president, vice-president, general manager, etc., may hang out. Equipment is generally a telephone, typewriter and some desks. The salesmen are not employed by the aluminum siding company. They are independent contractors; they are a group of meandering, fast-talking, quick-closing salesmen that may move from coast to coast.

A boiler room is used in connection with the aluminum siding fraud. The boiler room is usually a loft-type room in an older or run-down area of town up on a second floor. It is usually run by a party completely separate from the aluminum siding company. It has a big long table in it or sometimes a series of little temporary-type soundproof booths. It has a number of telephones with space for young girls or men to call prospective victims and make appointments for salesmen.

The personnel in the boiler room are provided with outlines of sales pitches on aluminum siding. They are given a supply of contact cards, and in the event they are able to make an appointment for a salesman to call, they write down the name, address and time of the appointment. The cards are turned over to the man operating the boiler room who in turn takes all the contact cards and turns them over to the man in the back room of the aluminum siding business or the girl. He or she then gives them to the salesman. These salesmen wander in and out as they see fit and let it be known that they are available to do some selling for the outfit.

Typical Victims: The aluminum siding cases necessarily require the victims to be home owners. The home owners are not low class because they do not have enough money or equity in their homes to buy anything or go on the hook for 84 months' credit. They are usually the low-middle-class or middle-class person. They appeal to the people that have a nice home in the older residential area of town where it is becoming a burden to keep up the exterior of a house.

Initial Contact of Swindler with Victim: In this case, the contact card is given to the salesman and an appointment has already been made for the salesman to meet the victim at the victim's home, usually in the evening. It is always made special that both the wife and husband be present. It should be kept in mind that this is necessary if they are looking for a binding deed of trust on the home, as they need the signature of both the husband and the wife.

The contact is by this wandering independent salesman. He usually has a younger fellow with him, one that is learning the ropes on how to bamboozle a victim, find the shortcuts, and practice the in's and out's of a fast-talking quick-closing aluminum siding sale.

They have a very friendly approach ("Hi! How are you!") and usually establish themselves on a first-name basis. They compliment the husband and wife on what a nice house they have. After some conversation, they sit down at a table where the salesman can spread out some of his papers. He proceeds, then, to give them an offer of making this very lovely little home of theirs a showplace of the community, covered with gorgeous aluminum siding at a very, very low-cut price as an introductory offer. He always names well-known national companies in the aluminum area, assuring them, "You've seen them on television." This company is just introducing this new product to the consuming market and they want to do it on a straight cost basis and they will make this house a kind of example in the community.

Establishing Victim's Interest and Willingness to Buy: He qualifies the victim by feeding his ego and telling him what a nice house he has. He nails him down with the promises of a very reasonable price, long-term benefits and that if other people in the community buy, he will get a rebate of 25 to 50 dollars.

The steps in the sale procedure under the next heading are to get the people hooked on the idea that they really like it, they now believe it is cheap, and they stand to gain. They have already been told that they have a long time to pay, there is a very small price involved, and so as soon as the salesman gets them on the hook, it is out with the papers and let's fill these things out. They tell the victims that they have got to move in a hurry because this is an introductory offer, and if they delay, they are not going to be able to give them this sales deal.

The papers are filled out in a hurry and written in longhand on lien contract and deed of trust forms. The lien contract and deed of trust is printed up at the top of the page but is not necessarily seen by the victim, particularly that language "deed of trust." The salesman gets their signatures down there right away and scribbles in some figures. He then checks the house and makes the estimate on how much this job is going to cost. The salesman goes outside and spends about five minutes walking around the house, supposedly taking measurements as to the cost of the job. He does not necessarily write down the true cost on the contract, but they are uncannily correct in figuring out what it really costs and then writing out the contract to insure a good healthy profit to the so-called aluminum siding company.

Paying for the Siding: The victims do not pay cash. They sign a lien contract and a mortgage. Experience indicates that only one out of every 25 people had knowledge that they were signing a mortgage on their home.

After the salesman gets the contract signed, he gets a description of the property so that the so-called company or mortgage firm that buys the paper can add the true legal description of the property. He gets a description from a contact in a title company or by checking out the deed at the county recorder's office.

The mortgage company buys this contract, secured by the deed of trust, from the so-called aluminum siding company and the mortgage company pays the aluminum siding company the contract balance. The contract balance is the amount of the contract as stated to the victim by the salesman. The contract balance is far less than the time balance, which generally runs anywhere from 48 to 84 months.

On an 84-month contract, the time price balance may be twice the amount of the contract balance. On a $2,000 aluminum siding job, the party may find himself with a time price balance of $3,900. The mortgage company pays the $2,000 to the aluminum siding company.

The aluminum siding company immediately contacts a small contracting outfit. They work on a piecework basis; therefore, the contractor's license is obtained by a fellow that sets up the aluminum siding company. He gets a B-1 general contracting license which entitles him to employ piecework or hour-by-hour workers. All it takes is somebody in the operation to be able to qualify as a contractor.

The carpenters, the small outfit contacted by the aluminum siding company, comes out in a truck that does not have any identifying marks or signs on it. They have a ladder, appropriate tools and the know-how to put aluminum siding up on the house and aluminum window frames in.

Soon after the contract is signed, the carpenters go out and measure the home accurately and then go and buy the necessary materials from one of the aluminum siding supply houses in the area. They then go out and put aluminum siding on the house. After the job is completed, they submit their bills with copies of the bills for the material to the aluminum siding company.

The aluminium siding company in our example case here has 2,000 dollars. In cost cases, the job costs about 1,000 dollars. The aluminum siding company pays the carpenters, these installers, the 1,000 dollars they need for their work and the aluminum siding company now has 1,000 dollars clear profit. The aluminum siding company so far has not done a thing. The man running the operation has not even left the little back room of his business front that he occupies with his girl-Friday sitting out front. He takes 1,000 dollars and gives 400 to 500 dollars to the so-called salesman. He does not give the salesman a wage; he just gives him a flat payment of this money. No report is made to the state or federal government; nothing is withheld for tax purposes.

If anyone claims fraud on the part of the salesman, the man that runs the so-called aluminum siding company says he was not his employee but was an independent contractor finding people interested in buying aluminum siding.

Many victims find out that the price they were charged was not as cheap as was represented. Others realize what occurred when they get their payment book and the notification from the mortgage company. They find out from this mortgage company that there is a mortgage on their home. The bulk of the victims are never told that there is a mortgage. They are not advised by the mortgage company that the contract is secured by a mortgage; they are merely told that the contract has been purchased by them and that enclosed they will find a payment book for their payments.

The most general manner in which the victims determine that they have been defrauded is by the Police Department, District Attorney's Office or the State Attorney General's Office. They undertook a general investigation into the so-called aluminum siding frauds, checking through the county recorder's office and getting the names of the individuals against whom or onto who's property deeds of trust have been recorded. After getting their names and addresses, they go out and interview and tell the victims that they have signed a deed of trust. This is when they first become aware that they have been defrauded.

When the victim calls and finally gets to see one or two of the characters in the back room, he is told that the salesman who sold the aluminum siding is no longer with them, and they get the victim to believe that the fellow was kind of a sharpie. They were a little embarrassed by some of his actions. They tell the victim that they will be out to see if they can take care of whatever the complaint is.

They go out to the home, and if the victim is really squawking and states that a person down the block bought some siding and wants to know why they did not get their rebate, they give the victim 25, 50, or 75 dollars to cool him off. In some cases, they came out and said they would add some pretty decorative stone in front of the house and that they would have the workman come out and do a little more work around the house. In another case, they would come out and give the victim a free electric frying pan or other cool-off gimmick.

Embarrassment and remorse greatly reduce the likelihood of a complaint. In most cases, the victims will not do anything about the fraud because they are too embarrassed and do not want their friends and neighbors to know about their stupidity.

Usual Outcome of Cases Where Complaints Are Filed. It must be understood that criminal actions taken do not alter civil relationship and or liabilities that may result from the aluminum siding cases. The criminal actions go only to criminal sanctions upon those individuals guilty of fraud, theft, forgery and offering forged documents for recordation, etc. The home owner victims must be made to understand that in all probability, further civil action will be necessary to clear the record on their real property and to resolve disputes with the purchasers of the lien contracts.

In some cases, it appeared as though the mortgage company had completed the contracts, as the print was different and more than one typewriter was used. The manner in which the deals were closed right on the scene the very first night makes it clear that the documents could not have been typewritten. However, by the time the documents were received in the county recorder's office, they were typewritten. The only explanation for that is that the salesman got the victim to sign paper including a whole blank set of contracts and deeds of trust which were filled in and typewritten later.

The usual outcome, then, is not too good on the civil side but has been pretty successful on the criminal side.

Illustrative Example

The victim had been contacted by phone on several occasions by the salesman, who offered to put aluminum siding on her home at a very reasonable price. The salesman informed the victim that the price was so reasonable because the company intended to use her completed home for advertising on television and in magazines.

The victim agreed to have the home covered with the aluminum siding for the price of $3,572.52 and signed the contract to that effect.

The victim was shown color prints of various styles and colors and was promised that her home would look just like the photo when completed. The salesman also promised that imitation flagstone was included for the front of the house. No mention was ever made of a mortgage on the property.

An elderly gentlemen finished the installation in a day and a half. However, it did not appear to be as complete and attractive as the prints that were shown. The imitation rock was never installed, and the corners were never sealed properly.

The victim complained to the company many times and the company made many promises but never took any action.

At a later date, the victim discovered a third mortgage on the home because of the aluminum siding. Victim had no knowledge that she had signed a mortgage on her home.

TRAINING SCHOOL

Typical Structure: The type and location of structure depends upon the type of material to be taught at the school. For example, if the school is designed to teach the trade of aircraft mechanics, the location will be near a large commercial airport. The building usually consists of a secretary/receptionist sitting at a desk in the front office, one office to house the president and a large room to supposedly house the aircraft parts and engines.

The school usually crops up when there is a demand for skilled labor or some new development or projects of large scale which require skilled help.

The school, in most cases, will use the first name only or initials of well-known organizations for the name of their school.

Typical Victims: The victims are usually persons who are engaged in the type of work that the school is designed to teach and are seeking promotions and a raise of pay in their general trade. The person, in some cases, is an unskilled individual who is seeking prestige in a new, fast-moving field of trade.

Initial Contact of Swindler with Victim: Names are obtained for a mailing list from persons who are working in the general line of trade that the school is teaching. In many cases, the school advertises through the newspaper with attractive ads. The cards or ads usualy state "Worldwide jobs paying up to $16,000 per year without loss of time from your present job if you qualify. Fill this card out right away and mail it in today to see if you qualify."

Establishing Victim's Interest and Willingness to Buy: After receiving the card, the victim fills it in and mails it to ascertain whether or not he is qualified for this school. Upon receiving the card, the secretary/receptionist sends back a standard form advising the person that the school is happy to announce that he has been accepted for training in their program.

Approximately two to three days after the victim receives his reply that he has been accepted, a man comes to the victim's home and advises the victim that he is a field representative of the school. The field representative, a fast-talking individual, informs the victim of a list of specialized jobs open to the people who complete this school course. He proceeds to get out brochures which lists possible salaries upon graduation from the school, ranging from 12,000 to 16,000 dollars yearly. He has the victim believing that upon graduation, the school personnel will arrange employment contacts with different companies that the school is affiliated with.

After psychologically getting the victim in the right frame of mind, the field representative presents several papers and asks the victim to sign them and to fill in the references so that a further background investigation can be made on the victim, as the school wants only qualified people who are interested in bettering their opportunities.

Approximately ten days later, the victim receives his first two lessons through the mail for his home-study purposes, and approximately two weeks later he is sent an examination test which anyone with brain one can pass. The victim mails his test questions and answers in and in two to three days receives his grade, usually of 93-95 percent. The high score now convinces the student that he is doing good work, and he is extremely enthused about the new school.

The next phase is that he receives through the mail a card

telling him to report for an introductory meeting and for him to also bring his wife. At this meeting an instructor again speaks to a group, now of about 60 people (husbands and wives), about their job opportunities. During this meeting they are all shown a film, which anyone can get at no cost for education purposes from various film libraries, to stimulate the students' interest.

The next step is that the subject receives through the mail a bill for approximately 450 dollars payable at 25 dollars a month over a long period of time while the training is going on. This bill is a copy of the contract that the victim signed the night he signed the papers for his background investigation. Only now, above the signature line, all of the data pertaining to the prices and payments of the course are filled in.

Paying for the Lessons: There is no down payment on this school. The money changes hands at the rate of 25 dollars a month or in some cases 50 dollars a month, depending on the person's ability to pay.

The subject usually becomes aware of the fact that he is a victim of a fraud when he only spends approximately two hours a month on ridiculous home-course studies that the average fourth grader gets at school. When the victim complains, he is told that the next lesson will be down at the shop and after this stall method has been employed for some time, the group is all brought together again and shown another film in an attempt to pacify these individuals.

Usual Outcome of Cases where Complaints Are Filed: The usual outcome in some cases has been prosecution and jail sentences ranging in time as high as seven years in jail. In some cases, persons have been successful in securing civil remedies from attorneys hired by them.

Illustrative Example

The victim received a postcard in the mail from a jet training institute advertising mechanical training in jet aviation. The victim filled out the card and mailed it in.

Approximately two days later, a man came to the victim's home and identified himself as a field representative for the jet institute. The field representative gave the victim a fast sales talk, informing and showing him a list of specialized jobs, advertising material, possible salaries upon graduation ranging from 12,000 to 16,000 dollars yearly, and told him that their school had the jet engines, tools and other necessary equipment to work with while attending classes one to two nights a week. The field representative also told the victim that upon completion of the course, the school would arrange employment and contact different companies the individual wanted to work for. The victim agreed to enroll in the course, and the field representative gave him several papers and asked him to sign them. He also asked the victim for one name of a person who could be used as a reference, so a background investigation could be made by the school to determine whether or not the victim was qualified.

Approximately ten days later, the victim received a notice that he had qualified, and shortly after that, the first two lessons were received through the mail.

During the following month, the victim received a card to report to an introductory meeting and also to take his wife. Upon arriving at the meeting, he saw that there were approximately 60 to 65 individuals attending. A male instructor spoke on the advantages, benefits, opportunities and the good jobs available upon their graduation. During this meeting, they were shown a film on military jet aircraft in flight.

The next month, the victim received in the mail a card instructing him to attend a class session. The victim attended the class, and the only subject presented was a tape recording on the subject of how a fuel system operated. Since attending that class, the victim had not been notified of any further classes but received lessons by mail.

At this time, the victim became suspicious of a possible fraud and contacted the local police authorities. The authorities visited the school and it was disclosed that no jet engines for classroom work were available, other than one engine that was completely inoperative. No tools or any other materials were available.

As a result of the visit to the school and the investigation made by the local police authorities, a case involving fraud was brought against the individuals involved.

HOME PHOTO SERVICE FRAUD

Typical Structure: The structure in this type of fraud is usually the suspect's home or a very small office somewhere in a low-rent area. In most cases when the suspect has an office, he employs an answering service. Thus he does not have to pay for the services of a secretary.

Typical Victim: The victim is always a new mother of an approximately two- to four-week-old baby.

Initial Contact of Swindler with Victim: The contact is made by obtaining information as to the new births from the vital statistics of the newspapers in the immediate area. The last name of the child and the address is used in searching the telephone book for the phone number.

The victim is usually contacted during the midmorning and is advised that her child has just been chosen as the baby of the month. They lead the victim on to believing that this baby-of-the-month selection could lead to the national recognition of the child's picture on some type of leading baby product. The caller advises the new mother that this photo service company has been selected to do the photographs of the child of the month.

Establishing Victim's Interest and Willingness to Buy: At this particular point, the mother becomes very elated with the good news that her child has been chosen baby of the month.

She is then advised that she will be contacted by a professional photographer from this studio who will bring his professional equipment to her home for taking the necessary pictures of the baby of the month. A midmorning appointment, when the husband is not home, is made for the photography work. After the appointment has been made, the woman is told that if she purchases two pictures, she can get one free.

On the day in question, the photographer calls at the home of the victim. He allegedly takes several shots of the baby using his floodlights and camera equipment.

The photographer then asks the mother if she would like her picture taken with the baby because now that he is there and his equipment is set up, he could give her a good deal. The mother agrees and again the photographer takes several more exposures.

After the photographer is finished taking the pictures, he tells her that when the proofs are done, he will be back to show them to her. At that time, if she purchases two or more, she will get one free.

The high-pressure salesman returns with the proofs and fast-talks the victim into a contract. The contract is usually twice the price of any normal photo studio.

If the victim wants only the one free picture, the salesman advises her that these are only proofs and that he will bring her the finished product when it is completed. The salesman leaves and the victim never sees him again.

Paying for the Pictures: After entering into the contract, the victim is then asked for a deposit of usually 10 dollars which will be applied to any of the purchases. In some cases, the victim is then given an ordinary receipt for the deposit, of a type which could be purchased in any stationery store.

When the victim attempts to contact the photographer, she is only given the runaround by clerks from the boiler room. She is advised that they are only an answering service and can only take messages for the photographer. At this time, the victim suspects a possible fraud and contacts the local authorities.

Usual Outcome of Cases Where Complaints Are Filed: Convictions are are almost unheard of in this area, other than for a business license violation.

Illustrative Example

The victim contacted the local police department and advised that she had been contacted by a photo service. The representative of the photo service advised her that her child had been selected as the baby of the month and that they wanted permission to photograph the child. She was led to believe that this picture would be sent in with other pictures and they would all be judged, and the picture with the best-looking baby could be selected and entered into a national competition. She was told that if she purchased two pictures, she would, in turn, receive one free photograph.

In contacting the police department, the victim was attempting to ascertain whether this was a legitimate organization.

Investigation failed to reveal that it was or that they had a business license to do business in the city limits.

The victim was then told to make an appointment for having the baby's picture taken. Arrangements were made with the victim to have a plainclothes officer in the home when the subject arrived for the appointment.

On the day in question, when the subject arrived, he explained the details of the contest to the lady while the plainclothes officer was in another adjoining room. She was to get one free picture if she purchased two, but no size was mentioned of the free picture she was to get.

At this time, the suspect was accosted by the plainclothes officer, and investigation revealed that he did not have a business license to do business in the city nor did he have any proper credentials or business cards showing that he was affiliated with any photography organization.

The subject was issued a summons for violating the business license code, for which he paid a 25 dollars fine.

Investigation of this firm in other cities revealed that when the woman would pick the three photographs of her choice and pay for the two as per contract, she would then be given the one free photograph which was a black and white or colored 2 x 2 photograph. It was also revealed that the victim paid an exorbitant price for the two photographs which she purchased as per contract.

BEAUTY PARLOR FRAUD

Typical Structure: In this type of fraud a personal-type contact is made. There is no phone call or any advertising by paper to attract the victim. The suspect does not work out of any type of business structure. His business is carried on in a door-to-door basis.

Typical Victims: This type of fraud has two kinds of victims. First, the owner of the beauty parlor is a victim; and secondly, the purchaser of the service card is a victim. In all cases, the victim who purchases the card for services at the beauty parlor is a female.

Initial Contact of Swindler with Victim: First, the subject who commits the fraud selects a beauty parlor in the community that is doing an average business. He personally contacts the owner and tells her that he can and will up the business by 200 percent. He talks the owner into letting him print up fifty cards which will entitle the bearer to six free hair services.

These printed cards will contain the business establishment's name and address and will entitle the bearer to the above-mentioned free services. The handing out of these cards, he explains, will promote business, as these 50 people will not only come back but will also send their friends in. The beauty parlor owner, wanting more business, enters into a verbal contract.

Establishing Victim's Interest and Willingness to Buy: The swindler has established the owner of the beauty parlor's interest by promising to increase business. After getting permission to print up fifty cards, the suspect has five hundred cards printed. He then goes out into the community and by means of door to door salesmanship, he sells these cards for $3.50 each. He tells and shows the person that they are getting the following:

* Shampoo and set
* Individually styled haircut
* Hair conditioning treatment or shampoo and set
* Shampoo and set
* Individually styled haircut
* Hair conditioning treatment or shampoo and set
* OR ANY SERVICE MAY BE SUBSTITUTED ANY MONTH AS FOLLOWS:

A: $5.00 off any $15.00 (and up) permanent wave.

B: $5.00 off on bleaching, frosting or virgin tint.

The subject will get these services for $3.50 and that without such a card it would cost 30 dollars.

The cards show that the listed services are only good on Monday, Tuesday or Wednesday. He sells as many of them as he possibly can on Thursday, Friday, Saturday and Monday for $3.50 each to 500 women and for a total of 1,750 dollars.

Paying for the Cards and Services: The suspect receives payment for the hair service cards directly from the victim at the time he peddles it. The victim, in return, gets the card.

The only money that changes hands between the beauty parlor owner and the suspect is the money the suspect gives to the owner which is her share of the profit from the cards. At best, she receives a dollar for each of the fifty cards.

Usual Outcome of Cases Where Complaints Are Filed: The beauty parlor is suddenly deluged with more people than they can touch at this ridiculous giveaway introductory price. The beauty parlor is unable to cope with it, so they start dishonoring the card or they will have to go out of business.

The owner tries to contact the salesman but is unsuccessful.

There has never been a prosecution because no one is able to identify the suspect.

Illustrative Example

An individual contacted the owner of the beauty parlor and told the owner that their business could be increased greatly by selling cards entitling the bearer of the card to six free services, one each month. The card would entitle them to two shampoos and sets, two individually styled haircuts and two hair-conditioning treatments or shampoos and sets.

The salesman stated that the cards would be sold for $8.95 and that part of the profit would be given back to the owner. He would keep the remaining amount for the cost of the printing and for his time and trouble. The owner agreed to have fifty cards printed up.

The suspect went out and had five hundred cards printed up. He then went from door to door and sold each card to a woman for $8.95 and told her what a terrific buy she was getting.

When one of the women went to the beauty parlor, she had some difficulty making an appointment with her service card; however, she was able to get one of the services offered. On her next visit, the victim was refused because the owner of the beauty parlor was no longer honoring the cards.

The victim notified police authorities, who checked into the case and found out that the beauty parlor owner agreed to have fifty cards printed up, but actually five hundred were printed and sold. At this time, it was also disclosed that the beauty parlor was no longer in business and had moved out of the area. They moved not because they were at fault but because they were forced to due to the contract they had made.

INDEX